HIGHLIFE GIANTS

WEST AFRICAN DANCE BAND PIONEERS

JOHN COLLINS

CASSAVA REPUBLIC

FEEDING THE AFRICAN IMAGINATION

John Collins is a naturalised Ghanaian of British descent who came to Ghana in 1952 when his father, the late Edmund Collins, began teaching at the University of Ghana. Collins plays the guitar, harmonica and percussion, and has worked and performed with numerous Ghanaian and Nigerian artists and bands, including the late Fela Kuti. He has worked, recorded and played in several other West African countries including Nigeria, Togo, Benin, Côte d'Ivoire and Liberia. Currently, Collins is a professor at the music department of the University of Ghana at Legon, co-runs the Local Dimension highlife band, is a patron of the Musicians Union of Ghana (MUSIGA) and is chair of Bokoor African Popular Music Archives Foundation (BAPMAF).

First published in 2016 by Cassava Republic Press
Abuja – London

A CIP catalogue record for this book is available from the British Library and the National Library of Nigeria.

UK ISBN 978-1-911115-29-8
Nigerian ISBN 978-978-50238-1-7
eISBN 978-1-911115-30-4

Editor: Chinelo Onwualu
Editorial assistant: Anthea Gordon
Production and layout: Jibril Lawal
Cover design art: Ashai Nicholas

Printed and bound in Great Britain by Bell & Bain Ltd, Glasgow.
Distributed in Nigeria by Book River Ltd.
Distributed in the UK by Central Books Ltd.

To my wife, Dovi Helen, and son, Thomas Kojo.

Contents

Introduction

The highlife of Ghana and Nigeria is one of the many varieties of urban popular dance music styles that have emerged in sub-Saharan Africa since the nineteenth century. It fuses African with European, American and, in some cases, Islamic influences. Other West and Central African trans-cultural music styles include: Sierra Leonean goombay and maringa; pan–West African ashiko (or asiko); Nigerian juju, fuji and Afrobeat; Cameroonian makossa; Ivorian ziglibithy and zoblazo; the Congo jazz or soukous of Central Africa; and the Afro-Manding, woussoulou and mbalax music of Mali, Guinea and Senegal. The emergence of highlife and these other African popular music styles parallels what happened in the New World where encounters between European and African American cultures resulted in musical styles such as Negro spirituals, ragtime, jazz, samba, blues, calypso, rumba, swing, R&B, soul, reggae, zouk, disco and hip-hop.

Music historians have noted that the two branches of black popular music, in both the Black New World and in Africa, have been in continuous contact with each other since the nineteenth century. This exchange was made possible through freed slaves returning to Africa, black colonial soldiers stationed in different parts of the continent, and black seamen crisscrossing the Atlantic. In the early twentieth century, the reconnection was enhanced by sheet music, film, records and visits to Africa by African American, Afro-Latin and Afro-Caribbean artists. Consequently, the music of the African Diaspora, like calypso, rumba, swing and so on, has had a long-term impact on the evolution of African popular music. This Atlantic musical exchange is what I call a 'transatlantic black musical feedback cycle' and what the writers Paul Gilroy and Robert Farris Thompson have called the 'Black Atlantic' and 'Afro-Atlantic' culture.[1]

The process of the popular music of the black Americas finding its way to Africa is a type of return; what the Ghanaian musicologist Atta Annan Mensah refers to as a musical 'homecoming'.[2] The earliest evidence in West Africa of such a 'homecoming' is the Jamaican goombay (or gumbe) drum and dance introduced by freed maroon slaves who returned to Freetown, the capital of the British colony of Sierra Leone, in the early nineteenth century. This laid the foundations for many early Anglophone West African popular music styles, such as maringa, ashiko, highlife and juju music.

Freetown Goombay group (*An Introduction to the Music of Sierra Leone* (1982) by Cootje van Oven)

Goombay frame-drum music was originally created by the Jamaican maroons (rebel slaves) during the late eighteenth century as a response to the suppression by the British slave masters of traditional African hand-carved peg-drums. African peg-drums were feared by the whites because they were associated with so-called pagan rituals, and because the drums could 'talk'. In fact, 'talking drums' were used in the successful black revolt of the neighbouring Caribbean island of Haiti. By the mid-nineteenth century, this Jamaican maroon drum-dance music had become a craze in Freetown. It later spread inland and along the coast to many other parts of West and Central Africa via migrant workers and fishermen. In Nigeria, for instance, it is called 'goumbe' or 'kumbeh'. It is 'gome' in Ghana, where these types of frame-drums were used by some early highlife ensembles.

This brings us to highlife, West Africa's oldest and most well–known popular dance music. Although the word 'highlife' was not coined until the 1920s, the music dates from the late nineteenth century, when three distinct streams of urban music emerged in Ghana. First, the colonial military brass bands triggered a local proto-highlife known as 'adaha' music that inspired an even more localised offshoot known as 'konkoma'. Second, visiting sailors stimulated the growth of the coastal guitar and accordion 'osibisaaba' style which later moved inland and resulted in the rustic 'palm wine' style of guitar highlife. Third, there were the local high-class African ballroom orchestras, which began playing the occasional local adaha, osibisaaba or other street melodies. It was in this elite context that the name 'highlife' was coined in the early 1920s, and it was these pre–World War II dance orchestras that laid the foundation for the post-war highlife dance bands of E.T. Mensah, King Bruce, Bobby Benson and other highlife giants who are discussed in this book.

1. Paul Gilroy, *The Black Atlantic* (Cambridge: Harvard University Press, 1993). Robert Farris Thompson, *Flash of the Spirit* (USA: Vintage Books, 1984).
2. Atta Annan Mensah, 'Jazz: The Round Trip', in *Jazz Research*, 3/4, (1971/2).

SECTION ONE:

The Origins and Spread of Highlife

1

Black Soldiers, Seamen and the Coastal Elites: Brass Bands, Guitar Bands and Ballroom Dance Orchestras

Highlife was born in Ghana in the late nineteenth century and from the late 1920s the word 'highlife' gradually became the generic name for Ghanaian popular music, whether played by brass bands, dance bands, palm wine groups or guitar bands. By the 1950s, highlife had firmly established itself in other West African countries, particularly Nigeria.

Early Brass Band Music in Anglophone West Africa

The earliest musical stream that fed into highlife developed out of the nineteenth century military brass-and-fife bands associated with the British settlements in Freetown, Cape Coast, Lagos, Calabar and, later, the American colony of Liberia. As will be discussed, the Africanisation of western regimental military music seems to be linked to the innovative role of coastal African ethnic groups, as well as African and West Indian soldiers and, in some cases, African sailors and stevedores.

In the case of Nigeria, Bode Omojola refers to the creation of brass bands in Lagos, Calabar and Onitsha from the 1860s,[1] whilst Waterman refers to the late-nineteenth-century bands of the Royal West African Frontier Force, the West India Regiment and the Hausa Police. Although these initially played only western music, local songs had been included by the 1920s and 1930s. According to Waterman, the most famous of these local marching bands was the Lagos-based Calabar Group led by Azukwo Bassey.[2] Omofolabo Ajayi-Soyinka mentions that the band moved to Lagos around 1930 from the southeastern town of Calabar in present-day Cross River State.[3]

The drummer Bayo Martins, who was born in Calabar in 1932 and is discussed more fully in Chapter 9, recalled seeing local brass bands playing for the local elites as a child. These bands played a selection of ballroom music as well as 'native blues' and 'itembe' music. The latter 'predated what is today's highlife' and was sung in Efik or Creole (i.e. pidgin English), which had 'spread all along the coast from Gambia to the Congo'.[4]

According to Christopher Fyfe, the militia of the British Sierra Leone Company had a drum-and-fife band in Freetown that, by the 1850s, began to give public Sunday concerts of European songs and hymns for the Krio elites, who were descendants of freed slaves. These Sunday programmes were subsequently taken over by the band of the West India Regiment in 1864.[5] Naomi Ware noted that, between the two World Wars, the band of the Royal West African Frontier Force, many of whose members were West Indians, provided popular music for dances and concerts.[6]

Brass bands were also popular in Liberia in the early 1900s. In 1984, the 67-year-old Monrovian musician David Kwee Bedell told me that, as a small boy, he watched quadrilles being played at public weekend picnics by the marching bands of the indigenous Kru (or Kroo) and Grebo inhabitants.[7] As will be mentioned later, the Kru were famous mariners who found their way to many West African port cities, carrying their musical influences with them.

Brass band music in Ghana can be traced back to a regimental 'native orchestra' the British set up at Cape

Coast Castle in the 1830s. This band played western military marches, polkas and dance music, but not local songs.[8] This changed after 1873, when the first of six to seven thousand black soldiers from the English-speaking West Indies[9] were stationed at Cape Coast and the neighbouring Elmina Castle to help the British in their 1873–1901 wars against the inland Ashanti Kingdom. These West Indian rifles had regimental brass bands and in their spare time they played early forms of calypsos and other Afro-Caribbean music. This music also utilised call-and-response, rhythmic offbeats, syncopated clave/bell rhythms and other African musical features drawn from their slave past. Not surprisingly, Afro-Caribbean music resonated with the young Fanti musicians who had obtained their brass band skills from military personnel. At first, these local musicians simply copied the West Indians' clave rhythms and melodies. For instance, according to Attah Annan Mensah, the early highlife tune 'Everybody Likes Saturday Night'[10] was based on a calypso melody.[11] Within ten years however, Ghanaian brass band performers moved on to develop their own distinct adaha music. Afro-Caribbean music therefore acted as a catalyst for Ghanaian brass band musicians to indigenise their own music.

Ghana Territorial Army Band, early 1900s (BAPMAF)

According to Atta Annan Mensah, two late-nine-teenth-century local brass bands from Elmina, the Lions Soldiers and Edu Magicians, included adaha music in their repertoires. Europeans, however, objected to adaha and its street parades. In 1888, Reverend Dennis Kemp described the sound of drum-and-fife bands as 'tormenting' and warned that allowing Sunday-school processions to be led by them would 'ultimately lead to the ballroom, the heathen dance and other worldly amusements'.[12] In 1908, the District Commissioner of Cape Coast, Mr A. Foulkes, curbed the town's five brass bands from playing their 'objectionable native tunes', as he claimed they led to competitive quarrelling, obstruction of roads, drinking and dancing.[13]

Despite European colonial and missionary protestations, these local marching bands spread from the coastal Fanti area into southern Ghana to both the urban and rural areas, where there was money coming in from the boom in cocoa.

Although adaha brass bands became popular in the early 1900s throughout southern Ghana, a 'poor man's version' of adaha called 'konkoma' or 'konkomba' surfaced around 1930, in villages where people could not afford the expensive imported brass band instruments.[14] Except for the occasional big brass band drum and sometimes a flute or bugle, only locally constructed hand-held goombay-type frame drums, modelled on the western military side drum, were used. They subsequently became known as 'konkoma drums' and 'pati drums'. Men were the instrumentalists but both men and women sang, marched and danced to this music. Though konkoma groups used mainly local instruments, they did keep the baton-waving conductors and the western-type synchronised marching of adaha brass bands. Also, like adaha brass bands, the konkoma groups played a cross-section of foreign and local popular music.

Konkoma became a Ghanaian craze in the 1930s and 1940s. According to Sackey, it was created by 'school drop-outs' and 'ruffian boys'.[15] K.N. Bame and A.M. Opoku, who were schoolboy members of the Kpandu town's konkoma group in the late 1930s and early 1940s, told me that the members usually marched to the performance venue, but then formed a semicircle for the dancers to perform either freestyle or in drill-like formation. According to the Ghanaian choreographer A.M. Opoku, the baton-wielding konkoma conductor would dramatically pass the baton 'under his thigh and catch it with his left hand – and as soon as it came down, the drumming would start'.[16] The instrumentalists and dancers, says Sackey, wore armed-forces-inspired uniforms.[17] Opoku described these as check shirts, shorts with 'many secret pockets' (for silk handkerchiefs) and peaked caps with tassels of varying colours that represented the particular konkoma group. These groups were highly competitive and expressed their rivalry by the use of all sorts of eye-catchers. This competitiveness was also reflected in the dancing itself. According to Opoku, the word 'konkoma' is part of the Akan expression 'me twa konkoma ma bo fum' (I cut konkoma and I fall down), which was used when the dancers purposely bumped into each other and tried to knock one another down on the phrase 'ko' of 'konkoma'.

Because of its marches and ranks of uniformed young men, the British decided to use konkoma to recruit Ghanaians into the British Army during the Second World War. Sackey for instance, refers to anti-German-Axis konkoma songs, such as the one that translates from Fanti that they are chasing him (i.e. the Japanese) out of Burma.[18] This connection between konkoma, Ghanaian soldiers and the Second World War is also reflected in the fact that konkoma music was used in the wartime African Theatre that entertained the tens of thousands of Allied African troops fighting against the Japanese in India and Burma from 1943–6.[19]

Uniformed member of Tsito Konkoma band, late 1940s (Senyo Adzei)

Although the konkoma variety of highlife gradually died out during the 1950s due to the rise of highlife dance and guitar bands, it influenced various forms of mid-twentieth-century Ghanaian traditional recreational music. These modernised or 'neo-traditional' drum-dance performance styles include the akyewa and asaadua of the Akan[20] and the borborbor[21] of the Ewe people of southeastern Ghana and Togo. Moreover, in its eastwards movement, konkoma highlife spread as far as western Nigeria. According to the Nigerian musician Segun Bucknor, konkoma music was an informal, 'low-class', percussion-based highlife that came to Lagos in the 1930s:

By the early thirties you had informal dance steps like konkoma. This was not like the dance bands but was what you would now call highlife, but without the guitar. During weekends labourers or carpenters would form a group to play at naming ceremonies for some few drinks, and a couple of pounds [...] this dance-step was later called agidigbo, as it took its name from a Nigerian box instrument with five strings [i.e. thumb piano with plucked metal lamellae].[22]

The Yoruba musician Adeolu Akinsanya was a pioneer of agidigbo music and was influenced by Ghanaian konkoma highlife music.[23] In the late 1940s and 1950s he formed his Lagos-based Rancho Boys and Rio Lindo Orchestra, which used five or six local instruments as well as Afro-Cuban bongos, maracas, congas and local percussion.

West/Central African Palm Wine Guitar Music

Although this book focuses on dance band highlife, I will say something briefly here about the guitar band variety. Although these two branches of highlife had different origins and social contexts, they shared similar instruments, songs, urban audiences and performance spaces.

The origins of Ghanaian guitar highlife and other forms of West/Central African guitar music – such as Sierra Leonean ashiko/asiko and maringa, western Nigerian juju music, Cameroonian makossa and the acoustic 'dry' guitar music of the Democratic Republic of Congo – goes back to palm wine and 'native blues' guitar music. These terms were used to collectively describe the various early-twentieth-century music styles that combined local percussion instruments such as tambourines, box drums, goombay-type frame drums, rasps and wooden claves (or a bottle struck by a nail or coin), with the portable ones of visiting seamen: the concertina, accordion, piccolo, penny whistle, harmonica, mandolin, banjo and guitar.

A particularly important formative group that pioneered African guitar playing was the coastal Kru or Kroo people of Liberia. The Kru were traditionally long-distance canoe men who knew the West African coast well and were therefore employed as navigators, surf-boat operators and seamen by the Portuguese, the British and the Americans.

The Kru were first employed as sailors on board British ships from the late eighteenth century, where they had access to some of the small, portable musical instruments mentioned earlier. The African style of playing these western instruments was thus pioneered on the high seas by the Kru mariners. Of particular importance was the Spanish guitar,[24] to which the Kru applied a two-finger (thumb and first finger) plucking technique drawn from the traditional African oppositional way of playing local lutes and harp-lutes[25]. During the late nineteenth century these West African seamen began spreading their innovations down the West and Central African coast.[26] Kru songs, guitar techniques and syncopated rhythms became an important influence on the emerging coastal popular music styles of many African countries.

In 1920, there were about five thousand Kru in Freetown, Sierra Leone and their music impacted the emerging local maringa music of the Krio population. Maringa emerged in the 1930s and was played on large thumb pianos (congamas), goombay drums, guitars, concertinas, cigarette tins, bottles and musical saws.

In Nigeria, both Waterman and Alaja-Browne refer to the 'Kru's bass' two-finger technique of Lagosian palm wine or native blues music in the 1920s and 1930s.[27] In fact, Lagos' largest interwar palm wine group, the Jolly Boys Orchestra, was based at this city's harbour-front area and was partly composed of seamen. Its leader was a Kru ex-seaman known as 'Sunday Harbour Giant'. Early exponents of Yoruba juju music, like Tunde King (who coined the term 'juju music'), Ojoge Daniel, Ayinde Bakare and Akanbi Wright all used the Kru two-finger guitar picking style.

Nineteeth-century drawing of Liberian Kru surf-boat operators
(A *History of West Africa* (1967) by J.B. Webster and A.A. Boahen, with H.O. Idowu.)

Congo paddle-wheel steamer, which plied the Congo River in the early 1900s (*The Congo and Coasts of Africa* (1907) by Richard Harding Davis, p. 38)

The introduction of the palm wine guitar techniques to DR Congo is linked to the five thousand coastmen from English-speaking West Africa who worked there as contract artisans, clerks and sailors between 1885 and 1908.[28] These West African coastmen, operating in the port of Matadi and up and down the Congo River, helped trigger Congo's earliest recognised local popular music style, called 'maringa',[29] which was played on thumb pianos, frame drums, guitars and accordions. As will be discussed in Chapter 13, maringa spread throughout the DR Congo (as well as neighbouring Congo–Brazzaville and Gabon) in the 1920s and laid the foundation for 'Congo jazz' (or soukous), the dominant style of Central African dance music during the 1950s, pioneered by the likes of Le Grande Kallé, Dr. Nico, Tabu Ley Rochereau and Franco Luambo.

Maringa band in Gabon (BAPMAF)

There is also a maritime factor in the emergence of the makossa popular music of the southern Cameroons. Makossa began as a low-class palm wine guitar band music that surfaced in the 1940s and 1950s in the port town of Douala, where local ambass-bey street music was blended with Congolese maringa and West African ashiko by pioneering artists such as Eboa Lotin, Misse Ngoh, Mama Ohandja and Ebanda Manfred.

Ashiko itself was a popular urban music in late-nineteenth-century Freetown, and was played on goombay frame drums, musical saws, accordions and guitars by the town's Krio population. Around 1900, these Freetown Krios introduced ashiko to cities like Lagos and Cape Coast,[30] turning it into a pan–West African accordion/guitar music style.

According to Ajayi Thomas, in Lagos 'asiko' was particularly popular in the early 1900s with the city's Christianised Saro (Sierra Leonean) inhabitants.[31] Ashiko was also introduced to the Cameroons by West African seamen, where, by the 1940s, it was being played in Douala by local artists like Jean Aladin Bikoko and Uncle Joseph Medjo.

In Ghana, the Kru guitar and accordion songs and Krio ashiko music were introduced to the low-class dockside drinking bars in ports like Cape Coast by foreign sailors and stevedores. These in turn influenced the local recreational music styles of the Fanti people, such as kununku, akrodo, adenkum, densim and the fishermen's osibi music, which involved wrestling displays by young men.[32] In the very early 1900s, this cultural blending resulted in the osibisaaba, a Fanti guitar/accordion music that used claves and the 'adakam' box drum to supply 4/4 or 6/8 rhythms for a local type of ring dance. The earliest recording of this music took place in 1927/8 by Fanti musicians such as Roland C. Nathaniels, George William Aingo and Jacob Sam. In June 1928, Jacob Sam (Kwame Asare), a twenty-five year old guitarist, took his Kumasi Trio[33] to London to record thirty-six guitar songs for the Zonophone record company, including one of the most important highlifes ever composed: 'Yaa Amponsah'.[34]

During the 1930s Fanti osibisaaba music spread from the coast into the agricultural heartland of southern Ghana where the guitar gradually replaced the local Akan stringed 'seprewa' (or seperewa) harp-lute. However, as it did so, the guitar players absorbed the modal playing style of the seperewa.[35] This resulted in a guitar (and occasionally accordion) music style known as 'odonson' or 'Ashanti blues'. Like seprewa music, this indigenised guitar music was accompanied by proverbial lyrics and was played at both funerals and village spots that sold palm wine. Thus, it was from this time that this local acoustic guitar music also became known as 'palm wine music'.

Fanti osibisaaba group in 1928. Leader Kwame Asare (right) was taught guitar by a Kru (Kwaa Mensah, via BAPMAF)

Early West African Ballroom Dance Orchestras

Besides the brass band and guitar varieties of early Anglophone West African popular music, a third musical stream that became involved in the highlife story in the early 1900s arose in the context of the balls and concerts of the local African elites of Sierra Leone, Ghana and Nigeria. The Sierra Leonean musicologist Christian Dowu Horton mentions that the Sierra Leone Weekly Times newspaper was reporting Freetown light concerts, operettas and choral performances as far back as 1830.[36] Flemming Harrev speaks of a Krio 'Dignity Ball' in 1883 at the West African Hotel in Freetown and a 'Grand Concert' there in 1892, performed by students of local educational institutes.

Late-nineteenth-century Lagos also had ballroom dances, concerts and recitals by European-trained performers who largely belonged to the Saro and the Aguda elites. The Saro people were descendants of Yoruba 'recaptive' slaves who were settled by the British anti-slavery squadrons in Freetown, and had returned home to Nigeria from the 1830s. As early as the 1860s, these Saros were staging western-type concerts and theatre. By the early 1900s the Lagosian Saros had introduced ashiko music and an accompanying dance that resembled the foxtrot.

The Aguda people are the descendants of freed Brazilian slaves who settled in Lagos (as well as Porto Novo in Benin and Accra in Ghana) from the 1830s. They brought with them the carata fancy dress, elaborate calunga masquerades, the bonfin festival and the samba drum.[37] In the 1880s, the Aguda elite established a Brazilian Dramatic Society that put on a 'Grand Theatre' for Queen Victoria's birthday in 1888.[38] According to Ebun Clark (1979), these Lagos elites enjoyed black and white minstrel shows and patronised 'Native Air Operas', cantatas and oratorios that were precursors to the Yoruba travelling theatre (of Hubert Ogunde and others) that emerged after the Second World War.[39]

Ghana also had its elite functions and one of the earliest documented examples is the 'Magic Costume Ball and Concert' held at the Cape Coast Castle's Great Hall in 1903 for a mixed audience of local and European ballroom dancers.[40]

Whether in Cape Coast, Freetown or Lagos, the local elites seemed to have loved refined ballroom dancing, and as a result, a number of local dance orchestras were formed in the early 1900s. These orchestras were large symphonic-type ensembles that sometimes played European light classical pieces, but with a focus on ballroom dance music such as the waltz, polka, foxtrot, quickstep, rumba, ragtime, tango and samba. In the 1920s and 1930s Sierra Leone had several ballroom orchestras: Henry Smart's Triumph Orchestra, Collingwoode Williams and Lawrence Nicol's Dapa Jazz Band and David Christian Parker's Danvers Orchestra.[41] Nigeria had its own bands favoured by the local 'Oyinbo Dudu' (black Englishmen).[42] They included: the Nigerian Police band, the Lagos City Orchestra, the Chocolate Dandies (formed in 1927), the Triumph Club Dance Orchestra (formed by pianist Fela Sowande in 1932),[43] Ezekiel Akpata's Lisabi Mills Orchestra,[44] the Sunnyside Hotel Orchestra of Calabar and the Broderick Orchestra of Port Harcourt. Indeed the musicologist Tundi Vidal says there were twenty ballroom outfits operating in Nigeria during the 1920s to 1940s.[45]

In Ghana, the two earliest were the Excelsior Orchestra and the Jazz Kings, set up in Accra in 1914 and 1916 respectively. The music of these elite outfits came from sheet music and from listening to imported western records of ballroom music, ragtime and Negro spirituals.

The Exelsior Orchestra's surviving members, 1959. Frank Torto is in the middle, with a baton. ('The First Orchestra', *Ghanaian Daily Graphic*, 1 September 1974, p. 10)

The Emergence of Highlife

The name 'highlife' was coined in the 1920s in Ghana, when local dance orchestras began including an occasional popular tune or street song in their repertoires. One of the very first written references to local Ghanaian music being given such a name comes from the 5 September 1925 progamme of the Cape Coast Literary and Social Club's 'Grand Soiree' held at Hamilton Hall.[46] The music provided by the Rag-a-Jazzbo Orchestra included waltzes, one-steps, foxtrots, 'high life' and a local variety of blues.

It should be pointed out that highlifes played at elite functions seemed to have been an occasional novelty feature for the elite dance fans. As a small child in the 1930s, Frances Ademola recalled looking out from a window of her house, which overlooked the partially open-air courtyard of the Rodger Club, and seeing well-to-do Ghanaians doing sedate ballroom dancing. However, when the orchestra struck up a highlife, the whole dance floor would fill with animated dancers, waving handkerchiefs or doing a follow-the-leader 'la conga' dance and generally, as Ademola put it, 'letting their hair down'.[47]

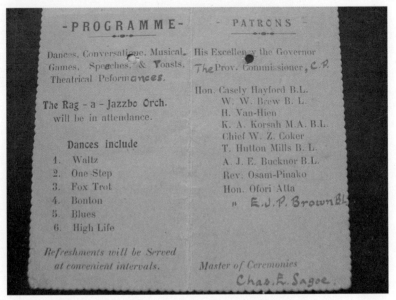

1925 Cape Coast Grande Soiree brochure, with the first known reference to the term 'highlife' (Cape Coast Archives via Nate Plageman)

Attah Annan Mensah observes that it 'was through the patronage of high-ranking merchants and other local elites enjoying the good life that the new musical type earned its name'.[48] Likewise, Ghanaba talks of the name 'highlife' being associated with 'middle-class Africans who wore tuxedos and played "the white man" for the night'.[49] However, according to Yebuah Mensah it was neither the well-to-do ballroom musicians nor their high-class clientele who actually coined the word 'highlife'. Rather, it was a catchword invented by the poor who gathered outside the exclusive clubs to enjoy a free show on the pavements outside.[50]

1. Bode Omojola, *Nigerian Art Music* (Nairobi: Institut Français Recherche en Afrique, 1995), as quoted in Godwin Sadoh, 'The Organ Works of Fela Sowande' (PhD dissertation, Louisiana State University, 2004), p. 22.

2. Chris Waterman, *Juju: A Social History and Ethnography of an African Popular Music* (Chicago: University of Chicago Press, 1990).

3. Omofolabo Ajayi-Soyinka, 'Calabar', in Carole Boyce Davies (ed.), *Encyclopedia of the African Diaspora,* (California: ABC-CLIO, 2008), p. 526.

4. Bayo Martins, interviewed by Wolfgang Bender in 'Bayo Martins: Voice of the Drum' (Lagos: Music Foundation Nigeria, 2004).

5. Christopher Fyfe, *A History of Sierra Leone*, (Oxford University Press, 1962), as referenced by Flemming Harrev, 'Goumbe and the Development of Krio Popular Music in Freetown, Sierra Leone', paper presented at the fourth International Conference of the IASPM, Accra, 12–19 August 1987, p. 6.

6. Naomi Ware, 'Popular Music and African Identity in Freetown Sierra Leone' in Bruno Nettle (ed.), *Eight Urban Musical Cultures,* (University of Illinois Press, 1978), p. 300.

7. David Kwee Bedell, personal communication, Monrovia, September 1984. Bedell told me that the Liberian variant of the quadrille involved a circle dance and that the music for it was supplied by guitar and accordion, two instruments that he played.

8. John Beecham, *Ashanti and the Gold Coast* (London, John Mason, 1841).

9. Festus B. Aboagye, *The Ghanaian Army* (Accra: Sedco Publishing, 1999).

10. The earliest recording of this old highlife tune was made in Lagos, 1942, by Akanabi Wright (Paul Oliver, 1990: 71).

11. Atta Annan Mensah, 'Highlife', unpublished manuscript (1969/70).

12. Dennis Kemp, *Nine Years at the Gold Coast* (Ghana: Macmillan, 1898), quoted in Robert Boonzajer Flaes and Fred Gales, unpublished manuscript, (1991), pp. 13 and 20, and f/n 20, 22 and 38. Also see Boonzajer Flaes, *Brass Unbound* (Royal Tropical Institute, 2000), p. 14 and f/n 23.

13. Letter from District Commissioner's Office, 16 March 1909, Ghana National Archives, no. 134e.

14. Chrys Kwesi Sackey, *Konkoma*, (Berlin: D. Reimer 1989).

15. Ibid.

16. K.N. Bame and A.M. Opuku, personal communication, 1970s. Both were teachers at the Institute of African Studies at the University of Ghana.

17. Sackey, *Konkoma*, 1989

18. Ibid.

19. Approximately 65,000 Ghanaians did military service during World War II (Fage, 1966), of which 42,000 Ghanaian servicemen fought in India and Burma as part of the 374,000-strong Royal West African Frontier Force. These figures are from Salm (2003: 66/7), referencing various Gold Coast Armed Services reports.

20. For more on the akyewa or 'aways', popular with the village youth of the 1940s and 1950s, see Opoku, (1966: 25). For the slightly later asaadua, see Nketia (1973: 66 ff).

21. This still-prevalent, Ewe, neo-traditional drum-dance was invented in 1950 in the town of Kpandu as a combination of the local akpase recreational dance with konkoma music (Collins, 1996: 101–3).

22. Segun Buckno, personal communication, Lagos, 21 December 1975. Ajayi Thomas (1992: 87), says the agidigbo was introduced to Lagos in the 1940s by palm wine tappers from the Yoruba town of Ila.

23. Both Waterman (1990: 84–5) and Alaja-Browne (1985: 65) say that konkoma was brought to Lagos by Ghanaian Ewe and Fanti migrants. Because of the Afro-Cuban influence, agidigbo was also known as 'mambo' music and Akinsanya and similar groups (like the Rosey Mambo Orchestra) began releasing records of this music on the local Jofabro label in 1952 (Waterman, 1990).

24. They also developed an early form of pidgin English and created the African-mermaid or 'Mammy Wata' cult.

25. It should be noted that this oppositional technique is also used with other African instruments, such as the thumb piano, in which the two thumbs play oppositionally.

26. These included 'Kru Towns' in Freetown, Sierra Leone; Accra and Takoradi in Ghana; Lagos (Tinubu Square) and Calabar in Nigeria; and Fernando Po (Bioku) in Equatorial Guinea.

27. Afolabi Alaja-Browne , 'Juju Music' (PhD dissertation, University of Pittsburgh, 1985). Afolabi Alaja-Brown, 'From "Ere E Faaji Ti O Paria" to "Ere E Faaji Alariwa"', paper presented at the fourth International Conference of IASPM, Accra, 12–19 August 1987. Waterman, *Juju: A Social History*, 1990. Chris Waterman, 'Juju: The Historical Development, Socio-economic Organisation and Communicative Functions of West Africa Popular Music' (PhD thesis, University of Illinois, 1986).

28. In 1908, the Belgian government confiscated their King's 'free state' for his cruel and counterproductive colonial policy and began developing a modern infrastructure of roads and railways for its mining industry.

29. Whether there is a link between Freetown maringa and that of the Congo is yet to be determined, but it is of interest to note that the Sierra Leonians were part of the group of West African coastmen who worked in Matadi and on the Congo River in the late nineteenth and early twentieth centuries.

30. Kwaa Mensah, interviewed in John Collins, *Music Makers of West Africa* (Washington, DC: Three Continents Press, 1985), p. 15. Waterman, *Juju: A Social History*, 1990, p. 39.

31. T. Ajayi Thomas, *History of Juju Music* (New York: The Orgnisation, 1992), p. 73.

32. Atta Annan Mensah, personal communication.
    Kwaa Mensah, personal communication.

33. The three young members were all coastal Fantis but were working in the inland town of Kumasi for the British Tarkwa Trading Company.

34. Released on the Zonophone 1000 series with H.E. Biney on second guitar and Kwah Kanta on percussion.

35. Akan melodies do not follow western I-IV-V chord progression but rather move between two centres, a full tone apart.

36. Christian Dowu Horton, 'History of Popular Bands', *African Popular Music*, 14 (1983), pp. 12–13.

37. Waterman, 'Juju: The Historical Development', 1986, p. 58.
    Alaja-Browne, 'From "Ere E Faaji Ti O Pariwo"', 1987, p. 3.
    Frank Aig-Imoukhuede, 'Contemporary Culture' in A.B. Aderibigbe (ed.), *Lagos: The Development of an African City* (Nigeria: Longman Nigeria, 1975), p. 213.

38. Michael J.C. Echeruo, 'Concert and Theatre in Late Nineteenth Century Lagos', *Nigeria Magazine*, 74 (September 1962), pp. 69–70. Echeruo mentions that some of the important Brazilian-Aguda concert names of the times were J.J. de Costa, J.A. Campos, L.G. Barboza and P.Z.S. lva.

39. Ebun Clark, *Hubert Ogunde* (Oxford University Press, 1979).

40. *Cape Coast Leader* 21 February 1903. Document donated to BAPMAF by Catherine Cole. Also see Catherine Cole 2001, pp. 64–6.

41. Horton, 'History of Popular Bands', 1983, pp. 12–13.
    Christain Dowu Horton, 'Popular Bands in Sierra Leone', *Black Perspectives in Music*, 12:2 (1984), pp. 183–192.
    Ware, 'Popular Music and African Identity', 1978, p. 300.

42. Waterman, 'Juju: The Historical Development', 1986.
    Waterman, *Juju: A Social History*, 1990.
    Atta Annan Mensah, 'Jazz: The Round Trip', *Jazz Research*, 3/4 (1971/2).
43. Acclaimed Nigerian art-music pianist/composer who also played jazz in Lagos and continued to do so when he went to the UK in 1935 to study music. He became a music director of the wartime Colonial Film Unit. He returned to Nigeria in in 1953 to become head of the music section of NBC, and then a professor at the University of Ibadan.
44. Waterman, 'Juju: The Historical Development', 1986. Waterman, *Juju: A Social History*, 1990.
45. Tunji Vidal, 'Africanism and Europeanism on Popular Music: West African Highlife Music and Culture in Retrospect', paper presented at the Jim Rex Lawson International Highlife Music Conference, University of Port Harcourt, 21–23 January 2015.
46. Document donated to J. Collins/BAPMAF archives by Nate Plageman in 2005.
47. Frances Ademola, owner of Loom Art Gallery, Accra, personal communication, 19 January 2009.
48. Atta Annan Mensah, 'Highlife', 1969/70.
49. Kofi Ghanaba, *Hey Baby! Dig Dat Happy Feelin'* (Self-published, 1995), pp. 27–8.
50. Yebuah Mensah, personal communication, July/August 1973.

2

Highlife Dance Bands and the
Early Independence Era

The Impact of World War II

The weakening of the colonial European powers following the Second World War of 1939–45 helped paved the way for independence movements in India and across Africa. Material resources from the Indian sub-continent and Africa became vital to the Allied war effort, as was the employment of tens of thousands of Indian and African soldiers. Around 375,000 Africans fought abroad. These included the Nigerian 'Boma Boys' as well as 42,000 Ghanaian servicemen who fought against the Japanese in India and Burma.[1] In fact, in Ghana, the trigger for independence was the famous 1948 march for backpay by ex-servicemen on the colonial administration at Christiansborg Castle in Accra. The protest resulted in several fatalities, the mass looting of European shops, and the British ulimately losing their colonial nerve.

The Second World War also had a big impact on the popular entertainment scene of many African countries. Servicemen returned home with new music and performance ideas and, more importantly, Allied troops who were stationed in some of these countries introduced their own homegrown music styles. During the war years, thousands of British and American troops were stationed in Ghana, Nigeria and Sierra Leone.[2] American swing and big band jazz was the favourite dance music of the Allied troops and, as a result, these servicemen brought with them swing-jazz records as well as the associated American slang, zoot-suit fashions, dark glasses and jitterbug and jive dances. A local nightclub scene opened up to cater for them, which led to local swing bands springing up in these countries.

Boma Boys in May, 1943. They were Royal West African Frontier Force Infantrymen who fought in Burma (UK Naval Historical Branch)

Allied troops drinking in a bar in Sierra Leone or Ghana, 1943 (www.flickr.com via Gbaku)

In Nigeria there were the Deluxe Swing Rascals, the Swing Rhythm Brothers, the Harlem Dynamites and Soji Lijadu's Chocolate Dandies, followed, just after the war, by Bobby Benson's Theatrical Party and the Sammy Akpabot Players. In Freetown, Sierra Leone, in the 1940s there was the Mayfair Dance Band, featuring the trombonist Boston Griffiths; Jacob Lewis's Cuban Swing Band;[3] and the Blue Rhythm Jazz Band, which specialised in swing music. There were also Ralph White's Melody Swingers, Charles Mann's Band and the Royal West Africa Frontier Force Band.[4]

The importance of Ghana to the war effort during the Second World War can be assessed from the fact that numerous Allied army camps were established in Accra, and that Achimota College in Accra was being prepared as a potential seat for an exiled British government, if Britain were invaded by Germany. Furthermore, American pre-fabricated planes were being assembled in Takoradi and, for a time, over a hundred American planes were stopping at Accra for refuelling every day.[5]

For entertainment, the Allied troops listened to swing records and numerous drinking bars sprang up to cater for them, often with American-sounding names such as the Weekend-in-Havana and Kit-Kat in Accra. Besides the availability of jazz and swing records, the foreign troops also brought in film shorts of Duke Ellington, Artie Shaw and Buddy Rich. Not content with records and film, some of the musically inclined Allied servicemen actually established swing bands that consisted of foreign soldiers and Ghanaian musicians who had passed through the local dance orchestras and could read music. The earliest of these bands was the Black and White Spots, set up in 1940 by a Scottish soldier known as Sergeant Jack Leopard, and which included the young E.T. Mensah (see

Chapter 3). After this band came the Tempos, formed in 1942 by an English engineer with two Ghanaians and some white army personnel.

Although both the wartime Black and White Spots and the Tempos were influenced by American big band jazz, these Ghanaian outfits were based on the smaller 'combo' size, due to problems of acquiring instruments and large numbers of trained musicians. Yet another, even smaller band that provided swing music for foreign wartime troops' army camps and local bars was the Fireworks Four, which consisted solely of Ghanaians, including the drummer Kofi Ghanaba (See Chapter 6).

When the foreign soldiers were demobilised these swing bands collapsed, except for the Tempos, which continued to operate with Ghanaian musicians. After E.T. Mensah took over the band's leadership in 1948, it went on to become the most important West African highlife dance group of the 1950s.

The Tempos

Besides successfully blending swing music with highlife, other important ingredients in the Tempos' repertoire were Trinidadian calypsos and Afro-Cuban music. Calypso melodies had been popular in Ghana from the late nineteenth century, when West Indian soldiers introduced the music. But the calypsos I speak of here are the later post–Second World War calypsos of Trinidadian musicians like Lord Kitchener, Lord Beginner and Lord Invader. Invader's song 'Rum and Coca-Cola' was popularised by the American Andrews Sisters' record in 1945,[6] triggering an international craze for this Caribbean music. Cuban music had also been popular in Ghana for many years – as far back as Don Azpiazu's international son-rumba record hit 'Peanut Vendor' first released by the American Victor Record Company in 1930.[7] It was then re-released in 1933 on the British HMV GV label that was aimed at the colonial West African and Indian markets.[8]

In the case of the Tempos, it was the introduction of Afro-Cuban instruments such as the congas and bongos that became important in the band's rise to stardom. As will be discussed in Chapter 6, it was Kofi Ghanaba who actually introduced Cuban drums. This was an important addition to the Tempos line-up as the pre-war dance orchestras did not use local African drums. The Afro-Cuban variety, in the form of instruments like the conga hand drums, helped pave the way for the introduction of almost identical local African hand drums in the 1950s and 1960s.[9]

The Tempos' successful post-war blend of swing and West Indian music with highlife became the model for scores of Ghanaian dance bands, like King Bruce's Black Beats, Tommy Grippman's Red Spots, Saka Acquaye's African Tones, Jerry Hansen's Ramblers, Sammy Obot's Broadway and Stan Plange's Uhuru.

Kwame Nkrumah at the Kit-Kat nightclub in the 1950s
(Ghana Information Service)

The Tempos also spread their brand of highlife to other West African countries such as Nigeria, which they first toured in 1951. They made another important innovation in the mid-fifties: by becoming the first Ghanaian dance band to put professional female singers such as Julie Okine on stage, as discussed in Chapter 5. And, as will be discussed in Chapter 4, E.T. Mensah and his Tempos were also staunch supporters of Kwame Nkrumah's Convention People's Party (CPP) that spearheaded Ghana's independence movement. The Tempos often played at CPP functions and released pro-Nkrumah records like 'Ghana Freedom Highlife' and 'Ghana Guinea Mali'. Many of the other bands that followed in the Tempos' wake, such as the Ramblers, Modernairies, Broadway and Uhuru, also released pro-Nkrumah songs.

One could say the Tempos' music became the zeitgeist for the early optimistic independence era in Ghana and elsewhere in Africa. For just as the Tempos successfully Africanised the western jazz combo ensemble, the inherited western Gold Coast sociopolitical system was also about to be Africanised.

The Spread of Ghanaian Highlife

I have mentioned the role of the Tempos in spreading highlife to Nigeria, but smaller waves of highlife had been sweeping into the country since as far back as the 1930s, with a countrywide tour by the Cape Coast Sugar Babies Orchestra and an influx of low-class Ghanaian konkoma highlife into western Nigeria.

According to Waterman (1986 & 1990)[10], by the late 1930s, Lagosian swing and ballroom dance orchestras, such as the Chocolate Dandies and Lagos City Orchestra, played the occasional highlife. Still, it was the Tempos that spread this Ghanaian music to Nigeria in a more substantial way through its extensive tours of the country from 1951. The

Tempos' up-to-date style of highlife, which brilliantly blended local music with swing-jazz and other contemporary western popular dance styles, really impressed Nigerian bandleaders, who mainly played imported swing, calypso, rumbas and ballroom music. They incorporated the Tempos' style of highlife into their repertoires. As in Ghana, this dance band style of highlife became associated with the Nigerian pre- and early post-independence era. Some of the key Nigerian highlife pioneers who were influenced by the Tempos' early fifties tours included Bobby Benson, Sammy Akpabot, E.C. Arinze, Victor Olaiya, Rex Lawson and the young Victor Uwaifo. Besides E.T. Mensah's influence, other Ghanaian highlife artists who made a significant impact on Nigerian music scene were the guitarists Stan Plange and Nat Buckle.

The Cape Coast Sugar Babies Orchestra (also known as the Cape Coast Light Orchestra) with fans in Enugu on their 1938 Nigerian tour (BAPMAF)

Not surprisingly, during the 1950s and 1960s Ghana became a Mecca for Nigerian highlife musicians. The trumpeter

Zeal Onyia and tenor saxist Babyface Paul Osamade were actually members of the Tempos in 1954, and for some months in 1952 Bobby Benson's band shared the same stage as the Tempos at the Weekend-in-Havana club in Accra. Moreover, the Broadway band in Takoradi as well as the Delta Dandies and Downbeats in Accra, were run by Nigerian bandleaders Sammy Obot, Jibril Isa and Bill Friday, respectively. Later, during the 1960s the young Fela Anikulapo Kuti often toured Ghana with his Koola Lobitos highlife band.

Victor Olaiya (middle, on trumpet) with his All Stars Band, 1960s
(BAPMAF)

By the early 1960s, highlife had come to dominate the local Nigerian dance band scene. However, everything changed with the 1967–70 Nigerian Civil War between the Yoruba and the Northerners of the Federal Government on one side and the eastern ethnic groups dominated by the Igbo, Efik and Ibibio of the oil-rich secessionist state known as Biafra on the other.[11] Because many of the top highlife bands in Yoruba-speaking western Nigeria had been run by eastern Nigerians (e.g. Rex Lawson, Raphael Amarabem, Sammy Akpabot, E.C. Arinze,

Bill Friday, Agu Norris, Enyang Henshaw, Eddy Okonta, Charles Iwegbue and Stephen Osita Osadebe), these bands broke up and their members had to return to their homelands. The only highlife dance bands left in the Lagos area were those of Bobby Benson, Victor Olaiya and Roy Chicago, who were Yoruba. Even Chicago's band collapsed when his musicians were drafted into army bands during the civil war. As a result of this highlife vacuum, Yoruba juju guitar band music came to dominate the western Nigerian popular music scene.

Despite the post–civil war demise of highlife in western Nigeria, it continued to be popular in the mid-west and eastern parts of the country, supplied by artists such as Victor Uwaifo, E.C. Arinze, Rex Lawson and the others who had relocated eastwards. In the Igbo-speaking east, however, there was a tendency to move away from the large dance band to the smaller highlife guitar band format that had already been established in the 1950s and 1960s by eastern Nigerian pioneers such as Okonkwo Adigwe, Israel Njemanze, Stephen Amechi, Stephen Osita Osadebe and Celestine Ukwu (as will be covered in Chapter 20). These musicians paved the way for the highlife guitar band explosion in southeastern Nigeria in the 1970s and 1980s led by the Seagulls, the Ikenga Super Stars of Africa, Oriental Brothers, Warrior, Oliver de Coque, Prince Nico Mbarga and many others.

Although I have mostly focused on the influence of Ghanaian highlife on Nigerian popular music, it also spread much further in West Africa. As I will discuss in Chapter 7, the Tempos played a crucial role in this. They usually played in the towns of Cotonou and Porto Novo in Benin Republic when en route to and from Nigeria. Their music influenced the young Beninese trumpeter Ignace De Souza, who is discussed in Chapter 13.

Ebenezer Calendar (middle, on guitar) and his Freetown Maringa
Group, late 1940s (Wolfgang Bender, sleeve notes to *Sierra Leone Music*
CD, 1987)

In October 1958, the Tempos went further afield on a
marathon five-month tour of West Africa that included Sierra
Leone, Guinea and Liberia. In Freetown, E.T. Mensah recalled
hearing local music that was similar to highlife music but with
a different name. What he heard was the maringa music of
the local Krio people, an offshoot of the local palm wine and
goombay music that had evolved in the late 1930s, and was
popularised after the Second World War by Ebenezer Calendar,
Ali Ganda, Famous Scrubbs, Chris During and Tejan-Se.

The most popular maringa musician was Ebenezer
Calendar,[12] whose Rokel River Boys released a string of hit
records in the 1950s and 1960s, like 'Double Decker Bus', 'River
Rockel' and 'Jollof Rice'. Another was 'Fire dey Come', which
was also a big hit in the Ghana of my youth in the early fifties.
The Sierra Leonean Krio musician Samuel Oju King comments
on this important figure:

Calendar originally played goombay and later formed his band, which was a brass band, with one goombay drum, two frame drums, guitars, flutes, recorders, trumpets and a sousaphone that you wrap around your body. By the time I quit Sierra Leone in 1967, he was a fairly old man and had stopped music and was made a producer on Radio Sierra Leone.[13]

By 1960, the influence of the Tempos resulted in highlife being played in Sierra Leone, as explained by Oju King:

Highlife was very popular, and we had a couple of groups that played this music. One was the Ticklers, which had saxes, trumpets, guitars and was patronised by middle-aged Sierra Leoneans. The Ticklers played highlifes, Latin numbers and meringues, which were a bit more polished than Calendar's. We also had the Female Police Orchestra, a big band with women vocalists, drummers, guitarists, sax and trumpet players.[14]

According to musicologist Christian Dowu Horton, the Female Police Band was led by Under-Superintendent of Police, Dowu Allen.[15] Other dance bands of the 1960s and early 1970s that played ballroom music, maringas and an occasional highlife were Chris During's Chris Na Case of the Sierra Leone Broadcasting Service and the Army Dance Band, under the directorship of Captain John Bangura.

On their 1958–9 tour, the Tempos also visited Monrovia, whose Americo-Liberian ruling elite had their own local dance called the 'quadrille', played on brass and guitar/accordion bands. Although E.T. Mensah saw first-class nightclubs in Monrovia that played swing and jazz on hi-fi amplifiers, he did not see any dance bands that played this music (although there was one local Liberian dance band – the Greenwood Singers). At the time, the local popular music of Monrovia was mainly supplied by palm wine bands like those of the guitarists Hanty Coleman and Tom Brown, and blind pianist Howard Hayes. E.T. would not have encountered these palm wine artists as they played at low-class bars rather than prestigious nightclubs.

At the time E.T. visited Liberia there were no recording studios in the country. However, by the 1960s and 1970s a number of studios such as Mr. Shaafi's ABC studio and Studio One were operating in Monrovia. Thus, it was only from this period that recordings of Liberian musicians began to appear. These included guitar band artists like Jones Dopoe, John Dweh, Morris Dorley (Sunset Boys), Sonny Halawanga and Jerome Paye (Music Makers), Robert Toe Emmanuel, 'Kruboy' Koffa and a rising generation of female singers such as Yatta Zoe, the Sherman Sisters, Fatu Gayflor, Hawa Daisy Moore, Christine Clinton and the internationally famous Miatta Fahnbulleh.[16]

Besides the Tempos, there were other Ghanaian dance bands in the fifties and sixties spreading highlife into West Africa through their tours. In the mid-fifties Dan Tackie's Havana Band took a trip to Monrovia and the Black Beats travelled to Lagos and Ibadan. Then, in 1959, the Koforidua Rockies went to Monrovia. Teddy Osei's Comets went to Nigeria to inaugurate the Ibadan television station around the same time. In 1960, the Stargazers toured Nigeria, Côte d'Ivoire , Togo and Burkina Faso. The same year Broadway played in Nigeria, Côte d'Ivoire, Togo and Mali. In the mid-sixties, the Ramblers travelled to Togo, Gambia and Sierra Leone. In 1968, the Uhuru big band and Kofi Ghanaba travelled even further, on a six-week East African tour sponsored by East Africa Airways.

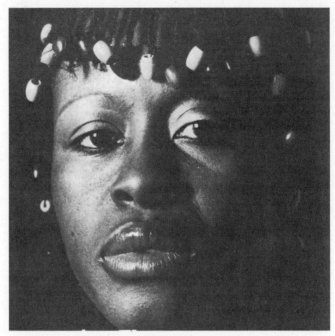

Miatta Fahnbulleh of Liberia (*West African Pop Roots* (1985) by John
Collins, p. 86)

In the following chapters, we will focus on the details
and life stories of the key pioneering highlife dance band
musicians of Ghana, Nigeria and Benin whose music provided
the soundtrack of the early independence era for many newly
emerging African nations.

---

1.   These Ghanaian servicemen were organised into six battalions according to Aboagye
     (1999). Two complete divisions of African infantry were involved in the East African
     Campaign against the Italians, who surrendered at Gondar in 1941. African troops also
     helped conquer Madagascar and were deployed in Burma to fight the Japanese.
2.   After Pearl Harbour in 1942.
3.   For the details of the Mayfair and Cuban Swing bands, see Christian Dowu Horton
     (1983, pp. 12–13).
4.   Naomi Ware, 'Popular Music and African Identity in Freetown Sierra Leone' in Bruno
     Nettle (ed.), *Eight Urban Musical Cultures*, (University of Illinois Press, 1978), p. 300.
5.   Wendell P. Holbrook, 'The Impact of the Second World War on the Gold Coast', (PhD
     dissertation, Princeton University, 1978), quoted in Steve Salm, 'The Bukom Boys' (PhD
     dissertation, University of Texas, 2003) p. 62.

6.   This was written by the Trinidadians Lord Invader and Lionel Belasco. The Andrews Sisters naively retained the lines commenting on the prostitution that accompanied the American wartime presence on the oil-rich Caribbean island. The lyrics state that the Americans 'gave them a better price' with 'both mother and daughter working for the Yankee dollar'.

7.   Scores of versions of this song were recorded over the years, including those by Louis Armstrong's New Cotton Club Orchestra in 1931, the London-based Edmundo Ros Rumba Band in the late 1930s, and Stan Kenton's American Cu-Bop band in late 1947.

8.   Ivor Miller, quoting the Senegalese scholar Garang Coulibaly, says that Afro-Cuban music may have been popular even earlier in Francophone Africa, as some recordings of the famous Septeto Habanero (formed in 1920, first recorded in 1925) were all the rage in Dakar during the 1920s. Personal communication with Miller, 2009.

9.   The shape and size of Afro-Cuban drums are similar to African ones, the main difference being that the imported ones use metal screws to tighten the drum-head, whilst the African ones use wooden pegs.

10. Chris Waterman, 'Juju: The Historical Development, Socio-economic Organisation and Communicative Functions of West Africa Popular Music' (PhD thesis, University of Illinois, 1986). Chris Waterman, *Juju: A Social History and Ethnography of an African Popular Music* (Chicago: University of Chicago Press, 1990).

11. The thee main contending groups were the southwestern Yoruba and peoples of the north, who allied themselves to fight the Igbo and other ethnic groups of the oil-rich east who tried, unsuccessfully, to break away from the Nigerian Federation to create a new country called 'Biafra'.

12. His father had been a ship's barber from Barbados.

13. Samuel Oju King, personal communication, 1970s. Oju King was the percussionist for the mid-sixties Echoes band in Freetown. In 1967 he relocated to Ghana, where I met and interviewed him in the mid-seventies.

14. Ibid.

15. Christian Dowu Horton, 'History of Popular Bands', *African Popular Music*, 14 (1983), pp. 12–13.

16. I was lucky enough to meet some of these performers, in September 1984, when the Ghanaian music producer Faisal Helwani invited me to interview the artists recording at his just-opened Studio 99 in Monrovia.

SECTION TWO:

Highlife Pioneers in Ghana and Nigeria

E.T. Mensah: Youthful Days and the Early Tempos

Emmanuel Tetteh Mensah was born on the 31 May 1919, in the Asare quarter of Ussher Town, Accra, where he and his six brothers and sisters lived with their mother in their maternal grandfather's house. His mother, Florence Adukwei Akwei, a cloth trader, had the main responsibility of bringing up the children. E.T.'s father, Robert Noi Mensah, was a goldsmith in Osu and a guitarist whose favourite song was the highlife 'Yaa Amponsah'. E.T. picked up some of his musical interests from him.

The house in which E.T. was brought up contained a number of ancestral shrines officiated by the head of the household, who fulfilled the function of the family's traditional priest or wulomo. Unfortunately for the musical members of the household (E.T. and his elder brother Yebuah), these shrines placed a taboo on whistling and playing music. It was believed that to break this ban would annoy the ancestors, who would appear as snakes in the house. However, this did not deter the musical brothers, who continued to pursue their interests despite beatings from the wulomo.

Both E.T. and Yebuah went to the old Government Elementary School in Jamestown where they met Joe Lamptey, popularly known as 'Agra', a young arts and crafts teacher who was also a keen sportsman and played with the local Standfast Eleven football team. In 1924, Lamptey formed a drum-and-fife band amongst the junior members of the school, later forming a school orchestra amongst the senior members. Both E.T. and Yebuah learned to read music and play the concert flute and piccolo in 'Teacher' Lamptey's junior fife band. The fife band was sixty–to–eighty–strong and would play marching songs at picnics, or lead street parades of children on important occasions such as Empire Day on 24 May. During this time they played side by side with the police band at the Old Polo Ground in central Accra.

Besides military music, the school orchestra also played local dance music and what was by then known as highlife. Highlife was, according to E.T., 'a music of free expression based on the native tunes picked from the streets'.[1] E.T.'s older brother, Yebuah, gives a fuller account of the origin of the term:

> The term highlife was created by people who gathered around the dancing clubs such as the Rodger Club, to watch and listen to the couples enjoying themselves. Highlife started as a catch-phrase for the indigenous songs played at these clubs by such early dance bands as the Jazz Kings, the Cape Coast Sugar Babies, the Sekondi Nanshamak and later the Accra Orchestra. The people outside called it the 'highlife' as they did not reach the class of the couples going inside, who not only had to pay a relatively high entrance fee of about 7s 6d, but also had to wear full evening dress, including top-hats, if they could afford it.[2]

Joe Lamptey himself belonged to a generation of Ga musicians who formed the Jazz Kings in 1916, one of the first Ghanaian dance orchestras. A teacher by profession, he loved music, especially marching songs. He could read music and played the clarinet. In 1924, he took out all his savings from the post office to buy flutes, piccolos and side drums for a school fife band. From 1927, he started building up the school orchestra by introducing new instruments such as brass, woodwind and strings. Two of Lamptey's contemporaries from the Jazz Kings, Briandt Ayiku and Frank Torto, came to him in 1933 to try and convince him to get older musicians into the orchestra. But Lamptey refused, telling them that he preferred teaching children. These two musicians were thus obliged to start their own band, which they called the City Orchestra.

The Accra Orchestra around 1930, with the uniformed Joe Lamptey sitting in the middle (BAPMAF, from E.T. Mensah)

The Accra Orchestra was formed out of Lamptey's school orchestra around 1930, although its official launching or 'outdooring' was not until 1932. It was at this time that E.T. managed to wangle his way into the orchestra as a 'gungadin' or general packer and carrier of instruments. In 1933, he became a fully-fledged member playing flute and piccolo, but only after considerable pressure on Lamptey from E.T.'s saxophone-playing brother, Yebuah. The Accra Orchestra itself was large and had a highly fluid membership. According to E.T., the orchestra 'was not limited in the number of players or the number of musical instruments – and players with any type of instrument were qualified to sit in with the band'.

Unlike the fife band of the junior school, which concentrated on marching music, the Accra Orchestra played a whole range of contemporary popular music: foxtrots, quicksteps, waltzes, one-steps, sambas, rumbas and, of course, highlifes. The orchestra played at a variety of different functions such as church picnics, charities and at both evening ballroom dances and the less formal 'flannel dances', where couples still had to wear jackets, ties, frock-dresses and other prestigious European attire. The orchestra also played at home soirees of the local elites such as those at Temple House in Jamestown, which was built by the Ghanaian lawyer Thomas Hutton-Mills.

The once-prestigious Temple House in Jamestown, Accra; a 1930s venue for the Accra Orchestra (John Collins)

The original Accra Orchestra finally broke up in 1936 when, after a week-long trip to the Volta Region, the young musicians grumbled that Lamptey had not paid them their full wages. Within a few months they formed the Accra Rhythmic Orchestra under the leadership of Yebuah Mensah. As a result,

45

the Accra Orchestra had to be reconstituted by Lamptey and in 1939 and it re-emerged with a batch of newly-trained ex-schoolboy musicians including Joe Kelly, Pop Hughes, Tommy Grippman, Okai Abossey and Moi Buckman.

In 1936, at the same time that E.T. left the Accra Orchestra, he finished elementary school and started attending the Accra High School. Whilst there, he joined the school orchestra and played at school functions such as Founder's Day. It was at his high school that E.T. began to play the organ, although he continued to play the alto sax with his older brother's Accra Rhythmic Orchestra.

Yebuah Mensah's Accra Rhythmic Orchestra in 1937 (BAPMAF)

Yebuah Mensah's orchestra differed from Lamptey's Accra Orchestra in several ways. It was smaller and did not contain a violin section. It was also the first dance band to use amplification and one of the first dance bands to use the plucked double bass. However, the music they played was similar to the Accra Orchestra: jazz, highlifes, waltzes, foxtrots and other popular western music of the time such as Joe Loss numbers, the Palais Glide and the Lambeth Walk. E.T. recalls some of the highlights of this band:

> During 1938 or 1939, the Rhythmic Orchestra won the Red Cross Dance Band Competition [The Lambeth Walk Competition] which was held at the King George V Memorial Hall – now Parliament House. The year 1939 was also notable for the earthquake, and during the fortnight of earth tremors our band conducted voluntary social work by playing every night free of charge, entertaining the homeless people who were encamped at various places in Accra.[3]

E.T. Mensah (right) and J.A. Mallet (left) of the Accra Rhythmic Orchestra in 1937 (BAPMAF)

By 1940, E.T. had obtained his School Certificate and enrolled at the School of Pharmacy at Korle Bu Teaching Hospital in Accra. This was also the year that problems began to arise in the Accra Rhythmic Orchestra over paying for the instruments, and so some of the members began to leave. E.T., however, continued to play in his brother's band while also joining the Black and White Spots created by Jack Leopard, a Scottish sergeant in the British army.

Leopard came to the Gold Coast in 1940 and prior to his army career he was a professional dance band saxophonist. Upon his arrival in Accra, he decided to form a band to entertain the soldiers. He recruited a number of musicians, and each one had to bring his own instrument. Because Sergeant Leopard's band was interracial he called it Leopard and His Black and White Spots. As E.T. explains, the international nature of the band helped the Ghanaian musicians to develop their musicianship: 'It was Sergeant Leopard who taught us the correct methods of intonation, vibrato, tonguing and breath control which contributed to place us above the average standard in the town.'

Although they sometimes played at private functions, the regular spots for Leopard's band were the European Club and army camps in Accra. As E.T. explains:

> We played from one army camp to another in the Accra district. Each of us got a pound after each engagement. Boy, oh, boy, that pound seemed a fortune to us in those days. For some years we had been playing in one of the other of the three orchestras in town, the Accra, Rhythmic and City. In these we used to get about two shillings for every engagement.[4]

The fact that they performed for a predominantly white audience was reflected in the music they played: jazz, swing and ballroom numbers, but very little highlife.

The presence of Allied army musicians stationed in

Accra during the Second World War not only resulted in swing becoming popular in Ghana but also had a more general impact on Accra nightlife, explained E.T.:

> When the Americans came it was the first time that I personally saw a whiteman holding a pick-axe and digging. Up to then it hadn't been natural to see a whiteman doing this. The Americans were building a bridge on the Korle Lagoon and when we went there we could see them digging and driving tractors. They usually came to town with wads of money, count so much of it and buy about two or three bottles of beer. When you wanted to give them the balance they would say 'keep the rubbish.' The whites, especially the Americans, often left their camps to patronise the local bars. Bars began to spring up during the war so that in any small corner there was a kiosk selling beer. They didn't mind sitting down at these bars from six at night to twelve midnight drinking, talking and listening to jazz and swing on the gramophone.[5]

In 1942 Jack Leopard was transferred, but the band continued for some time under the same name. An immediate result of Leopard's departure was that it was far more difficult for the band to get bookings at the army camps and the European Club. The Metropole Night Club and the Lisbon Hotel near the Airport Hotel became their new venues. The Black and White Spots finally broke up in 1944.

Once E.T. finished his pharmacy training in 1943, he was transferred the following year to Sandema, near Navrongo in northern Ghana, as a government pharmacist. In 1946, he was transferred south to Kumasi and while there he played for a band called the Philharmonic Orchestra. He returned to Accra in 1947 where he assisted his brother with the Accra Rhythmic Orchestra and then joined the Tempos, by then under the leadership of Joe Kelly. The Tempos had been in existence for some years and Adolf Doku, one of the first members, describes its formation:

> The Tempos band was formed by the late Arthur Leonard Harriman and me. Harriman was a good saxophone player having played with several European bands in Britain before coming out to West Africa. He met me at a private party where I was playing the piano and asked if I would allow him to play his saxophone with me at that party. Of course I agreed to his request and soon we were playing music to which the guests danced. After this we met several times and later we decided to include a drummer and trumpeter to the team. We drafted in two members from the Armed Forces who were in the Gold Coast at the time. It was in 1940 during the Second World War years and soon we started getting engagements to play at private parties only. Later on, however, the secretary of the then European Club in Accra approached us and engaged us to play at all mid-week dances, and also every Saturday.[6]

According to Horace Djoleto, an alto-sax player who joined the band at this time, there had been an all-white band resident at the club since the late 1930s called the Pop Hotshots. This band folded up and so the club needed a new one. Adolf Doku explains:

> It was at this juncture that I suggested the name Tempos for the band. The other members fell for this name, which we adopted thereafter. Harriman left the Gold Coast for

Britain on leave in the latter part of 1947, and in order to keep the band going, I drafted in an old friend named Joe Kelly, a brilliant musician who played the saxophone, clarinet and trumpet. He stood in fittingly for Harriman. However, on his return from leave, Harriman was posted to Takoradi. He induced me to resign from my work and join him at his new station. Of course, he was able to find me a job and we started a new band in Takoradi which we named the Takoradi Tempos. When leaving Accra for Takoradi, I left the Tempos in charge of Joe Kelly, who also brought in Messrs Guy Warren [Kofi Ghanaba] as drummer and E.T. Mensah as trumpeter.[7]

The final composition of the band under Joe Kelly in 1947 was as follows: Joe Kelly (tenor sax and vocals), E.T. Mensah (sax and trumpet), Guy Warren (drums and vocals), Pop Hughes (sax), James Bossman, and then Okai Abossey (double bass), Peter Johnson (guitar), Von Cofie and occasionally Therson Cofie (piano). The personnel of the band were now wholly African even though they still played mostly at the European Club (later known as the Accra Club).

By 1948, E.T. had resigned from government service and had started his own American pharmacy. This put an end to the continual transfers that had interfered with his musical career. The drugstore provided E.T. with both the premises for the band to practice and the money to buy his own instruments. It was also during this time that a money palaver developed between Joe Kelly and his musicians, which led to a reorganisation of the band. Guy Warren (later known as Kofi Ghanaba), took over leadership for a short while before E.T. became the leader. When Guy Warren and E.T. were running the Tempos, its line-up changed. The saxists Joe Kelly and Pop

Hughes were still with the group, but by then Serious Amarfio was on double bass, Baby Nelson on guitar and Dodds Schall on piano. In February of 1948, as E.T. explains, a disagreement at the European Accra Club led to Warren being banned from the premises:

> There was trouble between Guy Warren and a European. Guy fought the whiteman at the Club. He was the kind of guy who didn't like being bothered by any whiteman. He fought with the 'bigman' with the result that he wasn't allowed to play at the Accra Club. The band suffered through the loss of Guy, he was such a fantastic jazz drummer and to maintain him in the band we had to start playing more in different clubs.[8]

According to Warren, a Canadian had made a racial comment to him and so he beat him up. The band's new base became the Weekend-in-Havana and it was at this point that E.T. took over leadership of the band. He describes this venue:

> In those days nightclub life was unknown in the country. One of the first nightclubs which opened in Accra was the Weekend-In Havana. It was then a low, dingy bar. Its location in Jamestown made it a favourite hideout where the boys could retire in the evening after a hectic time. The late Mr. [Herbert] Morrison, the Nigerian proprietor of the place, had many ideas. He signed a gentleman's agreement with the Tempos to play every Friday evening. When we were underway we drew the crowds like Satchmo [Louis Armstrong]. Every Friday evening the Havana patrons came in hundreds to dance, to drink and cheer us. When I gave my solos they raved and shouted: 'Blow, E.T., blow'.

The girls would go out of their way to mop my forehead with dainty handkerchiefs. Our African crowds liked the jive numbers and the European fans loved the highlife.[9]

As will be discussed in more detail in Chapter 6, Guy Warren left the Tempos for a while in 1950 to spend nine months in the UK, playing Afro-Cuban music and working as a DJ for the BBC. On his return, he introduced calypso music and Afro-Cuban percussion instruments to the Tempos: two influences that enhanced the reputation of this pioneering highlife dance band.

The Tempos were becoming so popular that in 1951 E.T., Ghanaba, Joe Kelly and the rest of the band flew to Nigeria at the invitation of a society of Ghanaians in Lagos. They stayed there for one week, playing at two or three places before flying back. E.T. recalls that when they were there, highlife music was only really appreciated by the Ghanaians, since the Nigerians could not dance to it at that time. While in Lagos, E.T. met Bobby Benson, who was then the most popular Nigerian dance band musician, but he was only playing jazz and swing. It was shortly after their return from this trip that the Tempos split up.

Ghanaba left the Tempos with Joe Kelly, bassist Serious Amarfio, guitarist Baby Nelson and pianist Dodds Schall to form the Afro-Cubists or Cubans, that later in 1953, relocated to Liberia. After their departure from the Tempos, E.T. spent a year rearranging the band and recruiting new members such as Les Brown on guitar, Prince Bruce on drums, Tom Tom (Tom 'Thumb' Addo) on bongos and Tommy Grippman on trombone. For a time Saka Acquaye was on alto sax but soon left to form the Black Beats with King Bruce in 1952. E.T. recalls the Tempos at this time:

By this time the band had established a regular personnel. But because these players had not yet reached the level of proficiency to enable the band to play swing, jazz and the popular 'classicals' for which the old band was noted, I concentrated on the percussion instruments: the maracas, bongos, claves and congas. I changed the sound of the band and we specialised in South American rhythms, sambas, rumbas and mambos. Then came calypsos and plenty of highlife.

This caught on with our fans in a big way. The crowds were constantly crying for more of this new style. It became necessary to play throughout the week. The 'dough' was coming in and the boys were pleased with what they were making. The whole set of instruments were mine and I had managed to purchase two vans to cart the boys around. Our engagement fees were rising higher and higher as the public demand went up. Bookings were coming in from every corner of the country and the highest bidder got our prompt attention.[10]

In 1952, the Tempos, with the new line-up, were still based at the Weekend-in-Havana. That year Herbert Morrison, the club's owner, arranged for Bobby Benson and his Lagos-based Jam Session Orchestra to come to Ghana for a few weeks to play alongside the Tempos at the nightclub. At this time, Benson's band included the double-bassist Ajax Bukana (who stayed on in Ghana after the trip), trumpeter Zeal Onyia and saxophonist Babyface Paul Osamade.

It was also in 1952 that E.T. and his Tempos made their first recordings with Decca Records with songs such as 'Odofo Nuapa', 'Tie Ma Sem', 'Tea Samba', 'Shemi Ni Oya', 'You Call Me Roko' and also 'All For You', based on the old West Indian

'Sly Mongoose' melody. Consequently, it was from 1952 onwards that E.T. began to be acclaimed as the 'King of Highlife'.

E.T. Mensah (seated, middle) and the Tempos in 1952/3 (BAPMAF)

Despite their success, the Tempos split up yet again in 1953, just before a big Easter event. E.T. described it as 'the darkest hour of my musical career'. The split was caused by a disagreement between E.T. and Morrison, the club owner. Morrison wanted the Tempos to play only at his club during the weekends, while E.T. wanted to take outside engagements. So Morrison bought off the other Tempos musicians under Grippman and supplied them with instruments. Despite this sudden exodus of his musicians, E.T. explains how he managed to play:

The date had to be fulfilled. I was left alone with my trumpet and confused. The only chaps who clung on were Dan, Spike and Tom Tom. My secretary, Herbert Quartey, consented to play the congas and his girlfriend, Adelaide, agreed to shake the maracas. The engagement was at the Grand Hotel, Kumasi. I drove there in tears and managed to get local musicians to help me out, and somehow managed to get a group together. We spent the last three hours in intensive practice. The crucial moment came and I mounted the platform with wobbling knees. My heart sank.

We struck our signature tune 'Tiger Rag' and the crowd went hysterical. I played the trumpet as never before and the crowd kept on cheering and shouting for repeated encores. By some stroke of good fortune they didn't notice my drop in sound standard. My presence on the bandstand kept up their spirits until the end. A Lebanese named Shaffik, who promoted the dance, came up to extend his congratulations. He noticed tears running down my cheeks and was shocked by this and asked me what the matter was. I told him the whole story, but he waved this aside and said the band was great and wanted us to play the following night. He even offered us a few pounds extra and I took it and stayed on for the second engagement.

Even after the Tempos' successful Kumasi show with its rather impromptu line-up E.T.'s problems were still not over. He now had to reorganise and retrain his band with quality musicians. Furthermore, back in Accra, rumours were rife that the Tempos were finished. According to E.T., there were even posters announcing 'Tempos dissolved, Red Spots formed by Tommy Grippman'. Mr. Morrison of the Weekend-in-Havana was 'behind this sinister move'. When E.T. claimed his band was not yet dead Morrison threw down the gauntlet by requesting that the Tempos play at the Havana side by side with the Red

Spots. As E.T. describes:

> I said to myself that the boys who had deserted me must be
> after my blood. I had no band to match them, but the fans
> were excited and were all clamouring to see me compete
> with my old boys. I accepted the challenge. I drove through
> the length and breadth of the big towns in the country
> for artistes to help me save my good name. I got Tricky
> Johnson, the best guitarist then in the Western Region,
> and he agreed to help me. I approached Mr. Therson Cofie,
> an old pal from the Accra Orchestra days to back me up
> with the piano. I got Glen Cofie, a young boy fresh from
> school, to play trombone.
>
> On that memorable Friday, the Havana was packed
> full and even non-dancing fans turned up to watch the
> great competition. Throughout the whole morning of that
> day my boys and I practiced on some easy selections of
> calypsos, sambas, highlife and a few European numbers.
> We took our seats on the bandstand and as we waited I sat
> with my chin cupped in my hands. On my right were my
> old boys under a new name. We kicked off and declared the
> dance open with our old signature tune. We had so many
> repeats, and the crowd cheered so that at the end of the
> dance I had to keep sitting down on the stand out of sheer
> exhaustion. We had won the day and the other band was
> booed. But before the crowds dispersed I announced that I
> had finished playing at Havana and since April 1953, I have
> never set foot in the place.

The Tempos' line-up for the April 1953 Havana show became
the kernel of the Tempos for the next eighteen months when
the band settled at the Kit-Kat club. However, Therson Cofie

was replaced by Ray Ellis, whilst Tricky Johnson[11] was replaced by Bebop Aggrey. Julie Okine also joined up as vocalist. Finally, there came two Nigerian musicians from Bobby Benson's band: Babyface Paul Osamade on tenor sax and Zeal Onyia on trumpet.

With this line-up, a whole new series of recordings were made with Decca, including favourite hits like 'Saint Peter's Calypso', 'Nkebo Baaya' (I'll go with you), 'Donkey Calypso', 'Wiadzi' and 'Tro Va Phe'. The Tempos recordings were mainly sung in Ga and Fanti, but also included a few in Twi, Hausa, Ewe and pidgin English.

The band went professional in 1953 and, excluding the regimental and police bands, it was the only professional Ghanaian dance band at the time. Once or twice a year they travelled regularly to Nigeria, staying for up to three months on each visit. The band had become incredibly popular with Nigerians and was able to make more money there than at home. Indeed, their professional status depended on the revenue earned on these Nigerian tours and it was when they stopped touring there in the late fifties that the band reverted to its semi-professional status.

Towards the end of 1954, the Tempos split once again, leaving E.T. with only Dan Acquaye, Tom Tom Addo and Herbert Quartey. E.T. puts it this way:

Spike, Glen, Aggrey, Babyface Paul, Onyia and Ray Ellis left me to form the Rhythm Aces. It happened just after we returned from one of our Nigerian trips and like the previous split, came at a time when we had a big date coming up in Kumasi – the annual Revellers Dance. A Lebanese bigman wanted to invest in music so he bought some instruments and two cars just like my own [Morris Station-Wagons].

Even the colour was the same. He then bought my players off with the promise of fat salaries. Spike was made the leader. He [the Lebanese] also engaged one of my drivers who had been driving us around Nigeria and therefore knew all the tricks, such as where to take the Rhythm Aces and where to spend the nights. The audience could see the same musicians, only I was left out. The Lebanese did all this on purpose – same design car, same players – so that people who attended the dances would think the band was the Tempos.

So, in 1953, E.T. had to recruit new musicians. He brought in Amoo Dodo and Rex Ofosu Martey (alto saxes), Rich Kodjo (trombone), Dizzy Acquaye (guitar) and Joe Ransford (double bass). At about the same time, E.T. formed a second band called the Star Rockets, and Scorpion Mensah, a young guitarist who had just returned from England, became its leader.[12] These two bands, the Tempos and the Star Rockets (or Tempos No. 2), were represented by an umbrella organisation known as the E.T. Mensah Band Organisation. Thus, even when the Tempos were on their frequent trips to Nigeria, the other band could keep up engagements at home.

In 1955, E.T. made a three-month trip to England. He was accompanied by his girlfriend Christiana or 'Christie', a Ghanaian he had met earlier in the year whilst playing in the eastern Nigerian town of Calabar and who later became his first wife. On arriving in London, E.T. received help and hotel accommodation from the public relations officer at the Gold Coast High Commission, Mr. Addo-Ankrah, who later became the Ga chief, Nii Amposah II. E.T. managed to pack plenty of work into his short stay. He played in several clubs and performed as guest artist with the Chris Barber Jazz

Band at the Royal Festival Hall. He also featured in a BBC Commonwealth progamme playing 'Stardust', a UK hit at the time, and a Ghanaian highlife number. Whilst in London, E.T. was taken on a tour of both the Decca and the HMV studios. Although his contract with Decca prevented him from making any recordings with HMV, he did compose six highlife songs for them, including 'Happy Boy', 'My Sorrow' and 'Rolling Stone', which were recorded by a band called the West African Swing Stars. When E.T. left England, he stopped off one night in Abidjan, Côte d'Ivoire, and stayed with some Ghanaian friends with whom he arranged a short tour for the Tempos later that year.

While E.T. was in England, arrangements had been made for his two bands to become the resident bands at the Lido Night Club in Accra. However, an argument occurred between Dan Acquaye, who was standing in for E.T., and the proprietor of the club. Acquaye said 'the Lido manager supported the Star Rockets against us, so as to later entice them away.' By the time E.T. had returned, Scorpion Mensah and the Star Rockets had left en bloc. They became the Shambros, the resident band at the Lido owned by the Lebanese Shahim brothers, with Scorpion himself later moving on in 1957 to from his own Searchlites. As a result, E.T.'s Star Rockets band had to be reformed in 1955 under Rex Martey and Dan Tackie, though it still included the Tempos members Tom Tom Addo, Dan Acquaye and Herbert Thompson.

By 1956, E.T. had rented a club near the Central Post Office in Accra that had been known as Hyde Park and renamed it The Paramount Night Club, a name he had picked up from his English tour. He set up a resident band for it called the Paramount Stars led by Amoo Dodo. So, for a brief period, E.T. was running three professional bands simultaneously: his old

Tempos, the reformed Star Rockets and the Paramount Stars.

Unfortunately, in 1957 he had to sell The Paramount Club, but not before the famous jazz trumpeter Louis Armstrong, or 'Satchmo', came to play in Ghana and E.T. got to jam with him.

1. John Collins, *Music Makers of West Africa* (Washington, DC: Three Continents Press,1985), p.10.
2. I did interviews with Yebuah, E.T., and other members of the Tempos in 1973. They were later published in my book *E.T. Mensah: The King of Highlife*, published in 1986 and again in 1996.
3. E. J. Collins 1986. E.T. Mensah: The King of Highlife. London, Off The Record Press, p. 13.
4. Ibid, p.14.
5. Ibid
6. Ibid, p.15
7. Ibid
8. Ibid, p.16
9. Ibid, p.17
10. Ibid, p.18-95
11. Tricky Johnson went on to form his own band in his home town of Sekondi-Takoradi that included, at one point or another, the singer/tenor-saxist George Lee Larnyo and Mike Eghan, who went on to become a well known Ghanaian DJ.
12. He was taught guitar by Landeric Caton, the electric guitarist for Ken 'Snakehips' Johnson's West Indian Dance Orchestra, the first all-black swing band in Britain. On returning to Ghana in 1951, Scorpion spent three years with the resident band of the Wilbern Hotel Kumasi that included the young pianist Ray Ellis, before joining the Tempos.

4

Louis Armstrong and the Later Tempos

Louis Armstrong's First Ghanaian Trip

In 1956 the great African American jazz trumpeter Louis 'Satchmo' Armstrong brought jazz 'home' to Africa by playing in Ghana, then on the eve of its independence. Prime Minister Kwame Nkrumah had studied at an American college where he had become a jazz fan, and so facilitated the trip. Not surprisingly, Armstrong had a profound impact on Ghanaians and on highlife artists such as E.T. Mensah's Tempos in particular.

Armstrong's three-day visit took place in May 1956 and he was accompanied by his wife, Lucille, his All Stars band and the African American blues singer Velma Middleton. The trip was sponsored by the Columbia Broadcasting System (CBS) under the guidance of the American broadcaster Ed Murrow, who had made a feature film on Africa the previous year entitled *See it Now*. This film included shots of Accra, its nightlife and E.T. Mensah's club, the Paramount. Armstrong was already scheduled for a tour of Europe, which CBS studios was filming, and Murrow decided to lengthen it to include Accra and get Armstrong to jam with E.T.. The film, which included four weeks in Europe, the three days in Accra and Armstrong's return to America, was later released under the title *The Saga of Satchmo*.

Arrangements at the Accra end were in the hands of the British expatriate James 'Jimmy' Moxon, who was head of the Information Service and continued in this capacity even after Ghanaian independence in 1957.

The day before Armstrong's arrival, Moxon arranged for a meeting at his bungalow between E.T. Mensah and Gene de Poris, head of the CBS film crew. They had to decide what song they were going to use in the jam session, so Moxon pulled out his selection of Armstrong records and began to play them. One song was chosen and sheet music was given to E.T. and the few of his musicians who were present. De Poris asked them to play it even though the rhythm section was not present. As E.T. explains, this was no easy matter.

> They wanted us to play a song that we had never heard of at the time called 'St Louis Blues'. Unfortunately it wasn't the days when Guy and Joe were in, so they weren't very impressed with our playing.

James Moxon (wearing bowtie) standing behind the American photographer Willis Bell, the seated Nkrumah and his wife, Fatia
(Ghana Info Serv R-R-3075-17, via James Moxon)

The next day, 23 May, Louis, Lucille, Velma Middleton and the All Stars arrived. The All Stars were a five-piece band comprising Edmond Hall on clarinet, Trummy Young on trombone, Billy Kyle on piano, Barret Deems on drums and Jack Lesberg on double bass. A large group of local trumpeters, playing an old highlife tune 'All For You' were on hand to greet the band at the Accra Airport. When Louis, Edmond Hall and Trummy Young got off the plane they pulled out their instruments and joined in. The trumpeters fell in behind them and the whole group of musicians marched across the tarmac to the vehicles that were waiting for them. While the crowd had been waiting for the All Stars, they had been entertained by the Nigerian comedian Ajax Bukana, who worked for the Star Publishing Corporation in Accra and whom E.T. knew from his visits to Nigeria:

> He was originally a member of Bobby Benson's Band as a bass player and when he came here he liked the atmosphere and stayed. On any important occasion you see him dressed up as a clown, getting himself involved by making an unofficial floor-show. He even went to government functions in his peculiar dress. He was very well-known and could go almost anywhere freely. He paraded around that day and when the band arrived he joined us marching along with the trumpets.

The musicians were driven in a cavalcade from the airport to Accra, playing to the crowds lining the streets the whole time. Then Louis and the All Stars went straight to have lunch with Prime Minister Kwame Nkrumah.

Armstrong and the All Stars on arrival at Accra Airport in May 1956. On the left are E.T. Mensah and some Ghanaian musicians. The musical comedian Ajax Bukana is next to Armstrong, Trummy Young is on Armstrong's right, and Edmond Hall is on the extreme right (BAPMAF)

Armstrong, his wife, Lucille, and Nkrumah (1956 Ghanaian newspaper photo)

After meeting Nkrumah, Louis and the All Stars went to the Old Polo Ground to play at a free afternoon concert. By the time Louis and his band arrived, they were late and there was an enormous and restless crowd that the police estimated to be between 70,000 and 100,000 people. Unfortunately, the amplification was not very powerful and some of the speakers had been knocked over by the throng. When the band started playing, the crowd surged forward to hear better and broke through the police barrier to get close to the band. The police pushed the massed ranks back, flicking people's feet with the leather straps at the end of their truncheons, which was the normal method of crowd control in Ghana at the time. This happened several times and on each occasion Louis stopped playing in the mistaken belief that the police were truncheoning his audience in earnest.

The band played for about an hour and a half but, as E.T explains, the general impression of the music was poor:

> They were playing the sort of jazz that wasn't popular here then. Swing was popular but Dixieland was not. The crowd tried to listen to the music but the amplification wasn't so good and there was such a huge crowd that the music was drowned. The sound wasn't thick, the trumpet was pitched high so that the music was light and this wasn't popular with the African audience.

That evening the All Stars played with the Tempos at E.T.'s Paramount Club. Despite the expensive one-pound tickets, there was such a crowd inside that it caused problems for the film crew. Throughout the evening the dance floor got smaller and smaller as more tables and chairs were brought in. One small boy was even forced to dance on the roof. The Tempos opened the evening progamme and at about nine o'clock Louis Armstrong arrived. Dan Acquaye recalls that Edmond Hall was particularly impressed by the Tempos' rendering of 'A Stranger in Paradise'. Louis too, was impressed, as can be seen in this extract from the *Daily Graphic*:

> Mensah and his Tempos were certainly on top form when they played their signature tune, 'Tiger Rag'. This number nearly brought the house down. E.T. himself seems to have been inspired by the presence of the great Louis. His fingers moved over the valves of his silver trumpet to produce the best manipulation of this musical instrument by any West African trumpeter. Louis must have been surprised. He was moved. He was pleased. He went up to E.T. and shook hands with him.[1]

The All Stars then took the stage and started to play the 'St Louis Blues'. However, it was in a different key from the one the Tempos had practised in Moxon's house. Nonetheless, it took E.T. only a few moments to get the right key and shout it out to his musicians. E.T. was impressed by Louis's trumpet playing:

> Louis was a great player and when he was playing he put in all his energy, from his head to the tip of his toes. We could see everything quivering, sweating all round, saliva coming out and we could see that a portion of his lip had come out. I observed that if he wanted to play a note, he must force the note to come, come what may. So we could see him pitching high. He found my range and started above it so that his trumpet sounded like a clarinet. He was pitching high all the time and his lowest note was my top G. We jammed for about half an hour playing the 'St Louis Blues'. Then they left the stage and listened to us playing highlife. By then, the crowd was so huge that there was no chance of dancing. Afterwards, we talked to Louis; he liked our highlife as it was something he hadn't heard before. But it

was difficult to hear him talk as he was so choked up with his croaky throat.

On Thursday, the All Stars spent the day visiting schools, lunching at the University at Legon and being entertained at Achimota School by a display of cultural music and dancing. For the evening, a charity jazz concert had been arranged at the Opera Cinema. Tickets were three pounds each, and Kwame Nkrumah was there. The concert was compered by Beattie Casely-Hayford[2] and recorded by the Gold Coast Broadcasting Department. E.T. remembers the occasion vividly:

> When they started it was bad. The music was thin for us Africans and we wanted more rhythm, and so for about the first four numbers the audience would just look at them when they finished. The people did not know how to give heavy applause at the end of the music as it is done abroad, so the musicians were not getting that encouragement. Some of the audience was even going to sleep. It was Trummy Young, the trombonist, who saved the situation. He played reclining on his back using his legs to move the slide and got a huge applause for this. This raised the morale of the public and the musicians and from then on the people became interested. The show didn't close till midnight.

The next morning E.T. went to Moxon's to say goodbye to Louis and his band and stayed for lunch. E.T. had noticed that Louis was much thinner than his photographs suggested, and while eating, Louis explained that he was on a diet and was taking a special herb for weight loss. After lunch, everybody went to the airport to see the musicians off and as they left the Rakers Band broke into 'All For You', the same highlife song they had played to welcome Armstrong off the plane.

Although Armstrong only spent a few days in Accra, E.T. recalls that he made quite an impact on the local music scene:

> Before the advent of Louis Armstrong, people here didn't know that old people could be in the [popular dance band] music field. Musicians were always young men between the ages of twenty and thirty and old musicians weren't prominent. But when Louis came with the All-Stars we saw that some of them were old and we realised that music could carry on through one's life. We had thought that it was something we did as young men and then left it.

Another impact of Armstrong on Ghanaian musicians was that he introduced them to the New Orleans style of jazz, known in the 1950s as 'Dixieland' or 'traditional' jazz. Although jazz had been known in Ghana for some time it was more of the ragtime and later swing variety. As a result of the All Stars' visit, many Ghanaian trumpeters started using Armstrong's style of phrasing whilst local singers copied his gravelly voice. Some of the dance bands also began to play traditional jazz numbers and 'St Louis Blues' became part of the Tempos' repertoire.

E.T. also remembers that Louis and the All Stars were impressed by the standard of music in Ghana. Indeed, they liked the country so much that Armstrong expressed a wish to come back. According to the Australian Robert Raymond, a member of the Department of Information Services, Louis had seen a Ghanaian woman in the crowd at Achimota College who resembled his mother, which led him to believe that his ancestors came from Ghana.[3]

Although Armstrong didn't make it back to Ghana until

1960, clarinettist Edmond Hall did. He was so impressed by Ghana that he decided to relocate there. Hall and his wife, Winnie, left New York and moved to Ghana in October 1959 to form a band and open a music school in Accra, where they could give young local musicians an international training in jazz. However, as E.T. told me, Hall met problems.

> He came back to Accra and wanted to form a jazz band at the Ambassador Hotel. He got some local musicians together including one who had been with me for a time, Ray Ellis, a talented pianist. Ed went and bought instruments but he couldn't get the musicians to rehearse in the way he liked and therefore couldn't bring out the sound he wanted. He got fed up and went back to the States. The band was never even out-doored. The conditions are very terrible here for the musicians. In the United States or Britain, if you are a band-leader and you want to form a band, all you've got to do is to advertise and the musicians will come along with their own instruments. When you get an engagement, everybody brings their own instruments, so that task is easier there. But here, Ed could not understand why he should buy the instruments for the musicians to come and play – and then pay them, especially when the musicians needed more technical coaching to make them perfect.

Hall's dreams were dashed in just three months and on 7 December 1959 the Halls flew back to New York.

Independence and Nkrumah

On 5 March 1957, less than a year after Armstrong's visit, Ghana achieved full independence from Britain. E.T. remembers how his band played at a packed Lido nightclub to a jubilant audience to celebrate the event. The change of government, however, had some immediate negative effects on E.T. as a nightclub owner. First, the price of beer was suddenly raised by around 40 per cent, which cut deeply into E.T.'s profits. Second, the Nkrumah government introduced an entertainment tax. This meant that club owners and dance organisers had to estimate how many people would come to the event, then obtain official tickets from the Internal Revenue Service prior to the dance event, and pay the IRS one quarter of whatever the tickets would cost.

As a result, E.T. found it difficult to make his club economically viable, despite revenues from records and the Nigerian tours. One immediate consequence of these financial problems was that Dan Tackie and some of the members of the Star Rockets left E.T. in 1957 to form the Havana Dance Band, the resident group of the Weekend-in-Havana nightclub. E.T.'s Paramount Stars renamed themselves the Star Rockets to keep to E.T.'s original two-band format (Tempos and Star Rockets) to feed the public with a steady stream of ballroom music, Latin numbers, calypsos, swing, South American jives and, of course, highlifes. However, in the later part of 1957, E.T. was forced to sell his club, which was taken over by another proprietor and renamed Kyekyeku's.

Despite these problems, E.T. continued to be a staunch Nkrumah supporter and his Tempos still played at all of Nkrumah's Convention People's Party functions. From the mid-fifties to the early sixties the Tempos released a number of records in support of Nkrumah. One was 'General Election' in 1954 to encourage people to vote. Then came 'Kwame Nkrumah', sung by Dan Acquaye and, in 1961, 'Ghana, Guinea, Mali', which praised the attempt to create a 'great union' of these socialist West African countries for the 'redemption of Africa'.

However, his most famous political song was 'Ghana Freedom Highlife', which E.T. composed in 1957 to commemorate the country's independence. The lyrics, sung by Dan Acquaye, referred to the names of several prominent politicians who had, in some way, been connected with the independence struggle, including J.B. Danquah, Kofi Busia and Kwame Nkrumah.

James Moxon, who at that time was a government public relations officer, liked the song and gave it wide pre-publicity. However, one morning E.T. received a telephone call from one of the new government ministers, Krobo Edusei, who told E.T. that he had heard a pre-release copy of the song and wanted to see the bandleader in his office immediately. Not surprisingly, E.T. was excited, thinking that he was going to be commended, and so rushed through his breakfast and drove off to Government House.

But Krobo Edusei was in a boiling rage and told E.T. that Nkrumah was annoyed about the song, which linked him to Danquah and Busia, who were detractors of the government. He then went on to tell E.T. that he had to scrap the song altogether, or delete Nkrumah's name from the disc. By this stage, Edusei had got himself into a frantic state and was shouting loudly at E.T.. Then Edusei sent him on to another minister called Kofi Baako, who was a much quieter and more polite man. According to E.T., this minister told him that although he had done well to compose the song, Nkrumah was not pleased. He told E.T. that he had to remove the names of the other men or the government would be compelled to impose an embargo on the sale of the record. E.T. was then sent to Nkrumah himself, but when he arrived at the prime minister's office, E.B. Welbeck, the prime minister's secretary, told him that Nkrumah was so annoyed that he didn't even want to see the composer of the song.

Unfortunately, the song had been recorded in the Decca Studios in Accra and the master recording had already been sent to England for pressing. So, when E.T. left Government House, he went straight to the cable office and dispatched a long cablegram informing Decca of the situation. By this time over ten thousand records had already been pressed and packed, ready for shipment to Ghana. These all had to be destroyed and the Decca engineers went to work on the matrix to remove the names of Busia and Danquah. The new record, minus the offending names, was pressed and put onto the Ghanaian market.

Shortly after 'Ghana Freedom Highlife' was released, E.T. and the Tempos were invited to perform at a party in Nkrumah's New Town residence, where Nkrumah agreed to sponsor a UK trip for the band, and told E.T. to contact the minister of state, Kojo Botsio. A meeting was promptly arranged between E.T., Botsio and the Decca representative, Major Kinder, at the offices of the minister of state. It was agreed that Decca would look after the arrangements in Britain, such as accommodation and bookings, while the Ghanaian government would be responsible for the airfares, with the money coming from the Monuments Appeal Fund.

Although Decca had made all the necessary arrangements, weeks and months passed with nothing happening. Eventually E.T. rang Minister Botsio who was both a minister of state as well as chairman of the Monuments Appeal Fund. He informed E.T. that a sum of two thousand pounds had been allocated for the Tempos' tour in the UK. However, E.T. and the band had never received a penny as one of the other ministers had objected to the funds being used to finance a musical tour rather than a physical monument.

E.T. and his bandsmen had been preparing for months

for the trip and were bitterly disappointed by its cancellation. For E.T. it was an even greater blow, as it had been his life's ambition to take the band to England. However, since the tour had been widely advertised in the local press, he decided that the best thing to do was to organise a grand tour of West Africa himself. And this is how the idea for the four-month tour of Nigeria, Sierra Leone, Liberia and Guinea, described in Chapter 7, was born.

Another problem arose for the Tempos in the late fifties when the government started sponsoring its own dance bands:

> Besides the Army and Police bands, there were those connected with state-owned hotels, the Cocoa Marketing Board, the Black Star Line, the Workers' Brigade, the Builders' Brigade, the Farmers' Council and other agencies. The government could pay fixed salaries and most musicians wanted a regular wage. In fact, great competition quickly developed between the different wings of government, each one trying to outdo the other in producing a better band. As a result, E.T. lost many of his bandsmen. Dizzy Acquaye and Rex Ofusu joined the State Hotel Band; Dan Tackie and A.P. Mensah went to the Farmers' Band; whilst Glen Cofie joined the Builders' Brigade Band.[4]

E.T. was forced to dissolve his second band, the Star Rockets, and bring its remaining members into the Tempos. By 1962, he was in a difficult situation. Not only were his musicians constantly drifting away to state bands, but from 1958 he had discontinued his lucrative Nigerian trips due to pressure from some members of the newly-formed Nigerian Musicians' Union who wanted to promote their own nationals. So it was at this point that E.T. decided to go back into government service as a pharmacist and to run the Tempos on a part-time basis.

It was also at this time that Nkrumah, as part of his Africanisation policy, decided to try and change the term 'highlife' itself, to the older Fanti name 'osibisaaba'.[5] The move was ultimately unsuccessful. As E.T. himself noted: 'The new name never caught on as the name "highlife" had gone so deep that it couldn't be uprooted.'

One positive development was that Nkrumah encouraged the formation of music unions. E.T. had always considered a strong union to be a necessity in order to get higher royalties from recording companies. He also wanted to stop the perennial problem of nightclub owners wooing away musicians. E.T. explains in these edited extracts of a letter he sent to the *Daily Graphic* in October 1958 entitled 'The Need for a Musicians' Union':

A union of musicians is slightly different from a normal trade union. It is a union which comprises both employer and employee. Its organisation is complicated because it deals with different grades of musicians. There are professional musicians, and non-professionals. It will be entirely wrong to consider the professionals better than their non-professional colleagues. Some of our bandsmen have shown gross irresponsibility both to their leaders and to the bands that have trained them. There have been examples of bandsmen accepting outside contracts with their own bands, thus disappointing their colleagues and the public. Further, immediately a new band is formed, other bandsmen are attracted to leave their own bands overnight for the 'love of money'. There is a need to control bandsmen and check such acts. This is one of the reasons why all bandsmen should come together with the common aim of solving their problems.

By 1961, the climate was right for such a union, because by then more and more grievances had built up over the question of royalties from records. Later that year a meeting was called at the Accra Community Centre to work out the formation of the Ghana Musicians' Union. Most of Ghana's leading musicians turned up, and the proceedings were chaired by two CPP ministers. At the meeting a constitution was drafted, a chairman and a National Executive Council were elected, and a dance was planned in which seven of the top hands (including the Tempos) would play for free at the Community Centre to raise funds for the union. The first chairman was E.T. and the executive council included such names as King Bruce, Saka Acquaye, Guy Warren, Joe Kelly, Tommy Grippman and Philip Gbeho.

The aims of the union included a social-welfare benefit system for musicians, control and discipline of musicians, regulation of wages, fees from foreign artists playing in Ghana, and how to deal with copyright royalties. The union was able to make significant gains. At that time Decca had a recording studio in Accra, which was paying a two-pence royalty on each six-shilling record. The union was able to force this up to four pence per record. At its height, the union's membership reached about two thousand, with branches throughout the country. However, the union was affiliated with Ghana's Trade Union Congress, or TUC, and was dissolved in 1966 by the anti-Nkrumah military government because of its affiliation to the ruling party.

The Later Tempos

By the mid-sixties, with E.T. back in the pharmacy business and the Tempos having become a semi-professional outfit, the number of their engagements reduced. Moreover, except for a short trip to the University of Lagos and a few visits to Lomé in Togo, they had stopped travelling outside Ghana.

In 1967, Dan Acquaye decided to leave the Tempos to form the Planets Dance Band. Luckily, E.T. was able to reorganise the band with his son Nii-Noi Chris Mensah, who had developed sufficiently on the guitar, and another young musician called Bill Anobil, who had been learning the double bass:

> There was something good in this as Nii-Noi was, at that time, mostly interested in Congo music. By that time, Congo music was in fashion and he was very good at it. Dan and company couldn't play it so with Nii-Noi and his friends we became more flexible.

Another of E.T.'s sons, Edmund, joined them on trumpet. The band's guitarists were Kwao and Joe Bossman (who later joined the Black Berets army band) and its main vocalist was Jacob Awuletey who could sing in the Congolese Lingala language. E.T. was able to enlarge his repertoire to include Congo jazz (soukous) and imported pop music. But the difference in ages and in musical tastes led to problems between E.T. and his young musicians:

> The young boys in my band did not like to play waltzes, quicksteps, slow foxtrots and other Victor Sylvester–type numbers. They didn't like highlife much either. All they were interested in were Congo numbers and pop music. I nearly gave up my music because I was being compelled to play music that did not suit my taste, and to sit down with my own children and to be dominated by their taste in music was unbearable for me. I wanted to play both the old time music and the new as well.

With this youthful line-up the twelve-piece group left for a ten-week tour of the UK on 4 July 1969. Whilst in the UK, they played at the Battersea Town Hall, the Empire Hall, the Porchester Town Hall, the Police College, a West African Club in Manchester and numerous private parties. They also appeared on the *Top of the Pops* television show, played highlife on the African Service of the BBC and recorded an album at Decca studios called *The King of Highlife: African Rhythms*. Tempos vocalist Jacob 'Obi' Awuletey said, 'People really appreciated our music and everyone enjoyed the highlife. People were also surprised that Ghanaian musicians could play western music.'

The band finally returned home to Ghana on 28 October, the tour having lasted sixteen weeks instead of the planned ten. The extra six weeks were because the band became stranded in London, and had to be helped out by one of E.T.'s Ghanaian friends.

Back in Ghana, the Tempos were soon introducing their newest sound from the UK – Jamaican reggae. As Jacob 'Obi' Awuletey explains:

We played first at the Lab One Hotel and the Star Hotel for our welcoming dance. ... Before we went, we didn't know how to play it [reggae], but as we were playing to so many Jamaicans we had to learn it. We got to know some of the Jamaican musicians in London such as Desmond Decker. We felt that since we had been there, we should bring something new into Ghana. When we played at the Star Hotel some of our boys demonstrated the dance on stage. Although people had already begun to hear reggae on records, we were the first band to actually play it in Ghana.

In 1978, E.T. started to work with the Ghanaian-Lebanese music promoter and producer Faisal Helwani, who took him to Lagos to record an album on the Aphrodisiac label, a newly-created Nigerian offshoot of Decca Records run by Chief Moshood Kashimawo Olawale (M.K.O.) Abiola.

By the 1980s, E.T. was making only rare public appearances, and mostly with an All Stars band consisting of old Ghanaian highlife musicians. However, during the Christmas/New Year period of 1983–4, E.T. was invited to Nigeria to spend a month with his old friend Victor Olaiya, who wanted him to play at Olaiya's Papingo Club in Lagos and also record with him at the Polygram studio in Ikeja. This joint album of old E.T. and Olaiya hits was called *Highlife Giants of Africa* and was released in 1984 by Polygram. This was the last album E.T. Mensah made, though in the late 1980s, the British-based RetroAfrik Company released two CDs of old Tempos recordings remastered in digital form called *All For You* and *Day by Day*.

The All Stars Band of the Greater Accra Musicians' Welfare Association, playing at the Accra Arts Centre in November 1982. Line-up includes E.T. (wearing glasses, on sax), Tommy Grippman (seated, with trombone) and Jerry Hansen (saxist, right). ET.'s son Edmund is in army uniform on the extreme left (James Barnor)

Between 1980 and 1987 E.T. was president of the Musicians' Union of Ghana (MUSIGA, formed in 1974) and an executive member of the Ghana Musicians' Welfare Association, a mutual benefit club for older musicians linked to MUSIGA that also ran an All Stars band for veteran highlifers.

E.T. passed away in July 1996 after a long, incapacitating illness and was given a state funeral. He is musically survived by his sons, the most well known in Ghana being the trumpeter Edmund Narku Mensah, who began in his father's band.

1. *Daily Graphic*, 25 May 1956 (full reference unavailable)
2. Beattie Casely-Hayford was the son of the CPP Minister Archie Casely-Hayford and grandson of Sir Joseph Casely-Hayford, the famous early nationalist and Pan–Africanist writer and lawyer.
3. Raymond's 1960 book *Black Star in the Wind*, provides a detailed account of Armstrong's 1956 trip.
4. Trombonist Glen Cofie later led the Stargazers, which included a number of important musicians such as Eddie Quansah, Sol Amarfio, Teddy Osei, Pete Vanderpuie and Nat Buckle.
5. The old Fanti name for coastal guitar/accordion music, circa 1900, that combined traditional music features with maritime ones. At the time the word 'highlife' had not been coined.

5

Some Tempos Graduates

A large number of musicians passed through the Tempos band. As E.T. explains, two of the reasons for this perennial drift were the attitudes of some of his own bandsmen and the attitudes of leaders of competing bands:

> During the 1950s, if a boy finished elementary school, the only thing he could do was to become a messenger or clerk. But if a boy goes straight to music he is immediately put in the limelight, and so has to put on a fine appearance and meet high-up people and flashy girls. So [whereas] a messenger could only afford sandals, shorts and a shirt, the boy who had gone into music with me had to appear in fine shoes and be well dressed for his public. Also, he was better paid. He is automatically forced to lead a higher life, so he begins to demand more pay as his standard of living had changed. Consequently, if he found that there was an advertisement offering fabulous pay to musicians, naturally he would like to go. It's quite natural.

E.T.'s basic problem as a bandleader during the fifties and sixties was that he taught his musicians to such a high standard that they eventually left him, some going on to form their own bands. E.T.'s role in the Ghanaian music scene was like that of a teacher. Several musicians passed through his hands and he had a profound influence on dance band music in Ghana, Nigeria and other parts of West Africa. Some of the most famous artists who passed though the Tempos included Tommy Grippman, Julie Okine (one of Ghana's first female dance band performers), Dan Tackie (who ran a succession of highlife bands) and Kofi Ayivor (who went on to become involved with Afro-funk and Afro-rock musicians in the late sixties).

Tommy Grippman and the Red Spots

Tommy Grippman's Red Spots band recording at Decca Records, Accra, in 1952. Alex Brown is on guitar and Serious Amarfio is on double bass (Isaac Bruce Vanderpuie)

Alfred Adotei 'Tommy' Grippman was born in 1923 in Jamestown, Accra, and first became interested in music through the religious songs of the church that was attached to his Gold Coast Grammar School. His musical inclinations were further strengthened when he moved on to Government Senior Boy's School in Jamestown, where he was supervised by the school's famous music and sports teacher, Joe Lamptey.

After receiving his Middle School Certificate in 1939, he worked briefly as a bus conductor for the Gold Coast Omnibus Company, then joined the Gold Coast Regiment's Army Records Office. That year the young Grippman also joined

Lamptey's Accra Orchestra as a trombonist. As mentioned in an earlier chapter, this dance orchestra had been formed in 1930 and many Ghanaian highlife luminaries had passed through it, including E.T. and Yebuah Mensah. Grippman belonged to a later batch that included Joe Kelly, Pop Hughes and Moi Buckman. He continued playing with this orchestra after the war and in 1950 he helped tutor the trumpeter King Bruce with the imported stock arrangements of scored ballroom and jazz numbers that the Accra Orchestra played.

Grippman then joined the Tempos, which by that time was being led by E.T. Mensah. In 1953 when there was trouble between E.T. and Herbert Morrison, the Nigerian proprietor of Weekend-in-Havana club where the Tempos regularly played, Grippman left the Tempos and, with instruments bought by Morrison, formed the Red Spots as the Havana's resident band.

The Red Spots included former Tempos members Lex Brown, Serious Amarfio and S. Buckle. It became one of Ghana's top highlife dance bands and recorded many Fanti and Ga highlifes. In 1954, they released 'Essie Attah', 'Essie Mansah', 'Kumasi Aketesia Oriba' and 'Mipe Ntem Mekwo Kumasi', all on the Swiss UTC label. However, most of their hits of the 1950s and early 1960s such as, 'Alaba', 'Bra Me Jolly', 'Odo Handkerchief', 'Konkonsa Ni Bebere', 'Agyanka'[1] and the Nkrumah song 'Wu Onu Tsulu', were on records from the Decca label. They were also awarded a certificate by the Ministry of Social Welfare, for popularising highlife music. Between 1960 and 1966 Grippman was also an executive member of the Ghana Musicians' Union, which was affiliated with Nkrumah's Convention People's Party (CPP).

Whilst still playing with his band, Grippman earned a living by working at the Post Office, the Attorney General's Office and then the Stool Land Boundaries Settlement

Commission. He retired in 1978 and became a commissioner of oaths near Parliament House. During the 1980s, Grippman occasionally played with an All Stars band of veteran highlife musicians at venues such as the Arts Council. In the 1990s, he was active with MUSIGA and the affiliated Greater Accra Musicians Welfare Association of which he was chairman. He died in 2004 at eighty-one and left behind his wife, eleven children and thirty-nine grandchildren.

As the next section of this chapter focuses on Julie Okine, a graduate of the Tempos and a pioneering highlife singer and composer of the 1950s and early 1960s, the following is a brief discussion of the challenges women faced in trying to participate in popular music performances in Ghana and elsewhere in West Africa.

The Absence of Women in Early Highlife Music

Until the 1960s there were very few women in West African popular dance music. Both Ghanaian and Nigerian highlife were male-dominated with the few female musicians depicted as immoral and sexually loose.[2] Commenting on this situation, Aicha Kone, one of Côte d'Ivoire's top stars of the period, stated that 'not all families will accept a woman to be an artist and embrace her as a bride ... they think an artist cannot be a serious person, that she is never at home, traveling all the time'.[3]

The concert parties (highlife musical-drama groups) and highlife band practitioners' low regard for female performers is reflected in their reluctance to allow women to join their groups. Y.B. 'Opia' Bampoe, the leader of the Ghanaian Jaguar Jokers, a concert party group that operated from the 1950s to the 1970s, mentioned that when women approached him for jobs as actress-singers, he did not hire them. He explained that his female audience became annoyed at the idea that their husbands were admiring a real woman on stage, and since he did not want to displease them, Bampoe avoided employing women in his team.[4] For the pioneer concert party comic, Bob Johnson, 'a girl on stage would be branded as a girl without morals'.[5]

Vida Hynes (née Oparabea), who worked with concert parties as a teenager in the 1960s, says there was a similar reluctance to accept women into Okutieku's concert party. The band manager thought it would bring bad luck for the band, especially 'when females has menstruated and they touch band instruments – as the band may then not succeed,' states Hynes. She continues, 'a lot of men in Ghana think that if a female is having menstruation she should not cook dinner for her husband, nor should sleep with him just keep low.'[6] In the towns she played, Hynes encountered problems as she was often labeled 'ashao' (sex worker). The repulsion and anxiety around female performance was so great that Hynes's parents had her locked up in the police cells to prevent her from travelling with the Okutiekus concert party group.

Adelaide Buabeng, another female concert party artist, told me that in 1965, at the age of sixteen, she ran away from home to join the Worker's Brigade Concert Party.[7] Her family was unhappy with her career choice because she was part of the Akan royal family and they considered the concert profession unsuitable for a woman of her status. Her mother, however, supported Adelaide and each year gave a bottle of schnapps to the chief to allow her daughter to continue with her acting and singing career.

Although in many traditional African societies women were not forbidden to sing or dance, there were widespread taboos and restrictions on women's use of musical instruments.

For example, amongst the Akan of Ghana, women were not allowed to play horns and drums (except the donno pressure drum). They were, however, allowed to play light percussive instruments such as bamboo stamping tubes, adenkum gourds and rattles.[8] There is also a long tradition in African dramatic performance for female roles to be played by men. Examples can be found in the female impersonators associated with festivals like the Ga Homowo,[9] the indigenous theatre of the Mande people, and the Ibo 'okorakpo' theatre with its 'drag' parades.[10] However, women were not forbidden to play an active role in music making; rather there was a separation between the instruments that men and women played, although all danced and sang. Moreover, there were specific male genres related to warfare and hunting and female genres connected to funerals dirges and puberty rites.

The status of female artists was also exacerbated by issues arising from modernisation and the urbanisation process. These included the high ratio of urban male migrants (creating an increase in sex work), the influx of women into formal education and the introduction of individualistic sexual norms. Combined, these were seen as a threat to traditional male authority, which explains why popular texts so often dwell on the subject of sexual tension, marriage treachery, 'good-time' girls, witches and the 'duplicity' of city women.[11]

Another reason why female entertainers in African popular culture have been – and still are – belittled has to do with a general denigration of the entertainment profession itself. Entertainers were seen as leading a more itinerant life. They were assumed to be young 'drop-outs' and from the lower social classes. An association was also made between guitar playing, palm wine drinking and drunkenness.[12]

All of this was further compounded by imported, Western,

elitist attitudes that perceived 'popular' music as ephemeral, trivial and lowbrow. The combination of Western attitudes to popular music and traditional African attitudes towards women hindered women's participation in the production of popular music such as highlife. Despite the low participation of women in highlife, it should be noted that there were a handful of popular artists in the pre-1960 era. For instance, in Ghana, one of the earliest references to a female pioneer is in the 1929 Catalogue of Zonophone West African Records, which mentions the singer Akosia Bonsu, who accompanied George William Aingo's Fanti guitar and accordion osibisaaba (early highlife) recordings.

Kofi Ghanaba talks about Squire Addo's discovery in the late 1930s of Aku Tawia who had 'a voice like a nightingale'.[13] Addo, a Ga pianist, subsequently took Aku Tawia to London to record popular Ga songs, including one called 'Tiitaa Nmaa Wele' (Sweet Canary Write a Letter) for Zonophone. During the same period, the early Axim Trio concert party featured an actress called 'Lady Wilmot', but she was later replaced by the female impersonator E.K. Dadson when this group became a touring one. Except for Perpetual Hammond of Bob Vans' Ghana Trio concert party, female impersonators became the norm for the early itinerant concert parties that travelled the width and breadth of Ghana.

Likewise, in highlife dance bands in the 1950s there were just a few female names, such as the women who played with the Ghanaian Tempos and the later Rhythm Aces bands, as well as the Aikin Sisters, and Maud Meyer, who sang with Bobby Benson's band in Lagos.

The feminisation of highlife music only really took off post-independence with women being integrated into Nigerian and Ghanaian state bands, the rise of local television actresses and solo artists, the influence of foreign female pop stars and an influx of trained singers coming in from the gospel bands of the multiplying African separatist churches. But at this point we will turn to the E.T. Mensah's Tempos, the first Ghanaian dance band to employ females singers – the earliest being Julie Okine.

Julie Okine: Ladies Come on Stage

In 1953, the vocalist Juliana 'Julie' Ayeley Okine became the first female performer to join E.T. Mensah's Tempos as a full-time member. She was born in 1936 and began her singing career as a soprano in the Government Girls School in Accra. She then worked in a shop, where E.T. Mensah met her. She soon joined his band as a singer and maracas player. According to a DRUM magazine article, Julie Okine had a 'deep Eartha Kitt–like voice' and, according to E.T., she became a 'great attraction'.[14]

During her time with the Tempos, she went on Ghana-wide tours and made three highlife–calypso recordings. One of the favourites was 'Pretty Baby' and another, 'Nothing But a Man's Slave,'[15] could be considered Ghana's first feminist popular-music song. Below are some lyrics of the song:

VERSE: I went down town one Saturday night just for a bottle of beer,
I met a lovely Cape Coast boy looking so nice and sweet,
He stepped into a taxi-cab heading straight for me,
We went to a busy nightclub and he asked for table for two,
We went into a private saloon and he asked for gin-and-lime,
I searched into my breast pocket nothing was left for me.

CHORUS: He want to know my name, he wishes to know my game
If I died of a man's love, I'm nothing but a man's slave.

She also sang with the Builders' Brigade Band and in cabaret at the Coconut Grove Nightclub in Accra. Women rarely performed with popular dance bands due to a prevailing taboo of the times that labelled performing women as 'loose'. However, for Julie, there was little else she considered doing:

> A lot of girls have made a start, but they found they had to work too hard for the money. Then there are those that just make a few appearances just for the limelight. They usually disappear from show business with some charming beau even before they've learnt the key. You just can't last a minute unless you're mad about music. People in show business have got a terrific spirit ... I think I'd fade away and die if I had to do any other job.[16]

By 1961, Julie Okine was a busy person. Besides looking after a young daughter, she had a full daily music schedule, as explained by the DRUM reporter:

> Being a vocalist Julie will tell you, is very hard work, Julie's day never has an end or a beginning. At the wee small hours of 1:30 am she leaves the Accra's Coconut Grove nightclub, where she sings in cabaret. By 8:30 the same morning she is rigged-out in Builder's Brigade uniform and reporting for rehearsals with the Builders Brigade Band ... Said the Brigadier 'Julie's one of the boys – but she sings like an angel.'[17]

Julie Okine at the Coconut Grove in Accra in 1961 (*DRUM*, July 1961)

It is likely that E.T. was encouraged to include women in his band because he had been so influenced by American swing bands, many of which were being fronted by female superstars like Ethel Waters, Ella Fitzgerald, Sarah Vaughan and Lena Horne.

In fact, the Tempos had a number of female members including Agnes Aryitey, another singer/maracas player who played regularly with the Tempos at about the same time as Julie Okine. E.T.'s first wife, Christiana, also sang with the band.[18]

The Saxophonist Dan Tackie

Dan Tackie was born in Accra in 1937 and was exposed to music early, as his grandfather, D.W. Tackie, was an organist at the Freeman Anglican Church. Tackie attended the Adabraka

Methodist School from 1944 to 1951, where he learnt to play the flute. Around 1954 he was called in as saxophone player for E.T. Mensah's second band, the Star Rockets, led by guitarist Scorpion Mensah. Dan also played in E.T.'s third band the Paramount Stars, the resident band at the Paramount Club. Unfortunately, when the price of beer was suddenly raised in 1957, E.T. had to close his nightspot and disband the group. Luckily for Dan, his brother-in-law was running the Weekend-in-Havana club and invited Dan to form the Havana dance band with some other members of the Star Rockets.

The late Dan Tackie in 2001, when he played with Desmond Ababio's
Alpha Waves (BAPMAF)

Like the other highlife dance bands of the period, the Havana Band was considered a prestigious outfit in which the performers wore smart uniforms and the clientele had to attend in frocks and flannel suits.

In 2002, Dan spoke to Kwadwo Ofei about the status of highlife dance bands at the time:

> In those days it [playing] was done in style. It was a matter of class, especially in the fifties and early sixties. Performances like ours were meant for the comparatively high and middle class society. Both the musician and the audience were formally dressed and in conformity with decency. Commoners or the ordinary city-dweller dared not venture into the hall or club. If anything, they would stand at a reasonable distance from the outer wall and listen to the band perform under close police supervision, in case of any act of hooliganism.[19]

In 1957 the Havana Band travelled on tour to Côte d'Ivoire and Liberia and on returning home from Monrovia, Dan helped reorganise the Springboks Band. He was with this band for two years, and was subsequently invited to become the leader of the government's Farmers' Council Dance Band. It was while he was the leader of this band that he was injured in a bomb explosion meant for President Kwame Nkrumah at a CPP rally on 11 January 1963. As he narrated to Kwadwo Ofei:

> It took place at the Accra Sports Stadium when I led the Farmers' Dance Band on the occasion of a very important football match which was attended by President Kwame Nkrumah. The president had just sent for me and given me a handshake at the presidential dais – as a sign of appreciation of my band's performance. I had just returned to the bandstand and was cuing the band to strike our very last number when all of a sudden there was a loud bomb blast, followed by pandemonium. The bomb affected my

right ankle and I fell on the floor. I was just fortunate that a close friend, C.A. Quao, was around and transported me to the 37 Military Hospital. It was later found that the bomb was thrown by one Teiko Tagoe.[20]

This bomb attack occurred after a series of about ten other attempts on Nkrumah and the CPP that began in July 1961.[21] Until then, this type of assassination technique had been unknown in modern Ghana. It began after the country became a republic in 1960 and Nkrumah began to steer it towards a more socialist and 'non-aligned' path. As a result, Ghana was caught up in the machinations of the Cold War between the capitalist and communist superspowers. Capitalist agents were trying to remove him and, not surprisingly, Nkrumah became increasingly paranoid about the situation. As Dan goes on to explain, this negatively affected the country's nightlife:

It was around this time that Dr Kwame Nkrumah imposed a dusk-to-dawn curfew, and even though bands resorted to playing 'afternoon jumps' at the YMCA, Kit-Kat and Tiptoe nightclubs, these were not as effective as normal night-time performances.[22]

It took some months for Dan to recover from his injuries, but once he was well, he was invited to join another government parastatal band – the City Council Band, led by Joe Kelly. Whilst with them, he obtained a government scholarship to study in Cuba. Unfortunately, a few days before he was to leave, the anti-Nkrumah coup of 26 February 1966 took place and the scholarship was cancelled.

With the collapse of many governmental bands after the fall of Nkrumah, Dan was forced to look for employment with private bands. In 1966 he was invited to lead Nana Osei Poku's Caprice Band at the Caprice Hotel in North Accra. After this he went into semi-retirement, especially as it became increasingly difficult to operate live bands during the military regimes of the 1970s and 1980s. During the 1990s Dan had a comeback playing saxophone for Alpha Waves, the resident dance band at Bywels Club in Osu, Accra. Alpha Waves was set up in the 1990s by keyboard player Desmond Ababio, an ex-member of King Bruce's Black Beats. Their CD *Roko Party*, on which Tackie featured, was released in 2003.

The Percussionist Kofi Ayivor

Kofi Ayivor, highlife and Afro-fusion percussionist, Ewe master
drummer, in 1981 (BAPMAF)

Kofi Ayivor was born in 1939 and spent his first ten years in Gusau in Northern Nigeria, where his Ghanaian father worked. In 1949, his family returned to Denu, Ghana, on the border with Togo. It was here, in the Ewe region so famous for its cross-rhythmic percussion, that Kofi first started on drums. His uncle, Anthony 'Egle' Akakpo, was the master drummer of Denu and taught him forty or so local drumming styles. Kofi's father, who was a retailer, hated the idea of his son becoming a drummer and wanted him to be a doctor instead. But Kofi was so eager to play that he would walk a twenty-mile round trip to see top Ghanaian bands like the Black Beats and Tempos play in the neighbouring Togolese city of Lomé. As he told me in 1980, on these occasions, he would 'sometimes play the maracas, if the maracas player was in love with some girl and was gone'.

When he finished school in 1959, Kofi went to Accra, got a job as a lift operator and decided to try his luck by going to see E.T. Mensah at his pharmacy on Zion Street. As he explains:

> Fortunately E.T.'s wife, who is from Calabar, knew my father as she used to buy things from his shop. In fact, she started to cry and said my dad was a real human being and a beautiful person – always helping people. So she told E.T. he had to take me. So E.T. had to buy me some heavy clothes, for in those days musicians had to wear trousers, white shirts and bow-ties.[23]

Kofi consequently became the youngest member of the Tempos, playing bongos for them and being their 'gungadin' (packer). He toured the whole of West Africa with this band. In 1961, Kofi left the Tempos when he was offered a job as conga player by Tommy Grippman's Red Spots dance band and they gave him a chance to play solo. This was a busy time for Kofi as he was also playing with several other bands, including the Gagarin Band set up by the Ghana Trade Union Congress and named after the Russian cosmonaut Yuri Gagarin. He also teamed up with four Italian musicians who played Latin American music at cabaret spots in town. They got on so well that in 1963 the Italians decided to take the band home on tour, and asked Kofi to choose three more Ghanaian musicians to accompany them. The eight-piece band spent three months in Italy. Then they drove a car to Yugoslavia, Greece, Turkey and even Baghdad in Iraq. In fact, they got lost for a time in the desert on Christmas Day, but they got lucky as Kofi explained to me:

> By the grace of God we met one of these camel drivers. They can just look at the sun and tell us exactly which direction to go. So we got to Baghdad and played at the Ali-Baba Club. We were a big success, as Cuban music was popular there.[24]

Trouble eventually arose between the Italian and Ghanaian band members. The Italians already had trouble playing highlifes, but as Kofi explains, Turkish music completely floored them:

> Turkish music was in 6/8, 9/8, and 12/8 time but the Italians were unable to adjust to the new syncopation. Then Princess Amina, a Turkish dancer, joined the band. Yet, the Italians couldn't play for her – even after twelve days of practice. However, the Ghanaians were playing it within three minutes. This led to friction and the band scattered.

Kofi stayed with Princess Amina for four years and toured the Far East, Europe, and West Africa with her, finally parting company in Sweden. There, Kofi taught music and rhythm at the National Ballet School and, along with some West Indian friends, put together a band called the Modern Sounds which toured all over Scandinavia. In 1973, after a jam session in Oslo, he was invited to join the Osibisa Afrorock band whose leaders, Teddy Osei, Mac Tontoh and Sol Amarfio he knew well from Ghana. He recorded on four of their albums and wrote the two songs 'Somaja' and 'Kilele'. Kofi was also involved with the *Che Che Kule* album produced in 1977 by the Ghanaian highlife trumpeter Eddie Quansah for Island Records.

In 1980, Kofi and his wife moved to the Netherlands. Two years later, he collaborated on an album with Angelique Kidjo of Benin. Then between 1987 and 2000 he started drumming classes for children in schools and gave drumming lessons at Amsterdam's Royal Tropical Institute. In 2004, on the Dutch Otrabanda label, he released the *Rhythmology* CD that encompasses his vast musical range: traditional African drumming, big band highlife, Middle Eastern music, jazz, Afro-rock and funk.

---

1. This song featured the singer Jos Aikins and the British pianist Robert Sprigge..
2. Mosunmola A. Omibiye-Obidike, 'Women in Popular Music in Nigeria', paper presented at the fourth International Conference of IASPM, Accra, 12–19 August 1987, pp. 4 and 25–6).
3. Aicha Kone, quoted in John Collins, *West African Pop Roots* (Philadelphia: Temple University Press, 1992), p. 237.
4. Opia Y.B. Bampoe, personal communication, 1974.
5. Efua Sutherland, *The Original Bob* (Accra: Anowuo Educational Publications, 1970), p. 15.
6. John Collins, *Highlife Time*, (Ghana: Anansesem Press, 1996), p. 182.
7. Adelaide Buabeng, personal communication, May 1991.
8. J.H.K. Nketia, 'The Instrumental Resources of African Music', *Papers in African Studies*, 3 (1968), 1–23.
9. Evan M. Zuesse, *Ritual Cosmos* (Ohio University Press, 1979), p. 116.
10. Ruth Finnegan, *Oral Literature in Africa* (Oxford University Press, 1970), pp. 500–517. Simon Ottenberg, 'The Analysis of an African Play', *Institute of African Studies Research Review*, 7:5 (1971).
11. Yankah Kwesi, 'The Akan Highlife Song: A Medium for Cultural Reflection or Deflection?', *Research in African Literatures*, 15:4, (Winter 1984), 568-582. Waterman, 'Juju: The Historical Development, Socio-economic Organisation and Communicative Functions of West Africa Popular Music', (PhD thesis, University of Illinois, 1986), p. 135.
12. See Akyeampong (1996) for a discussion on drink and youth in colonial Ghana.
13. Kofi Ghanaba, unpublished manuscript, 1975.

14. 'Ghana's Sweetest Singer' *DRUM*, July 1961, pp. 16–17.
15. Released on Decca (WA 808) around 1957/8.
16. 'Ghana's Sweetest Singer', 1961, pp. 16–17.
17. Ibid.
18. African American female swing stars also provided role models for aspiring African dance-band singers in other African countries. For instance, the Zimbabwean singer Dorothy Mazuka, whose career began in the late 1930s 'specialised in African versions of American jazz favourites' (Makwenda 1990: 5–6), whilst South Africa's famous Miriam Makeba began singing with the local swing and close harmony group the Manhattan Brothers in 1952. Likewise, in Nigeria, Bobby Benson's swing-influenced Modern Theatrical Group (see Chapter 8) featured his British–West Indian wife Cassandra, the Aikin Sisters singing group and even, at one point, female saxophone and trumpet players. In the case of Ghana a further stimulus to the feminising of dance band music may have been the two trips of Louis Armstrong in 1956 and 1960, which featured the blues singer Velma Middleton.
19. Dan Tackie, quoted in Kwadwo Ofei, 'Long Essay' (University of Ghana, 2002). Ofei was one of my University of Ghana music department students.
20. Ibid.
21. The most serious, when Nkrumah was actually injured, occurred on 1 August 1962 in the northern Ghanaian town of Kulungungu, when he was returning from Burkina Faso and was offered a bouquet of flowers by an innocent schoolgirl. There was a bomb hidden inside the bouquet.
22. Ofei, 'Long Essay' 2002.
23. Collins, *Highlife Time,* p. 83.
24. Ibid. p. 84.

6

Guy Warren/Kofi Ghanaba: The Accra Orchestra and the Tempos

The musical career of Ghanaian percussionist Kofi Ghanaba (Guy Warren), who died aged eighty-five in 2008, spans both highlife and jazz, as he was a key member of the Tempos and later developed his own unique Afro-jazz style.

Ghanaba's Youth and Early Musical Influences

Kofi Ghanaba was born on 4 May 1923 in Accra. His birth name was Gamaliel Kpakpo Akwei, to which his father, a lawyer and headmaster of a local school, added 'Warren' after the then president of the United States, Warren Gamaliel Harding. The young Warren later added the nickname 'Guy' and then, in 1974, changed his name to Kofi Ghanaba.

According to Ghanaba, his mother's father was a Scottish mining engineer who had worked in the Kyibi and Akim Abuakwa area of Ghana's Eastern Region[1]. Kofi Ghanaba was brought up in a prosperous Ga family and so was influenced by many different local and foreign music styles. He attended the Government Elementary Boys School in Jamestown with its famous Accra Orchestra led by Joe Lamptey. Ghanaba was also exposed to traditional music as his mother lived near the Zongo quarter of Accra, a neighbourhood of Muslims from northern Ghana. The young Ghanaba saw Hausa people playing calabashes, odonno squeeze drums, rattles and flutes:

> In the house where I lived, there were some Ewe people, a very musical tribe and every Saturday night they would

hold a traditional drum-session. We also used to have masquerade parades in Accra every Christmas and everybody would dance a sort of poor quadrille to the sound of a bass-drum, flute and pati [a local side drum].

Another early musical impression came from the Empire Day marches and parades held every 24 May, which featured the Jamestown Salvation Army's band. Ghanaba, in an unpublished autobiography that he wrote in 1975, recalls that this marching group consisted of snare drums, big bass drums, tambourines, shakers, euphoniums and a preacher who played trumpet. Ghanaba also saw the brass bands that paraded around town advertising local cinemas such as Bartholomew's and Alfred Ocansey's Palladium, where he watched films that included American ragtime, jazz and tap-dancing acts.

In my August 1973 interview with him, he told me that he was also exposed to jazz by hanging around bars that played this type of music:

We lived in downtown Accra where they had this Gold Coast Bar that catered to seamen, prostitutes and pimps. They had a combo there and every night they would play and we would hear them from where we were [living]. They played ragtime and I learned to tap-dance. There was this great drummer who died called Harry Dodoo, a jazz drummer and comedian who used to juggle with the sticks and joke around, just like a little Baby Dodds. Harry was my hero and I used to go to the bar and watch him play and dance. When I was young it was jazz that dominated me. I was naïve and thought that was the thing.[2]

The Gold Coast Bar was near Bartholomew's Cinema on the

Accra High Street in Jamestown. It had swing doors and was the haunt of American and British merchant marines 'who had come into Accra for fun from ships anchored from offshore' (Ghanaba, 1995).[3] The small local jazz band there played popular American songs like 'Tiger Rag', 'St Louis Blues', 'Yesterday's Kisses' and 'You'll Never Miss the Water till the Well Runs Dry'. Dances included Charlestons, the black bottom and tap-dancing by Harry Dodds, the band's trap-drummer.

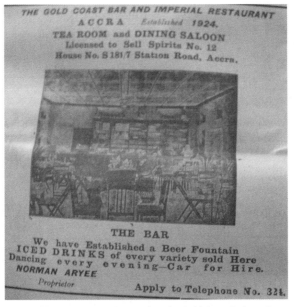

The Gold Coast Bar, as advertised in the *Gold Coast Independent*, 2 January 1932 (Nate Plageman)

The young Ghanaba was also a choirboy at Holy Trinity Church. He would accompany his family to watch the prestigious dance orchestras that played at the huge Easter picnics held annually in Mamprobi, in a field that was then on the outskirts of Accra. In 1939, after completing his elementary education, Ghanaba went to the Odorgonno Secondary School, where he joined the Accra Rhythmic Orchestra, his very first band, as a support trap-drummer. The orchestra was led by the clarinettist Yebuah Mensah. This fifiteen- to twenty-member dance orchestra had been formed in 1936 as a breakaway from Joe Lamptey's Accra Orchestra and it played a cross-section of ballroom styles: foxtrots, tangos, waltzes, ragtimes and occasional highlifes. Among its members were the young E.T. Mensah, and Clifford Quaye whom Ghanaba described in a 1996 letter as 'the greatest Ghanaian trumpeter of them all'.[4]

In 1941, at the age of eighteen, Ghanaba won a teacher's training scholarship to the prestigious Achimota College in Accra, where he met the composer Ephraim Amu. Amu is considered to be the father of Ghanaian art-music and composed scores of vernacular choral works and nationalist anthems, including during the 1920s 'Yen Ara Asase Ni' (This Land Is Ours) that has become Ghana's second National Anthem. Despite its excellent teachers, however, Ghanaba never completed his course and dropped out of Achimota in 1943 because he disliked the 'stern discipline which attempted to change me into an Englishman'.[5]

The American Influence

Fortunately for Ghanaba, at the very time he was rejecting his 'Englishness' the Americans were providing him with a new role model. Following the bombing of Pearl Harbour in 1942, large numbers of American GIs came to Ghana to join the British Allied forces. These soldiers brought American jazz records and films to the big cities. Ghanaba and his friends had access to a gramophone through Joe Kelly's father, who had a collection of ragtime and Negro-spiritual records in the house, and Ghanaba began to call himself by the American nickname 'Guy'. The songs the youngsters liked were the new wartime jazz-swing numbers by artists like Benny Goodman, Count Basie, Jimmie Lunceford, Glenn Miller and Lester Young. Also popular with them were the British jazz records of Jack Hylton, Billy Cotton[6], Harry Roy, Geraldo,[7] Bert Ambrose[8] and Jack Payne. Later Ghanaba got his own Victrola gramophone and a record of clarinettist Artie Shaw's *Non-Stop Flight* from a British army captain. Through American musical films called 'shorts' the Ghanaian youngsters were also able to watch as well as listen to other American artists, such as Artie Shaw and Buddy Rich playing 'Deep Purple', Duke Ellington with the tap-dancing Nicholas Brothers, Al Jolson in the film *Sonny Boy* and Harry Roy in *Everything is Rhythm*.

Swing music became so popular that in 1942, Ghanaba decided to form a small band called the Fireworks Four with his friends Joe Kelly (sax), Von Cofie[9] (accordion/piano) and Eddie Stanley Yebuah (guitar). This quartet played at army camps and a 'wild bar for American army boys' on the Accra High Street known as the 'Bucket of Blood' or 'B.O.B.'. Sometimes the Fireworks Four were accompanied there by the Ghanaian jazz singer Dinah Attah.

After Ghanaba left Achimota College only two years into his course, his furious father kicked him out of the house. Then he went briefly to Nigeria where he met Majekodunmi, the foremost jazz pianist in Lagos. On returning to Accra, Ghanaba enlisted in the American Army's Office for Strategic Services (OSS), the wartime precursor of the CIA. In 1943 he got his heart's desire to go to the States, the home of jazz. Whilst there he studied journalism at the Wabash School of Broadcasting in Chicago and learned the art of DJ'ing. He also played in New York's Greenwich Village with the jazz trombonist Miff Mole who was playing with Benny Goodman's swing band.[10]

On returning home that year, Ghanaba re-established

the Fireworks Four and began working as a crime reporter with a series of nationalist Ghanaian newspapers, such as the *Spectator Daily*, the *Gold Coast Independent* and the *Cape Coast Star of West Africa*. In 1944, Ghanaba became a DJ and the first jazz critic for the Gold Coast Broadcasting Service (previously the wartime Radio ZOY). This placed him in a good position to be an American intelligence agent. In 2005, Ghanaba told his daughter, Mawuko, that he was an undercover agent for the US army and his Area Commander was Captain Diamond.[11] Ghanaba gathered information from the bars he frequented about who was trafficking in contraband, who was a homosexual, who was frequenting prostitutes and other possible security risks.

Ghanaba Joins the Tempos

In 1947 Ghanaba was invited by Joe Kelly to join the seven-man Tempos band. As mentioned in Chapter 3 it was formed in 1942 by the English engineer Arthur Leonard Harriman (drums and saxophone), the Ghanaians Adolf Doku and Horace Djoleto, as well as some white army personnel who later left the country in 1945/6.

Although the Tempos band was much more to Ghanaba's liking than the earlier colonial dance orchestras, his main interest was jazz, not highlife. As E.T. Mensah once told me, whenever the Tempos played waltzes, foxtrots and highlifes, Ghanaba would play his trap drums half-heartedly with only one hand, but as soon as it came to a hot jazz number he would play full pelt.

At that time, Ghanaba was a total Americophile and even developed a perfect American accent. Many people thought he was African American. This misperception caused him trouble when, in February 1948, the Tempos were playing one of their regular gigs at the European Club in Accra:

> During the intermission I went over to see a white guy who, like myself, was in publishing. This guy's Canadian friend said, 'What's an American nigger doing here?' He thought I was an American and I thought he was one. He pushed me and I nearly saw red, as I had come to dislike the American whites intensely. By then I had been over there and had found all the propaganda about GIs being friendly a pile of horse shit. I thrashed his arse out. You see, this was the sort of club where Africans were only seen padding about gently, dressed in white tunics, and here I came beating this guy up. It was a sensation. Just about the same time the CPP was forming, and I was the editor of a daily paper. So James Moxon of the Colonial Public Relations Department talked to me afterwards in my house, and he rushed to the Governor's Castle and told him that the Canadian must be sent away immediately, which he was.

The British were worried by this confrontation because 1948 was the same year that three Ghanaian ex-servicemen,[12] protesting over backpay, were killed by the British in a shooting near Christiansborg Castle on 28 February, sparking five days of rioting and large-scale lootings of European and Syrian shops:

> This was a time when the temperature in the Gold Coast was in high register. The whole country was screaming 'white man, go home' and Kwame Nkrumah was roaring 'we want self-government now.' The [Ghanaian] ex-servicemen were also in the fray and the boycott of British stores and their goods was in motion. And here I was pumping one of

them at the 'sacred' European Club. The next day, I had an urgent message from the Public Relations Department, then headed by Major Lillie Costello, to 'kill' the happening at the European Club. The Governor had so instructed R.J. [James] Moxon, the PRO representative, to contact my step-father lawyer Adumoa Bossman to have me 'kill' the news.

The same day, Kofi Baako, Kwame Nkrumah's trouble-shooter, also came to see me with an urgent request to see him. I met with him [Nkrumah] and he asked me about the event at the Club. I told him I could not say anything because the Governor had had me 'swear' not to say a thing. The old man [Nkrumah] pressed me to tell him and he convinced me so well that I 'swore' him into secrecy, and he kept his promise. Years later, I was told by James Moxon that my word not to tell had saved the British government from a very critical political position.

By 1948 some of the original Tempos members – the pianist Von Cofie, the bassist James Bossman, Okai Abossey, the alto-saxist Horace Djoleto and guitarist Pete Johnson[13] – had left. Ghanaba took over the Tempos' leadership from Joe Kelly in early 1948 and the same year he handed over to E.T. Mensah. It was this 1948 Tempos line-up that Ghanaba says was the strongest. Besides himself and E.T., it consisted of Kelly on tenor sax and clarinet; Baby Nelson on guitar; Dodds Schall on piano; and Serious Amarfio on double bass.

Ghanaba Goes to the UK

In 1950 Ghanaba decided to go to London and re-form the Fireworks Four there. One of its ex-members, Von Cofie, was already working at a London post office and together they teamed up with the Ghanaian guitarist Eddie Johnson, who was studying electronics at Wembley Westinghouse. However, when Ghanaba got to London, the Cu-bop style of Dizzy Gillespie, Chano Pozo[14], the Machito Afro-Cuban Band and Stan Kenton[15] was all the rage amongst jazz fans. There was a Cu-bop band in London at the time called the Afro-Cubists, led by the tenor saxist Kenny Graham.[16] Ghanaba told me that the band consisted of 'trumpet, tenor sax, bass, piano, drums, Afro-Cuban maracas, bongos and congas. Graham's Afro-Cubists was the resident band at the basement Club Flamingo near Leicester Square. Ghanaba got to know Graham and started playing bongos with his band. Ghanaba also set up a number of Afro-Cuban combos to play at parties, such as the Afro-Cuban Eight which included Von Cofie, Eddie Johnson, a couple of West Indians and, on occasion, the Nigerian tenor saxist Chris Ajilo.

The Tempos in 1948. Ghanaba is on the extreme left. From left to right are Joe Kelly, Dodds Schall, Serious Armafio, Pop Hughs and Afan. Below, holding a trumpet, is E.T. Mensah (African Heritage Library)

Ghanaba, holding bongos, with Johnny Dankworth (right) and Don
Rendell (left) in London, 1950 (Val Wilmer collection)

Ghanaba also met many local jazz artists, like the singer/
guitarist/pianist Cab Kaye, son of British music-hall singer Doris
Balderson and the Ghanaian dance orchestra musician, Caleb
Jonas Quaye. At the time, Cab Quaye was playing with his
own band, the All-Coloured Orchestra, which regularly toured
Europe. Ghanaba also met members of the Dankworth Seven, a
leading British bebop band that had just been set up in 1950.[17]
It was led by the clarinettist/saxist Johnny Dankworth and
included the tenor saxist Don Rendell, with whom Ghanaba
was to work in 1968. Ghanaba also got to know calypso and
steel-band music through Bosco Holder, a West Indian who,
with his troupe, performed at the Caribbean Club in Central
London. At the same time Ghanaba was also a DJ for the BBC,
for whom he played jazz and a new wave of Trinidadian calypso
music being pioneered by Lord Kitchener and Lord Beginner.

This post-war variety of calypso had become big in Britain from 1948, when the *Empire Windrush* ship had arrived, bringing with it the first of many shiploads of West Indian immigrants.

Ghanaba spent nine months in London and when he went back to Ghana at the end of 1950 he brought many songs and musical innovations with him that he wanted to share with the Tempos:

> When I came back from London I brought bongos and Cuban percussion to Ghana for the first time. Whilst in London, I went to the Caribbean Club, somewhere near Piccadilly, the haunt of a lot of West Indians. It was calypsos every night and I played these records on a BBC programme I had. When I came back I brought some of these records and we [the Tempos] learned to play them, as I knew straightaway that the musical inflections were so highlife-ish. I lapped up calypso music. I learned to play the bongos, an essential drum in calypso music. And when I returned to Accra I introduced calypso to the Gold Coast. I broadcast it on my Station Z.O.Y. jazz programmes and played it with the Tempos.[18]

In 1951, Ghanaba, E.T. Mensah, Joe Kelly and the other Tempos members went to Lagos for a week-long trip organised by a group of Ghanaians residing there. This was the first of many Tempos visits to Nigeria, where the band introduced Ghanaian highlife to artists like Bobby Benson, E.C. Arinze and Victor Olaiya.

It was also an important year for Ghanaba as a journalist. On 12 February 1951, Kwame Nkrumah was released from Jamestown Prison, where the British had locked him up during the country's first general elections, in order to prevent him from winning. As a leading journalist who had been working for Dr Nanka Bruce's *Daily Echo* newspaper for three years, Ghanaba was invited to the 'sherry party' thrown at Christiansborg Castle in March 1951 by the British governor, Sir Charles Noble Arden-Clarke, to welcome British parliamentarians coming to assess the political climate after Nkrumah's stunning election victory. In Ghanaba's African Heritage Library and his 1995 booklet (p. 3) there is a group photo of those at this sherry party. Besides Arden-Clark and Ghanaba it also included the British members of Parliament W.T. Proctor, Ernest Kinghorn and G.F. Stevens, Sir Henley Coussey (chairman of the Coussey Constitution Committee), Kwame Nkrumah and the Ghanaian lawyer Thomas Hutton-Mills. This event began a long-lasting relationship between Ghanaba and Kwame Nkrumah.

Ghanaba Leaves the Tempos in 1951

After the Tempos trip to Lagos, Ghanaba and Joe Kelly split from the group to form their own band, the Afro-Cubists (or Afro-Cubans), which specialised in jazz. There were a number of reasons for this. First, E.T., who owned the Tempos instruments, wanted a bonus for their use. Second, E.T. wanted to enrich highlife with calypso, swing and Latin American music, whereas Ghanaba was more interested in fusing jazz with Afro-Cuban drumming. As Ghanaba explains in his unpublished 1975 autobiography or 'testiment', E.T.'s band had become 'stagnant' because it had 'slipped into nothing but highlife with a two frontline combo which had a lot of rhythm to it':

> We had three different angles. Joe Kelly's thing [he had lost interest in the band since relinquishing its leadership], E.T.'s bonus and then me with my idea of a new sound for

the band. There was nothing to hold the band together. So myself, Joe and Dodds [Schall] left together, taking almost everybody away. E.T. carried on and we had our Afro-Cubans. As E.T. had instruments he was able to recruit musicians like Tom Thumb [Tom Tom] Addo, Saka Acquaye and Spike Anyankor. He didn't want to get hung up with a load of musicians who would give him headaches.[19]

Yet another problem that was worrying for Ghanaba was the recording deal that E.T. had struck with Decca Records, which had just opened a large pressing plant in Accra:

At this point Decca Records wanted to record us, but their negotiator, an ex-British army officer called Major Pinder [Kinder] offered us cash-payment. I advised the band to accept only royalties agreement. This man recorded E.T. profusely and poured his music all over West Africa and the rest of the world. Major Pinder made his millions whilst E.T. straggled along. It's on record that Major Pinder bought himself a castle on the coast of Devon, England and died a millionaire. E.T. lived in a small estate house in Mamprobi, Accra and did not die a millionaire. In our brotherly relationship I always advised and warned E.T. of booby-traps in the music business, but he never listened.

According to Ghanaba, E.T. continued to use the name 'Tempos' for his band for the Decca recording even after the departure of Afro-Cubists members. The guitarist Scorpion Mensah told him he was infringing the copyright law and he advised him to the change the name to 'E.T. Mensah and his Tempos', which E.T. agreed to do.

In a 1996 letter, Ghanaba noted that several of E.T.

Mensah's early hits were not his own compositions.[20] Dan Acquaye was the composer of most of E.T.'s tunes. The song 'All for You' 'was brought to the Gold Coast from the West Indies by Liberian and Sierra Leonean seamen'. According to Ghanaba the original West Indian title was 'Sly Mongoose' but the seamen named it 'All for You, Titi'. 'Titi' was seamen's slang for a pretty woman. The famous Tempos song 'Calabar' was an Igbo tune from Nigeria that his first wife picked up when she lived there. Ghanaba also claims it was Odartey Lamptey, the drummer of Yebuah Mensah's Accra Orchestra, who composed 'Te Mi mah Ni Oya' (Get Away From Me). This was recorded and renamed by the Tempos as 'Mi Ke Bo Baaya' (Me and You Will Go Together) with new words by Dan Acquaye and Tom 'Thumb' Addo, a 'most talented jazz drummer and vocalist'.

Despite their differences, Ghanaba remained fond of E.T.:

E.T. loved music and was always faithful to his muse. He rose to dizzying heights and plummeted into the deepest chasms. He loved and played highlife with a matter-of-fact gesture. He did not play anything spectacular, but what he played and how he played, it grooved with the people. He was the 'King of Highlife'. No one should begrudge him this. But he was one of the many 'Kings' of highlife music. We still have giants like King Bruce, Tommy Grippman, Osibisa. They all deserve the 'King' appellation.

Ghanaba and the Afro-Cubists Go to Liberia

Ghanaba and his Afro-Cubists went to Liberia in February 1953 when Liberia's President Tubman invited Nkrumah on a two-week state visit in honour of the Ghanaian leader becoming Prime Minister in March 1952.[21] On this trip, Nkrumah was accompanied by thirty-five Ghanaians, including Ghanaba and the highlife musician E.K. Nyame. Afterwards, when everyone else went home, the Afro-Cubists remained in the country's capital city of Monrovia.

However, the Afro-Cubists did not remain together in Liberia for long. Joe Kelly soon returned to Ghana to join Tommy Grippman's Red Spots and then formed his own highlife dance band at the Seaview Hotel. Ghanaba stayed on, working for two years as a DJ and assistant director with ELBC Radio, Liberia's national broadcasting service. Ghanaba's access to the station's gramophone library made him even more familiar with American jazz, as well as with the classical works of Ludwig van Beethoven, Johann Sebastian Bach, George Fredric Handel and Pyotr Ilyich Tchaikovsky.

Ghanaba eventually left Liberia to follow his jazz muse, around February 1955. He moved to the United States, where he lived in Chicago and New York for a number of years. In New York, between 1958 and 1960, he ran his experimental Afro-jazz trio called the Guy Warren Sounds with two African American musicians: bassist Ray MacKinny, and vibes player Ollie Shearer. Although this is a topic for another book, it was in the United States where he got to know and played with many top jazz musicians like Charlie Parker, Red Saunders, Max Roach, Miles Davis and Thelonius Monk.

It was also in the USA that he met his 'muse'. As he once explained to me, this was the realisation that he would be the 'African musician who re-introduced African music to America'. So it was while he was in America during the late 1950s that he produced a whole series of revolutionary Afro-jazz LPs such as 'Africa Speaks, Africa Answers', 'Theme for African Drums', 'Africa Sounds', and 'Third Phase'. On returning to Ghana in the 1960s he continued his jazz experimentations, became

rather reclusive and established his African Heritage Library
music archives some distance outside of the busy city of Accra.

Ghanaba with Charlie Parker (wearing Ghanaba's Kente cloth) at the
Chicago Beehive Club in 1995 – just before Parker's death (*Hey Baby!
Dig Dat Happy Feelin'* (1995) by Kofi Ghanaba)

Ghanaba with granddaughter Lila, jazz percussionist Jim Riley/Juma
Santos (right), John Collins and son Thomas Kojo (left) at the African
Heritage Library in Medie, 2001.

1. There is some confusion about this as Ghanaba (1966, p. 42) says his maternal grandfather was a Canadian auto engineer, while his 1995 booklet (p. 3) states that Mr Moore was an English mining engineer from London.
2. John Collins, *Music Makers of West Africa* (Washington DC, Three Continents Press, 1985), p. 68.
3. Kofi Ghanaba, *Hey Baby! Dig Dat Happy Feelin'* (Accra, self-published, 1995).
4. This letter is in Ghanaba's African Heritage Library Archives.
5. Kofi Ghanaba, *I Have a Story to Tell* (Accra, self-published, 1966).
6. This band included the London-born singer/guitarist Cab Kaye, the son of Caleb Jonas Quaye, who had played for the Accra-based Jazz Kings before going to the UK, where (under the name Ernest Mope Desmond) he played with the Five Musical Dragons, the Southern Syncopated Orchestra and the American alto-saxophonist Sidney Bechet. Quaye died in 1922.
7. Ghanaba is referring to the British pianist and bandleader Gerald Bright who, in the 1930s, ran his Guacho Tango Orchestra and Geraldo Orchestra.
8. A British violinist who, in the 1920s–1940s, led ballroom dance orchestras at London's Embassy and Mayfair Club.
9. Called Vron Kofie by E.T. Mensah.
10. Miff Mole had earlier played with the Paul Whiteman Orchestra and, after working with Goodman, joined the band of the jazz guitarist Eddie Condon.
11. Mawuko Ghanaba, personal communication.
12. Sergeant Cornelius Frederick Adjetey, Private Odartey Lamptey and Corporal Attipoe.
13. Ghanaba says that Johnson was a good rhythm guitarist but too shy to take solos. He later went to London to study radio mechanics. When he returned to Ghana he went insane, burnt his guitar and died (personal communication).
14. Chano Pozo came from Cuba to New York in 1947 and played with Gillespie in 1946, before being shot to death in 1948.
15. Stan Kenton began playing with members of the New York–based Machito's Afro-Cubans mambo band in 1948, Machito himself having moved from Cuba to the United States to form his Afro-Cuban band in 1941.
16. Kenny Graham ran his Afro-Cubists between April 1950 and March 1952. His group combined influences from bebop with Latin music and Cuban mambos.
17. The Dankworth Seven operated between 1950 and 1953..
18. John Collins, *Music Makers of West Africa* (Washington, DC: Three Continents Press,1985), p. 66.
19. Notes on this document are with the J. Collins BAPMAF archives, Accra
20. The letters are in Ghanaba's African Heritage Library Archives in Accra.
21. Nkrumah was first made Leader of Government Business. This title was converted to Prime Minister a year later.

7

The Tempos' Travels in West Africa

E.T. Mensah and his Tempos undertook various West African tours between 1955 and 1959, exploring the music scenes of Sierra Leone, Liberia, Guinea and Côte d'Ivoire. However, E.T.'s travels to Nigeria started with a one-week visit to Lagos in 1951, when Joe Kelly and Kofi Ghanaba were still members of the group. E.T.'s next trip to Nigeria was in 1953. On this occasion the band drove to Lagos and stayed for two weeks at Bobby Benson's brother's house. However, instead of going straight back to Ghana, the band decided at the last minute to go to Ibadan, Warri and Sapele in Delta State. The band returned to Nigeria again later that year, stayed for three months and travelled as far as the then Eastern Region, covering Enugu, Onitsha, Port Harcourt and Calabar.

E.T. found that on both these trips his band received a tremendous welcome. Although dance band highlife was becoming popular in Nigeria through records, there were no bands in the country that focused on this type of music. So the Tempos began to make regular trips to Nigeria from 1953, travelling once or twice a year by station wagon, usually stopping off at Lomé in Togo, and Cotonou and Porto Novo in Benin along the way. They could stay for up to three months at a time without infringing on Nigerian immigration laws. These trips proved very successful financially for E.T. and his musicians, and enabled the Tempos to turn professional in 1953.

When E.T. first went to Nigeria in 1951, highlife was hardly known outside the boundaries of Ghana. At that time, Nigerian dance bands such as Sammy Akpabot's and Bobby

Benson's were playing mostly swing and ballroom music. There were, however, varieties of westernised indigenous music being developed by Nigerian guitar bands, which were similar to highlife. For example, there was Yoruba juju, but at that time this was considered a low-class street music that was rarely played at respectable nightclubs and hotels. However, by the mid-1950s the Tempos' continuous touring in Nigeria was beginning to influence dance orchestras there and they started to incorporate highlife into their repertoires.

Bobby Benson and E.T. Mensah (left to right) in Lagos in 1952
(BAPMAF, from E.T. Mensah)

Bobby Benson's Jam Orchestra is a case in point. Victor Olaiya, originally a trumpeter with Benson, also began to play the Tempos' style of highlife when he formed his Cool Cats. Eddy Okonta, also formerly with Benson, followed suit when he formed the Top Aces dance band. Others influenced by the Tempos' brand of highlife were Rex Lawson and E.C. Arinze, who both split from the Empire Hotel's dance band to form their own groups. In fact, Lawson used one of E.T.'s numbers as his signature tune. Dan Acquaye, vocalist for the Tempos, remembers how on occasion, Nigerian musicians would come to the Tempos for tuition:

> Agu Norris, leading the Empire Band, always used to visit us, taking lessons from E.T. on the trumpet. In Benin [City], Victor Uwaifo, then a school boy, would rush down to our hotel after school to watch my cousin, Dizzy Acquaye, on the guitar. He was determined to play the guitar and used to help Dizzy pack and clean his instrument.[1]

Nevertheless, the relationship between the Tempos and the Nigerian dance bands was not entirely one-way; and when the Nigerian bands started to write their own highlife, E.T. brought some of the tunes back to Ghana, like the Yoruba highlife 'Okamo' and 'Nike, Nike', composed by the trumpeter E.C. Arinze.

Eleazor Chukwuwenta Arinze himself was from Anambra State in eastern Nigeria and went to Lagos in 1952 to play for the Roving Orchestra, the resident group at the Empire Hotel. In 1959 he formed the E.C. Arinze and His Music band, which was based at nightspots like the Kakadu, White Horse, Ikeja Arms Club and Lido Bar. This is what Arinze told the journalist Jahman Anikulapo in 2000 about the time he played side by side with E.T. Mensah at the University College of Ibadan, just prior to Nigeria's independence in October 1960:

> Before then, if Nigerians wanted to hear the best music they'd go to Ghana to invite bands and the number one choice used to be E.T. Mensah. That night I saw Zik [the Nigerian leader Nnamdi Azikwe[2]] standing with James Robertson [the last British governor-general of Nigeria]

and E.T. Mensah already set. Mensah used to play at the Empire Hotel Lagos: everywhere. He used to play this number at that time 'Oh My Papa' and Dan Acquaye, his vocalist, was the most popular in West Africa. I was lucky enough to have come across a record at Kingsway Store, Lagos, which contained 'Oh My Papa'. I had studied and worked hard on it and started playing it at my regular shows. So when we met that day no trumpeter had ever played it in Nigeria because it was so difficult. I said to myself: 'today it is between E.T. Mensah and I.' If he plays the vocal I will play the trumpet version. When I finished playing it Mensah came and shook my hand. That number gave me a contract to play at the European Club.[3]

The Tempos made an enormous impact on Nigerian dance bands and E.T. made many friends there. However, it was not all plain sailing for – as is usual amongst musicians – there was an intense competitive spirit between the two nationalities. Dan Acquaye gives his own rather one-sided opinion on the matter:

If we make a record, after the recording we often improve the song and sing it better. To the Nigerian audience, even if we sang better they didn't like it. If we made a mistake in the recording they expected us to make the same mistake in the performance.[4] Some of the Nigerian musicians were very jealous, since whenever we went there we captured the market and all the fans would follow us. They [the Nigerian musicians] used to put word around that we could only play highlife. They wanted to distract the attention of the people from us.

Once when we were playing, a man from the floor told

us not to play highlife, as some people were suggesting that we couldn't play western numbers, we could only play highlife. This man was annoyed by the musicians who had suggested this and wanted us to show the audience that we could play all types of music. So I sang 'Unchained Melody' and 'Answer Me' and the audience was so impressed that they wanted more. Another incident was in Lagos in 1958 when the union officers [of the Nigerian Musicians' Union] rushed down to the place we were going to play. They actually prevented us from playing. I remember that one of the officers was from Ghana and was then on the Union's Executive Committee. He was also a member of Bill Friday's band at the Ambassador Hotel in Lagos. At first Bobby wasn't with them but later he sided with them. It didn't entirely stop us from playing on that tour but it was their way of showing their resentment.[5]

Bobby Benson was in fact the president of the Nigerian Union and had been a long-time friend of E.T. Mensah's, but even he was unable to prevent the Union from making a ruling to keep the Tempos out of Nigeria. Consequently, from 1958 onwards, the band had to stop their regular tours to Nigeria and hardly went there again apart from a Nigerian pre-independence visit in 1960 and an invitation by the students at the University of Lagos in 1964. Things had been getting more difficult for the Tempos in Nigeria for some years, partly due to the increased competition from local dance bands and partly due to the diminishing returns from these trips. According to E.T. 'at first, bar owners would give their places to me for about one third of the profits and then the next time I went conditions would have changed to the owners benefit.'[6]

The most extensive tour the Tempos made of West

Africa was the Grand Tour they made from October 1958 to February 1959. At that time the band consisted of E.T., his two vocalists Christiana Mensah and Dan Acquaye, as well as Joe Ransford, Tom Tom Addo, Dizzy Acquaye, Rex Ofosu and two new musicians who had come into the band: A.P. Mensah on trombone and Alex Martey on congas. They first travelled to Nigeria, where they stayed for three weeks in Lagos playing at many of the leading nightclubs: the Lido, Ambassador, Lagos Arcade, Chez Peter's, the Savoy Hotel and Bobby Benson's Caban Bamboo. It was during this trip that the trouble with the Nigerian Musicians' Union occurred.

From Lagos the band took a boat to Freetown, the capital of Sierra Leone, where they had some difficulty in finding a hotel. Fortunately, they met a Lebanese man who owned a nightclub in Juba, the army residential area just outside the town. He provided the band with a house to stay in and they played at his club every weekend. On this tour, the band met the prime minister of Sierra Leone, Dr Milton Margai, at a party. There, they discussed the idea of a free concert, which was later organised by the Municipal Council of Freetown.

On the day of the concert, almost the entire population of Freetown packed into Victoria Park, with the band playing under a pavilion. As the band did not have sufficiently powerful amplifiers, the crowd surged forward, practically mobbing the stage. After a while, they were forced to stop playing, although everybody agreed that it had been a great success. Except for a short tour to Bo and Kenema in the interior and a week-long visit to Guinea, the band stayed in Freetown for about six weeks. E.T.'s impressions of Sierra Leone are vivid:

The houses of Freetown were made of wood and zinc so we could see a lot of rusted roofs. It was something peculiar to my eyes, like a slum or shanty town and not an impressive place at all. However, at Juba, the residential area, we saw a lot of good estate houses. Another peculiar thing we saw was a very small passenger train that ran right through Freetown's main market. When the market people heard the train whistle they would quickly get their things off the rails and after the train had passed they would put their stalls back.

There was much grumbling over the trade depression caused by the stoppage of local people pinching diamonds. Sierra Leone is very rich in diamonds and there was a time when these were being openly sold on the black-market. At that time they did not have self-government, so the rulers or imperialists made stringent laws to forbid this black-marketeering. For instance, if you were living in a diamond area and wanted to build a house, you were not permitted to dig more than three feet down for the foundations.

There was a far greater number of Lebanese in Sierra Leone, right inside the small villages, than we could see in Ghana. They were shop-keepers and traders but really they were dealing in diamonds. There were no dance bands in Sierra Leone and at the clubs they danced to gramophone records. Highlife was there but not under that name. We didn't see any guitar bands although we did meet one boy who was popular for his guitar playing. We heard some local 'highlife' records [in fact, maringa songs] sung in Pidgin with the vocalist being backed by one guitar. We picked up some of these songs from the town and later recorded two of them. One of them was about a river and we called it 'Volta' and the other was 'Fire, Fire, Fire, Dey Come'.[7]

Another thing we noticed during our stay was that there was class distinction, with the upper class consisting of lawyers and doctors who did not like to mix with the working class. If we wanted this upper class to attend our dances we had to raise our entrance fee, or charge two separate fees and provide two separate dance floors to accommodate the two classes of dance fans. They didn't like the free mixture as it was in Ghana or Nigeria. So if we called a dance and charged seven shillings and sixpence the upper class would not like to come; they would prefer to pay three pounds for double.[8]

The Tempos spent the New Year in Conakry, Guinea, and as the road was pretty rough Dan Acquaye and Alex Martey flew while the rest went by car. The two who flew, arrived first and Dan takes up the story:

Alex spoke a little French so he told a man at the airport that we were musicians – an international word – and the man took us by taxi to a restaurant. The restaurant manager phoned the Parliamentary Secretary to the Minister of Information who came around and gave instructions that we should be fed. He then took us to the Ghanaian Embassy which had just opened in Guinea. The late Mr. [N.A.] Welbeck, the Ghanaian Minister of State and Mr. E.K. Dadson, a Parliamentary Secretary, were there. They questioned us, thinking we had taken advantage of the Guinea–Ghana Union and that we had turned up without proper notice. I told him that we didn't normally do this and that we were expecting E.T. any time from that moment. I told him that it was an official visit and that Sékou Touré [the president of Guinea] was in the know.

Actually, the way he was putting questions to us was just as if we were ruffians and didn't know what we were in Guinea for. They took us to a military camp where we could sleep. But on the way we saw E.T. in the station wagon. I told Welbeck to stop and E.T. showed him the papers and cables concerning the trip. This seemed to satisfy everyone and we were all taken to a hotel for the first night on the instructions of Sékou Touré himself.[9]

E.T. continues the story:

When we first reached the border we were very well received as they hadn't seen people from Ghana come that way before. The swish [laterite] road wasn't so good and the area was complete savannah. But when we got to about sixty miles from Conakry we found a first-class road. Six miles from the town the way was lit by an array of lights, as it was getting dark. Very luckily we met the boys we had sent by air. At that time there were certain Ghanaian ministers on holiday in Guinea, including Mr. Welbeck and Mr. [E.K.] Dadson. They took us to the house of one the Guinean 'bigmen', a Mr. Diallo Telli, who got in touch with Sékou Touré by telephone. It was arranged that we should stay at the very posh Hotel De France for the night and the following day they fixed up a school for us to stay. They brought in beds and took us to restaurants where we could eat. We were well cared for.

The Tempos had arrived in Guinea at a critical time. The Guineans had said 'No' to DeGaulle's September referendum and had therefore been given independence by France in October 1958. But before they pulled out, the French had made a thorough job of attempting to wreck the new state. E.T.'s immediate impressions of Conakry reflect this state of affairs:

The city, like all French West African cities, was first class. However, when independence was given to them overnight, the French took all the guns from the police and army and dumped them into a river. They also took all the files from the secretariat and burnt them so there could be no identifications. So the Guineans were left just like that. And we happened to arrive just at that very time.

The whole town was very strange. People were sweeping the streets without any pay and some of the army people were using bulldozers to clear certain unfinished work, again without pay ... When we went to the harbour we could only see one bunch of bananas in the whole place [the harbour front] and we felt very sorry for them because there was nothing inside.

At the Secretariat, although the people were dressed for work, they were roaming around as there was no work for them to do. The French did not train the Guineans and then handed over the country to them in a way they could not carry on ... Up to then all the wages for government employees had been sent each month from Dakar. This was stopped and all the French officials were flown out of the country. There was great confusion, since when the French left, the local people had to take over immediately. For instance, the young man who was serving his master at the airport had to suddenly take over immigration and didn't know what do to. So what he was doing at the time we arrived was to collect the passports from those coming by plane, give each of them a small note, and ask them to come back after three days to collect their passports. All the relevant documents had been dumped by the French.[10]

Dan Acquaye's comments run in a similar vein:

> My impression of the town was that the people were determined. They were working for months without pay and although food was being supplied, the army and civil servants were working without pay. There was however no sign of grievance. Stealing had actually disappeared for if anyone stole it was serious, because the country had been left naked and if you stole the little that someone had, you were considered a saboteur.[11]

E.T. and his musicians spent most of their visit touring the city and the only time they played was on New Year's Eve. On that day, they first played at a private party at the residence of the minister of defence. Afterwards, they performed at a dance packed with people organised by the Workers Union, of which Sékou Touré had been the former president and which he naturally attended. The popular styles of music in Conakry at the time were the cha-cha, the bolero and the samba. Dan and E.T. do not remember seeing any dance bands with African musicians, although they did see several European trios of piano, drums and violin playing French music in the Conakry nightclubs.

The Tempos returned to Sierra Leone and stayed in Freetown for a week while arranging for a boat to take them to Liberia. On arrival in Monrovia they went straight to an old school friend of E.T.'s, Ayi McCarthy, who owned a nightclub there. He put them up and the band started making money at the club. It is interesting to compare E.T.'s impressions of Monrovia with those of Freetown:

The town is similar to Freetown with houses made of wood and zinc, many of them storey buildings. Many of the roads are untarred and some of the houses are put on stones so that when it rains, the water goes underneath. Outside Monrovia is a sister town of fine houses where the rich live; whereas in Freetown the rich live in the town itself. The cost of living [*in Monrovia*] is very high and they have extremely rich people there. Class distinction in Monrovia is based just on money, so that even a poor man can move about freely. In Freetown, however, the class distinction is different. There, the respectable, rich class looks down on certain classes of people and don't like to mix with them. They have first class nightclubs in Monrovia but no bands. Music such as swing and jazz is played on hi-fi amplifiers.

Tempos guitarist Dizzy Acquaye and bassist Joe Ransford after the band returned from its marathon five-month 1959 West African tour
(BAPMAF, from E.T. Mensah)

As E.T. points out, the popular music was American, but the Americo-Liberian ruling elite had their own dance called the quadrille. This was originally Creole music brought to Liberia from the Southern United States, and when the Tempos were in Monrovia they learnt to play it. They stayed in the town for six weeks, but before leaving they played at a function at which President William Tubman was present. He was so impressed with the band that he told them he would invite them over for the inauguration of the next president.

The Tempos returned from Liberia to Accra by boat and on arrival received a cablegram from President Tubman inviting them back for his second-term presidential inauguration. As a result, E.T. returned to Liberia a year later. This time things were made easy for them as the Liberian government supplied the band with a three-storey house and free food. In fact, things were so good that the band stayed for three months, long after the ceremonies were over. President Tubman wielded enormous power in the country and was well known for his paternalistic method of governing. E.T. comments on this:

> Tubman was doing all the work which you could expect to be done by his ministers and secretaries. If you wanted to hire chairs for a large function you could go and see the president and hire chairs from his mansions. We wanted to service our car so we needed another one and were told to go and see the president at his executive mansion. We saw his secretary who sent us to his waiting-room where you could meet all sorts of people going to see the president over some personal matter or other. You could meet old women from the town who were having trouble with their husbands or households and so on. They all took their problems to the president who would solve them by meeting them one by one. His word was law.

My problem was that I wanted a car to use, so he took me down to a compound full of brand new unlicensed cars and told me to choose one. I chose one and drove it away. Later when we were about to leave we began to have difficulties because no passenger boats were passing through, except cargo boats which had only a few places for passengers. I wanted the whole band, the instruments and the car to be taken home at one go, so we saw the president and he somehow personally fixed it up for us all to go together as deck passengers on one of the cargo ships that was passing through to Ghana.[12]

The above description of the band's travels in West Africa brings out many of the differences between Francophone and Anglophone West Africa at the time. E.T.'s reflections on his two-week trip to Abidjan, the capital of the Côte d'Ivoire, in 1955 also highlight some of these differences. In terms of music E.T. says:

They had white musicians from Paris. And since the African musicians were not up to standard, there was little dance music from the Africans.[13] They [the white Ivorians] also ran the nightclubs and were importing European musicians and actors. We saw more whites in the clubs than the blacks. The whites could afford the nightclub life. The white bands were playing boleros, cha-chas, tangos and French music. When we played highlife only a few of the Ghanaians there got up and danced, although by the end of the tour some of the whites had begun to catch on.

From his experiences in Abidjan, E.T. makes more general comments about Abidjan and the other ex-French colonies:

The French were treating the country [Côte d'Ivoire] as their own, so you could see European taxi and bus drivers. In the markets were black and white butchers as the French had shops side by side with the Africans. They did not want to leave the town to the blacks, so they raised Abidjan to the standard of a European city. On the British side Africans had gone far ahead socially, but in the French territories there were only a few blacks who were far above everyone else. In 1955, at Abidjan, we were shown the mansion owned by Houphouet-Boigny. It was thirteen stories high. This was the first time I had seen such a tall building. A few blacks were very rich but the vast majority were far below the social standard of the Africans in the British areas. The French people dominated the blacks socially and this affected the music, as the whites were doing everything. The development, both social and musical, in the French territories has occurred mainly since independence and now they want to catch up.[14]

In the French West African colonies there was a clear demarcation between indigenous music and urban music, with the latter being dominated by the whites. It is interesting, however, that many of the dances played by these French bands, such as the tango, samba, rumba and cha-cha, are in fact partially derived from Africa, or rather the descendants of slaves taken from Africa to the Americas.

In Anglophone West Africa the British colonial policy of 'indirect rule' operated through the traditional chieftaincy system and was therefore more amenable to cultural and musical blending than the 'direct rule' system of France.

The French system operated out of Paris and therefore treated the traditional African chieftaincy and cultural systems as archaic and irrelevant. As a result, it was only after independence that local popular music really began to surface in Francophone West Africa, encouraged by the first generation of leaders who were embarking on Africanist cultural policies. For instance, around 1960, Guinea's Sékou Touré assisted the development of local manding, a popular musical idiom, by establishing six state dance bands including the Syli National Orchestra, Les Amazons and Bembeya Jazz.

I recently discovered E.T. Mensah's role in Sékou Touré's *authenticité* policy in the area of popular music. In a 2002 interview by Gérald Arnaud with Achken Kaba, the trumpeter and chef d'orchestre of Bembeya Jazz, Kaba said that the idea of forming modern bands to play in traditional mode occurred after two Ghanaians – the independence leader Kwame Nkrumah and the musician E.T. Mensah – visited Cotonou in 1958.[15] In the Christmas/New Year of 1958 Nkrumah attended the presidential investiture of Sékou Touré whilst, as mentioned earlier, the Tempos played for the Workers Union. According to Kaba, when Sékou Touré heard the Tempos playing home-grown African music on modern western band instruments it gave him the idea of creating Guinea's own local popular music and he set up state bands to initiate this.[16]

Although it is recognised that the Tempos had a profound influence on Nigerian music, it is not so well known that the Tempos also made musical waves in Guinea. Indeed, E.T. himself did not know about his huge impact on this Francophone West African country, but it is remembered by the local musicians there.

1. John Collins, E.T. Mensah: *The King of Highlife*. (London, Off The Record Press, 1986), p. 30.
2. He was the Premier of Nigeria's Eastern Region from 1954 and took over the governor-generalship of Nigeria in November 1960. He went on to become the country's first President in 1963.
3. E.C. Arinze, interviewed in *Great Highlife Party* (Lagos: Goethe-Institut, 2000), pp. 10–14.
4. The Tempos had exactly the same problem with Ghanaian audiences who also insisted they play any mistakes they made on records.
5. Collins, E.T. Mensah, p. 30.
6. Ibid. p. 31
7. Both these songs are of the local Sierra Leonean 'maringa' variety of popular music. The one about a river is called 'River Rockel', and has a refrain that goes 'River Rockel, me no savvy swim, water de carry me go.' E.T. changed the words to 'River Volta'. According to the Ghanaian journalist Godwin Yirenki, it was later again changed into the Ghanaian 'Abongo' marching song 'River Congo' by Ghanaian soldiers who were with the U.N. Peace Force during the 1960s Congolese Civil War.
8. Collins, E.T. Mensah, p. 31–2
9. Ibid. p. 320
10. Ibid. p. 33
11. Ibid. p. 33-4
12. Ibid. p. 35
13. When E.T. says African music was of low standard, he is only referring to western-type dance music and not to the indigenous traditional dance music.
14. John Collins, E.T. Mensah: *The King of Highlife*. (London, Off The Record Press, 1986), p. 35
15. Achken Kaba, quoted by Gérald Arnaud in 'Bembeya se Réveille', *Africultures*, 1 November 2002.
16. Ibid.

8

Bobby Benson and the Jam Session Orchestra of Lagos

Bobby Benson was one of the most important dance band musicians in West Africa. He helped pioneer a distinct form of Nigerian highlife and many top Nigerian musicians obtained their musical training through his various bands. Some of these Benson 'graduates' went on to revolutionise highlife music in the country.

The Story of Bobby Benson

Robert Olabinjo Shobowale Benson was born on 11 April 1921, in Ikorodu, Western Nigeria. After secondary school at the CMS Grammar School in Lagos he went into tailoring, did some boxing and then, during the Second World War joined the British Merchant Navy as a fireman and cleaner. In the Atlantic, his ship was hit by a torpedo fired from a German plane. Benson and some other survivors hung on at sea in lifeboats for thirty-two days until they were picked up and deposited on the Cape Verde Islands. There he met a lady called Thunderlio who taught him to play guitar.

From Cape Verde he was taken to an Italian prisoner-of-war camp and when the Italians capitulated to the Allies in 1943, he was released and moved to Britain in June 1944. There he joined the Entertainment's National Services Association (ENSA) that supplied light relief for the troops across Europe. This gave Benson the opportunity to learn to play various musical instruments. Benson then left the UK for the United

States where, for a while, he appeared in films and on stage. As he explains in an interview with *DRUM* magazine in October 1957:

> I'm a showman, not a musician really. This thing called music I had to pick up as I went along. In school I was good at playing the harmonica and this came in useful when I joined a touring troupe called E.N.S.A. and we toured all through Europe entertaining troops. I would not have left E.N.S.A., but had to scram to the United States when the British started conscripting fellows to go and fight. I had seen enough of war.[1]

However, by 1947 he was back in London where, because of his natural artistic talent, he made his theatrical debut with the Playhouse Group at the London Piccadilly Theatre. He also joined Les Ballets Nègres, Britain's first black ballet company, under the West Indian choreographers Petro Persuka and Miss Fisher. Benson toured Europe with this theatrical cabaret group. It was around this time that he met his Scottish–West Indian wife, Cassandra, who was a professional dancer. Benson and Cassandra decided to form a show team that put on comedy sketches, blackface acts and dances accompanied by music from records.

Benson's brother was so impressed by these shows that he bought a set of instruments for the performing couple so they could take their act to Lagos. Benson and Cassandra returned to Lagos on 9 September 1947 and began their rehearsals at Molete Street, Lagos. They subsequently launched the Bobby Benson and Cassandra Theatrical Party during the Easter of 1948. At first they continued their London format of using records to back 'black and white minstrel-type shows for Lagos audiences'.[2] Cassandra and the extroverted Benson dressed in tails, danced the jitterbug and kangaroo to jazz and boogie-woogie music. As mentioned in a 1957 *DRUM* article, Benson's shows introduced many other novelties to Lagosians:

> The short man with a goatie beard hit town in 1947 with a coloured girl about his height and size. They brought to town new fashions for the boys and girls – zoot suit and the Cassandra hair-style.[3]

It should also be noted the Bobby Benson and Cassandra Modern Group also involved female performers for novelty effect. These included female saxophone and trumpet players and the local Aikin Sisters singing group. According to Ebun Clark and M.A. Omibiye-Obidike, Benson's Troupe was the first Nigerian popular music group to introduce cabaret-type dancing girls on stage.[4]

Despite all these acts, the new American dances, the female performers and the fashionable zoot suits of the jazz-swing generation, Benson's shows were unpopular with Lagos audiences, and Cassandra eventually left Nigeria because of it. Benson explained another problem with his original theatrical group to *DRUM* magazine:

> My brother told me to come home for three months holiday and perhaps show my countrymen what we could do. I came home only to be disappointed because … we had no good band that could accompany our performance. The few shows we put on we had to use gramophone records. This was no good.

As a result of these problems with his cabaret format and lack of a live band, Benson set up his Jam Session Orchestra to accompany his theatrical performances instead of gramophone records. The band's music leader was the saxophonist Ezekiel Akpata, with Benson singing and playing sax and guitar. In fact, Benson used an electric guitar he had brought with him from Britain in 1947. It was the first time this amplified instrument had been used in Nigeria.

The Jam Session Orchestra ended up as an eleven-piece group including a frontline of seven horns. According to the musicologist Austin Emielu and musician Bayo Martins, the first generation players included the alto saxist Audu or Awudo Kano, Dele Bamgboye (or Bamgbose) on tenor sax, Bill Friday on trumpet[5], Jibril Isa on tenor sax and clarinet[6] and Magnus Iworare and Ladipo Benson on double bass.[7] The orchestra's percussion section was composed of the trap-drummers King Roberto Maduka and Lebato, with Sunday Eze and Ajax Bukana[8] on maracas and assorted light percussion. Four others who came into the group a little later were the fifteen-year-old trumpeter Zeal Onyia, the percussionist Bayo Martins,[9] alto-saxist Babyface Paul Osamade[10] and trombonist Philip Ugbogu.

Another reason for Benson's switch from records to a live band may have been competition with other theatrical groups like that of Hubert Ogunde, the pioneer of the Yoruba Travelling Theatre. In the late 1940s Ogunde was also using jazz, swing and calypso to accompany his popular drama shows, which involved some of his actors wearing blackface minstrel make-up and even a number of female saxophone players. Ogunde's theatre visited Ghana twice in 1948, when local concert parties were also using blackface and playing ragtime and swing, so it is likely that Ogunde borrowed some of his ideas from them.

Indeed, the Ghanaian influence was so marked that for several years Ogunde called his Nigerian group a 'concert party', before dropping this minstrel and dance band format and moving onto to the more indigenous Yoruban popular plays for which he became so famous.[11]

Despite the introduction of a live musical component to his Modern Theatrical Group, Benson continued to use blackface minstrel acts for a time, according to Ajax Bukana who was with him until 1952:

Anytime we had a show, we would make a concert and Bobby Benson would give me a part. He used to make some funny top hats and tails for us and I painted my face white and had a walking-stick. I used to make short comedies just like in Louis Armstrong's shows. I used to dance jazz and do tap-dancing. It was Bobby Benson who gave me the name Ajax Bukana.[12]

Bobby Benson (centre, with sax) and his Jam Session Orchestra in 1952.
Trumpeter Bill Friday is on the far left and the kit-drummer is King
Roberto Maduka. On Maduka's left is Ajax Bukana with Cuban maracas,
and on his right is the young Bayo Martins playing claves (BAPMAF,
from E.T. Mensah)

During the fifties, Benson performed at venues like the Empire Hotel and Lido Bar, where his band played ballroom numbers, Afro-Cuban music, jazz, jives and calypsos. According to Bayo Martins, Benson also liked to sing an occasional folksong, such as the Yoruba 'Oni Dodo, Oni Moi Moi'.

Besides his Jam Session Orchestra, Benson also ran another group at the time called Alfa's Carnival Group that, according to Benson Idonije, played at carnival shows as well as nightclubs.[13] At one point in the early 1950s, this second outfit was run by the trumpeter Victor Olaiya[14] before he went to the UK in 1952. In fact, Benson continued operating a stable of additional bands throughout his musical career, including Babyface Paul Osamade's Top Spotters in the late 1950s, and The Strangers (run by one of Benson's sons) in the late 1960s.

From 1951 the Jam Session Orchestra also began playing some highlifes, as by then this Ghanaian music was being introduced to Nigeria in a big way through E.T. Mensah's Tempos tours. However, as Benson told Chris Waterman (1986), he had already been exposed to highlife as a boy when Ghana's famous Cape Coast Sugar Babies Orchestra toured Nigeria in 1938. Although Benson could not recall the name of the band, he told Waterman:

> They came to Lagos with bigger musical instruments … they played in the West Indian Quarters opposite Clifford Street, now called Murtala Mohammed Way. A big band from Accra. They really hit it. They were the best when they came down. I was very young and we had to peek through the fence to see them. The Gold Coast something Dance Band. A big band [of] almost fourteen or seventeen pieces.[15]

However, it was E.T. Mensah's Tempos who were really influential on the older Benson, and in 1952 he went to Ghana for a few months when his band was contracted to perform in Accra by Herbert Morrison, the Nigerian owner of the Weekend-in-Havana nightclub in Jamestown. Whilst there, Benson played side by side with the Tempos, who were the club's resident band. Not only did this trip encourage him to include more highlifes in his repertoire, but later Zeal Onyia and Babyface Paul Osamade quit Benson's group to join the Tempos in Ghana. As will also be discussed later, other members of Benson's band, such as Bill Friday and Jibril Isa, also found their way back to Accra where they formed their own bands. Ajax Bukana was so impressed by Ghana that after Benson's 1952 trip, he stayed behind in Accra to reside there permanently.

Bobby Benson at the Weekend-in Havana nightclub, Accra, when his Jam Session Orchestra was in Ghana for a few months in 1952
(BAPMAF, from E.T. Mensah)

In 1957 Benson renamed his band the Hep Cats. By this time, his Jam Session Orchestra had already released his popular highlife record 'Taxi Driver', which in 1952 was a big hit. Its lyrics complain about Nigerian women only wanting to marry men like professional drivers who make money. The song, which had a distinctive beginning with the honk of a taxi horn, was not only a hit in Nigeria but in Ghana and elsewhere in Africa. In fact, this catchy song has became one of the great evergreen highlife standards.

In 1958 Benson became the president of the newly-formed Nigerian Union of Musicians (NUM) that was affiliated with the Nigerian Trade Union Congress, with Victor Olaiya as its social secretary. An unfortunate side effect of this new union was that despite Bobby Benson being a long-time friend of E.T. Mensah's, he was unable to prevent the union from making a ruling to keep the Tempos out of Nigeria. Consequently, from 1958 onwards, the Tempos stopped their regular tours of Nigeria.

The NUM, which Benson had helped found, went on to become a powerful force in Nigeria. Indeed, by the time of Nigeria's independence in 1960, its collective muscle was enough to influence the new government. By this time Chris Ajilo had taken over the union presidency, with trumpeter Zeal Onyia as its vice-president, Ghanaian guitarist Stan Plange as its treasurer and Amaefule Ikoro as its secretary. That year, NUM staged a demonstration over the musical preparations for Nigeria's independence celebrations. This is what Stan Plange told me about the matter when I interviewed him at the Napoleon Club in Osu, Accra, 1977:

It was in 1960 when the preparations for Nigeria's Independence were going on. The Nigerian government was intending to invite Edmundo Ros[16] to come and play at the National Independence Dance, as Princess Margaret was coming and we understood she liked Edmundo Ros. Victor Olaiya's band was to play second. So the Nigerian Musicians' Union organised a demonstration to protest against the bringing of a foreign group. About eight or nine hundred of us marched with placards from the Empire Hotel, Idi Oro, to Government House to petition the Prime Minister, Tafawa Balewa. Myself, Zeal, Chris and Amaefule went inside and told him that the contract should be given to the union, who would then form a mass band and select musicians to form a national orchestra for the Independence Dance. He agreed.[17]

As a result of the protest, two groups of musicians were asked to play for the event. One consisted of Victor Olaiya and Zeal Onyia, who co-led the Nigerian All Star Band. The other was the mass band that Stan Plange referred to above, composed of a 22-member national orchestra that was created around the Nigerian Broadcasting Corporation Band that had just been set up in 1959 under the leadership of Chris Ajilo.

In spite of all the activism concerning a Nigerian musical presence for the independence celebrations, by the mid-1960s the NUM collapsed and there was no musicians' union again until 1971, after the Nigerian Civil War.

The civil war changed the whole highlife scene in Nigeria. During the war, which lasted from 1967 to 1970, the oil-rich eastern portion of the country tried to break away as the independent Biafran state. As a result, many of the top highlife bands run by easterners in Lagos broke up, as any members who belonged to the breakaway Biafran ethnic groups returned to their homelands. The only highlife dance bands left in the Lagos area were those of Yoruba bandleaders like Victor Olaiya, Roy Chicago and Bobby Benson. Indeed there was a shift in taste by Yorubas away from highlife and towards their home-grown juju guitar band music, popularised then by Ebenezer Obey and Sunny Ade.

Nevertheless, Olaiya and Benson managed to to survive these difficult years following the civil war as they built up well-patronised hotel-nightclubs where their bands could regularly play. Benson's own club was a large multi-storey affair that he called the Caban Bamboo.[18] Tony Benson, Benson's oldest son from his marriage with Cassandra, and a talented keyboardist, became a prominent fixture at the Caban Bamboo from 1968, when he set up the soul-influenced Strangers band and, later, his Jazz Sextet.

Bobby Benson also left a huge musical legacy in Nigeria due to the number of musicians who passed through his various bands. These include the trumpeters Eddy Okonta, Roy Chicago and Rex Lawson who are discussed more fully in Chapters 9 and 19. Others who played with his early outfits include the trumpeter Sharp Mike[19], and vocalists Godwin Omabuwa[20] and Maud Meyer.[21] A newer generation of Nigerian artists who passed through Benson's band in the 1960s and 1970s includes the percussionists Remi Kabaka[22] and Friday Jumbo; the saxophonists Eric 'Showboy' Akaeze, Dele Okonkwo and Loughty Lasisi Amao; the singer Ezekiel Hart; and guitarist Monday Olufemi John.

Over the years, Benson's various bands acted as a college through which musical graduates obtained a well-rounded experience in all sorts of dance music forms that included highlife, jazz, swing, samba, calypso, Afro-Cuban, and the type of ballroom dance music that had dominated the colonial era.

However, Benson had a reputation as a no-nonsense taskmaster as he made clear in some comments to Charles Anyiam in 1982:

> Many musicians passed through my band. Some simply came in, tried themselves and left if they could not fit in. I see myself as an artist primarily. I sculpt, mould and even work as a draughtsman. You see, I understand what art is about and I have the additional ability to recognise a good artist when I see one.[23]

Bobby Benson on drums with some of his Hep Cat bandsmen in 1967
(*DRUM*, October 1967)

In 1971, Bayo Martins and Benson, along with Chris Ajilo and Fela Ransome-Kuti, formed the Musicians' Foundation. Then in 1981, Benson became an executive for the Performing Musicians Association of Nigeria (PMAN) whose main aim was to put an end to the music piracy that constituted 60 per cent of the Nigerian market at the time. PMAN included many of the country's top musicians including Sunny Ade, Ebenezer Obey, Sonny Okosun, Christie Essien, Nicholas Mbarga, Victor

Uwaifo and Laolu Akintobi 'Akins'. Sadly, Benson died in 1983 just two years after the formation of this important musical body.

1. Bobby Benson, 'Bobby Benson Hot Showman', *DRUM*, October 1957, pp. 7–8.
2. Ebun Clark, *Hubert Ogunde* (Oxford University Press, 1979), pp. 127–8.
3. 'Bobby Benson Hot Showman', DRUM, October 1957.
4. Clark, *Hubert Ogunde*, 1979.
   Mosunmola. A. Omibiye-Obidike, 'Women in Popular Music in Nigeria', paper presented at the fourth International Conference of IASPM, Accra, 12–19 August 1987.
5. See Chapter 9.
6. Jibril Isa (also Assah or Asa) left Benson and travelled to Ghana to form his own band in the mid-fifties called the Delta Dandies, based at the Palmcourt Club in Accra. With this band made up of local musicians (like George Lee) he released highlifes and Afro-Cuban mambos sung in Hausa on the HMV label.
7. Austin Emielu, 'Nigerian Highlife Music' (PhD thesis, University of Ilorin, 2009). Bayo Martins, 'Zealinjo, Zeal Onyia, "The Hip Cat", 1934–2000', *Ntama Journal of African Music and Popular Culture*, 23 January 2004.
8. The late Ajax Bukana was born in Lagos in 1920, joined Bobby Benson's Orchestra in 1948 and quit when Benson's group was on a visit to Ghana in 1952. Ajax then became a naturalised Ghanaian citizen and was popular with Kwame Nkrumah, who sent him to Russia to be trained as a clown. Indeed he became Nkrumah's 'personal jester' and, in 1988, was officially recognised as a 'state comedian' by the Ghanaian Provisional National Defence Council.
9. For details on Zeal Onyia and Bayo Martins see Chapter 9.
10. Paul Osamade left Benson in 1954 to work with the Tempos in Ghana, then moved on with Zeal Onyia to join the Rhythm Aces and Melody Aces. Osamade returned to Lagos in 1958 when he formed the Top Spotters, one of several bands managed by Bobby Benson.
11. For Ogunde's use of blackface, jazz and calypsos see Clark, 1979 (pp. 124–8 and Biographical Notes xviii).
12. Ajax Bukana, personal communication, Accra, 1988. Also see Collins, 1996, p. 27.
13. Benson Idonije, 'Echoes of the Sixties', *Lagos Guardian*, 1 October 2009.
14. See Chapter 10.
15. Bobby Benson quoted in Chris Waterman, 'Juju: The Historical Development, Socio-economic Organisation and Communicative Functions of West Africa Popular Music (PhD thesis, University of Illinois, 1986).
16. A Trinidadian-born black Venezuelan/Scottish percussionist who, in 1940, set up his famous Rumba Band that was to release 800 records for Decca.The group also played at high-class London clubs like the Coconut Grove and Bagatelle Club, where the future Queen Elizabeth danced to his music.
17. John Collins, *Highlife Time* (Accra, Anansesem Press, 1996), p. 252.
18. It was there that I met Benson in January 1977, when I was acting in Fela Anikulapo-Kuti's *Black President* film. Fela's partner in the movie, Faisal Helwani, introduced me to Bobby Benson at the Caban Bamboo where the Northern Pyramids and the visiting South African Ipi Tombi musical group were currently featured.
19. He left Benson in 1958 to join the Ghanaian Stargazers, a Kumasi-based highlife band led by Glen Cofie, Eddie Quansah and later Adlib Young Anim. Later, Sharp Mike was

in a Nigerian band called Outer Space. In 1965, he moved to Freetown to join the Leone Stars dance band.

20. After doing a stint with Benson, this calypso specialist formed the Casanova Dandies in the fifties, and later created the Sound Masters.

21. Mayer was of mixed Efik and Sierra Leonean parentage and was a teacher and dance artist from Port Harcourt. This jazz lady sometimes featured with Bobby Benson and was also a member of the Jazz Preachers discussed in Chapter 8 (Bassey Ita (1984), quoted in Omibe-Obidike (1987)).

22. This Nigerian drummer began his career in Accra in the early seventies and joined Bobby Benson, before working with Fela Kuti, Hugh Masekela, Osibisa and the British rock musicians Paul McCartney, Steve Winwood, Mick Jagger and Ginger Baker.

23. Bobby Benson, quoted in Charles Anyiam, 'Life and Times of Bobby Benson', *Africa Music*, 11 (September/October 1982) pp. 12–13.

SECTION THREE:

Highlife's Golden Age: Nigeria, Ghana and Benin

9

Veterans From Bobby Benson's Band

Some of the most important musicians who passed through Bobby Benson's bands in the 1950s were the ace trumpeters Bill Friday, Zeal Onyia and Eddy Okonta. They were all with Benson's Jam Session Orchestra in the early part of that decade, as was the percussionist, trap-drummer and later renowned musicologist Bayo Martins. The trumpeter Roy Chicago was a later addition; he was a member of Benson's Hep Cats outfit from 1958 to 1960 and went on to become a major figure in the Nigerianisation of highlife.

The Trumpeter Bill Friday

Bill Friday, the trumpeter in Benson's original Jam Session Orchestra, was, according to the Nigerian music journalist Benson Idonije, 'one of Bobby Benson's greatest sidemen'.[1] It was Friday who played the trumpet solos in Benson's big 1952 'Taxi Driver' hit and it was Friday who set the pace for the subsequent great solo trumpeters in Benson's band, like Zeal Onyia and Eddy Okonta.

In 1952, Friday, together with some other members of the Jam Session Orchestra, left to form Jibril Isa's Delta Dandies, which later relocated to Ghana. However, it was the grounding that he obtained with Benson that enabled him to form his own band in Ghana in 1956 called the Downbeats. Some of the local musicians who passed though his outfit there included the guitarist Okyere, the guitarist/double-bassist Oscarmore Ofori, Eddie Quansah (who later became known as the 'black trumpet'), and Stan Plange, who gravitated from double bass to guitar whilst with the band. Another member was the tenor-saxophonist George Lee Larnyo.[2] Friday's group was based in Accra but toured Ghana and neighbouring Togo.

In 1958, Friday returned home to Lagos where he was based at Nat's Club de Paris in Surulere. There, he put together a new version of the Downbeats. That year, he asked Stan Plange to rejoin the group in Lagos. This was what Plange told me about the Downbeats, with whom he played until 1961:

> There were only four Nigerians in the group; the rest were Ghanaians. Later, one of the Nigerians left and was replaced by the Ghanaian trombonist Pete Kwetey, now with the Armed Forces Band. In the Downbeats, I was the arranger and second leader, Joe Mensah was inside as a singer, George Emissah [Amissah] who is now leading Uhuru on alto sax, Nat Hammond [Lee Ampoumah] on bongos and Akwei 'I Zero' on congas.[3]

Within one year, Friday had relocated the Downbeats to the Ambassador Hotel in Yaba, Lagos. The band was resident there for some years and was particularly popular with the public at the hotel's 'Tea Time' dance session on Sunday afternoons. Indeed, in 1961 this group was rated as one of the top West African highlife dance bands by the University College of Ibadan, after playing at one of its 'Havana' dance sessions. Friday became so popular that the general public began to acclaim him 'Chief', and 'Chief' Bill Friday is considered to be the greatest trumpeter and Nigerian bandleader of the 1950s and 1960s. However, unlike his rival Victor Olaiya, another Bobby Benson graduate, Bill Friday only recorded one song for posterity. This was entitled 'Rosina' and was released on a 78 rpm record single.

The Trumpeter Zeal Onyia

The famous Nigerian trumpeter Zeal Onyia was born in Agbor in then Bendel State on 12 June 1934. He was the son of Chief J.I.G. Onyia from Asaba, the capital of Delta State. At just four years old Onyia learnt to play the six-hole fife and then became a member of his Asaba Government School band. When he moved on to the Aba Government School he began to play cornet, and it at was at this time that Onyia first became interested in the music of the legendary Louis Armstrong. In 1949 Onyia began his secondary education at the New Bethel College in Onitsha and played for the college band with which he toured eastern Nigeria. His trumpet playing so impressed Bobby Benson's saxophonist, Ezekiel Akpata, that in June 1949 he took Onyia to Lagos. As he was only fifteen, Onyia attended Kings College secondary school during the day and only played with Benson's Jam Session Orchestra in secret in the evenings. Onyia was with Bobby Benson for five years – at the very time when Bill Friday was the Jam Session Orchestra's main trumpeter.

In 1951 the Tempos came to Nigeria, boosting the popularity of highlife in the country. Tam Fiofori, writing about Zeal Onyia, said this about the Ghanaian group:

> The Tempos played highlife with an identifiable harmonic progression, good tone, organised solo work and rich rhythms ... Added to this, there was the political movement mobilising Nigeria's demand for independence. Mazi Mbonu Ojike had said that 'Nigerians should boycott the boycottables' and Dr Nnamdi Azikiwe was preaching that Nigerians should be proud Africans. This was the political climate when Joe Kelly, E.T. Mensah and Guy Warren came ... people who had been abroad and seen

the so-called civilised worlds came to Nigeria and played African music. This influenced lots of bands in Ghana and Nigeria and everybody started playing and enjoying highlife music. Before this, Nigerian highlifes were only played once or twice by a band during a normal seven-hour playing engagement.[4]

Zeal Onyia accompanied Benson and his band on their short residency in Accra in 1952, where they played side by side with the Tempos at the Weekend-in-Havana club. Then in 1954, Onyia and fellow Benson member Babyface Paul Osamade returned to Ghana to join up with the Tempos. But the Tempos split up within three months of their joining and Onyia and Osamade ended up following alto-saxist Spike Anyankor who, along with trombonist Glen Cofie, guitarist Bebop Aggrey and pianist Ray Ellis, went to form a new band called the Rhythm Aces.[5]

Young Zeal Onyia on trumpet with the Ghanaian Rhythm Aces, led by tenor-saxist Spike Anyankor, at the Weekend-In-Havana club, Jamestown, Accra, in the mid-1950s (photo courtesy of Isaac Bruce Vanderpuie)

Onyia and Osamade were also involved with a second band formed around 1954 or 1955 called the Melody Aces. The name may have been something the band used for copyright purposes when recording, as their group included many Rhythm Aces members, like Spike Anyankor, Bebop Aggrey, Glen Cofie and Freddy Tate – as well as a musician called Rex Ofosu Martey. The Melody Aces released several highlife hits like 'Mensu' and 'Bongo Lorry'. It was in these releases that Onyia first introduced his characteristic technique of holding a high note on his trumpet over many bars of music.

In 1955, Onyia left Ghana to go to London to study dance music at the Central School of Dance Music (what later became the Eric Gilder School). Onyia became quite active as a jazz trumpeter in the UK, sitting in with the top British 'trad jazz' bands (which played in the New Orleans Dixieland style) of Chris Barber, Terry Lightfoot and Humphrey Lyttelton, as well as the modern jazz group of Ronnie Scott. Onyia also played highlifes, swing and calypsos at the London Club Afrique with fellow Nigerian Ambrose Campbell and the West African Rhythm Brothers. It was during this 1955–7 stay that Onyia first met Louis Armstrong.

After two years in Britain, Onyia returned to Nigeria and, in 1957, started up Zeal Onyia's Band, which was based in the Ambassador Hotel in Yaba, Lagos. Bayo Martins says the band's personnel included Bata Hanger on trombone, Humphrey on alto sax, Abel Abu on congas, Easy Kabaka on guitar and, for a short while, Bayo himself on drums. This band was mainly a recording outfit and released such hits as 'Odziaze' and 'Vicky Yeme Afum', in which Zeal again demonstrated his instrumental novelty of using a long drawn-out dominant trumpet note. Other top songs that he released on Decca West Africa Records were 'Dibia A'buro Chukwu', about a car accident Zeal survived, 'Odiasi', and the 1958 'Egwu Jazz Bu Egwu Igbo', in which Onyia musically traced the history of jazz to Igbo-land.

Onyia featured various important singers for his releases. One of the first was Stephen Osita Osadebe from Atani near Onitsha who was with him for quite a while. Osadebe sang on some of Onyia's late fifties Decca recordings like 'Lumumba', about the first DRC head of state, Patrice Lumumba,[6] and 'Lagos Life Na So So Enjoyment'. Then, in 1961, Osadebe sang the Igbo highlifes 'Wabu Ifeukiti' and 'Oyim Kotan'. As will be covered in Chapter 14, Osadebe went on to became an important highlife musician who released around five hundred songs.

In 1960, Zeal became vice-president of the Nigerian Union of Musicians (NUM). He was among the delegates who petitioned Prime Minister Abubakar Tafawa Balewa, opposing the government plan to bring the British Edmundo Ros Orchestra for the country's first independence celebration. The petition was successful and resulted, as mentioned earlier, in Onyia and Victor Olaiya co-leading the Nigerian All Star Band that played for the Independence Ball on 1 October 1960.

In 1960 Zeal Onyia met Louis Armstrong for the second time when Armstrong, Velma Middleton and the All Stars Band visited Nigeria on the first leg of a three-month African tour.[7] Onyia and a group of local musicians played as Armstrong came off the plane. Afterwards, Onyia accompanied Armstrong to his hotel. Later that day Onyia, along with Olaiya and some other Nigerian musicians, played for Armstrong at the National Stadium in Surulere. According to Bayo Martins, 'Louis lost no time in recognising a protégé. "Who is that hip cat?" he enquired.'[8] This acquaintance translated into a lifelong friendship between the two, until the great Satchmo passed in July 1974.

By 1961, Onyia was becoming increasingly active in the Trade Union movement. However, these activities did not allow time for Onyia to operate a regular performing band, and so he formed studio groups that concentrated on recordings. It was around this time that another important singer, besides Osadebe, became attached to the Zeal Onyia's recording band: the Ghanaian highlife singer Nat Buckle. Buckle had sung with many top 1950s Ghanaian dance bands like the Rhythm Aces, Red Spots, Rakers, and Stargazers and also wrote the popular highlife song 'Abele' that E.T. Mensah's Tempos popularised on a record. In 1960, Buckle moved to Nigeria where he joined up with Zeal Onyia's recording group and one of the songs they released together was 'Onyema Echi'. After leaving Onyia in 1963 Buckle moved on to sing with many other Nigerian bands and artists.[9]

The Ghanaian highlife singer Nat Buckle, who operated in Nigeria for many years. (*Ghana Showbizz*, 8–14 July 2000)

In 1962 Zeal Onyia teamed up with the drummer Bayo Martins, pianist Wole Bucknor, double-bassist Ayo Vaughan and percussionist Apollo Aramide to form the short-lived Koriko (Wolf) Clan Jazz Group. This Afro-jazz band broke up due to Onyia's commitments as a trade unionist, which often involved visiting communist countries. Instead of running his own group, Onyia opted to join Art Alade's Jazz Preachers in 1964; it included some of the same members as his Afro-jazz group, though the pianist Wole Bucknor was replaced by Art Alade.

In 1966, Onyia was invited to Germany after he met members of a German chamber orchestra that was in Nigeria on an African tour. As a result of the meeting he won a scholarship from the Goethe-Institut to study classical music with Adolf Scherbaum at the conservatory at Hanover. Due to the civil war raging in Nigeria at the time, Onyia decided to stay on in Germany after completing his courses. In 1969, he joined a band in Germany called Dobs Ladykillers. Finally, in 1977, he returned to Nigeria when he was invited to become a producer for the Nigerian Broadcasting Corporation in Lagos.[10] Onyia remained with the Radio Nigeria External Service for many years and was its head of music until he retired in 1984. During his Radio Nigeria days he still had time to continue his musical career, playing classical music with Femi Bucknor and releasing highlife records like 'Zeal Anata' on the Tabansi label in 1981. Zeal Onyia died on 30 April 2000.

The Trumpeter Eddy Okonta

The highlife trumpeter Eddy Okonta was born in either Akwukwu or Asaba in Delta State. He began his musical apprenticeship with Sammy Akpabot's Sextet, which was formed in 1952. Sammy Akpabot[11] was one of the first vibraphone players in West Africa and his Sextet included a number of musicians who inspired Okonta. One was the great alto- and tenor-saxophonist Funso Adeolu, and another was Bala Miller, who, in 1966, formed the Harbours Band, before moving to Kaduna to run the Sahara All Stars and Pyramids or Pyrameeds of Africa.

Okonta left Akpabot's Sextet in 1954 and spent a few years with Bobby Benson's Jam Session Orchestra. According to Bayo Martins, Okonta considered Benson 'a good master, teacher, father and disciplinarian [who] made me through his hard lectures'.[12] Like trumpeters Bill Friday and Zeal Onyia, Okonta developed the ability to play around with high notes for long periods of time. In short, he became one of Benson's great trumpeters. According to Benson Idonije writing in 2008:

> Eddy's trumpet is perhaps the clearest and strongest on the scene, playing around with the topmost notes of the instrument with ease as often as he wishes – a phenomenon that is traceable to Harry James and Louis Armstrong, two influential traditionalists who are Eddy's source of inspiration. Another attribute which sets him apart is the propelling force of his rhythmic concept which makes dancing irresistible; and it is no wonder at all that he stole the show a few years ago at a highlife night organised by veteran musician and impresario, Steve Rhodes at the Glover Memorial Hall, Lagos.[13]

Having learnt the ropes in Benson's orchestra, Okonta was ready to run his own band, which that he called the Top (or Star) Aces. It became the resident band of the Paradise Hotel in Ibadan from the late 1950s to 1960. Okonta played trumpet and rhythm guitar. The Top Aces also featured the Ghanaian singer

Nat Buckle and saxophonists Orlando Julius and Etim Udo. In 1960, Louis Armstrong played in Ibadan on his second African tour and was so impressed by Okonta that he gave him his white handkerchief and a trumpet with a golden mouthpiece.

Towards the end of 1960, Okonta relocated his, by then, seventeen-piece band to the Central Hotel in Yaba, Lagos. His Top Aces became one of the top highlife bands in the city until the Nigerian Civil War of 1967–70.

Over the years, Okonta produced a string of hit records including 'Asili', 'Oriwo', 'Okokoko' and 'Abele', a highlife that had earlier been popularised by E.T. Mensah's Tempos. Although Okonta reduced his active band-playing after the Nigerian Civil War, he continued to release record albums like his huge West African hits *Victory, Fire Back to Town* (in 1978) and *Eddy Okonta: The Obi of Trumpet* in the 1980s.

The Percussionist Bayo Martins

Adebayo Santos Martins was born on 24 November 1932, in Calabar. His mother was a local Efik and his father was descended from a Yoruba 'recaptive' – a freed slave rescued by British navy – who settled in Fernando Po (now called Bioko and part of Equatorial Guinea) in the Gulf of Guinea. Bayo Martins' family moved around and so, as a youngster in 1946, he became the maracas player for Inyang Henshaw's Weekend Inn Orchestra in Enugu. In 1951, he joined Bobby Benson's Jam Session Orchestra in Lagos, first as its maracas player and then in 1952 as its trap-drummer. Bayo got this chance when Benson's drummer King Roberto, together with Jibril Isa, Bill Friday and Dele Bamigboye, left to form the Delta Dandies, which subsequently relocated to Ghana.

According to the German musicologist Wolfgang Bender, Martins himself moved to Ghana in 1955 to join the Delta

Dandies and the Gold Coast Radio Band directed by Adolph Doku, one of the Tempos founders.[14] A year later, Martins returned to Lagos to join Chris Ajilo's Cubanos band, leaving them in 1957 to join E.C. Arinze and the Empire Orchestra.[15] It was when he was with Arinze that Martins released a number of highlifes and calypsos records for Decca Records. When Zeal Onyia returned from his two-year stay in the UK later that year, Martins joined him to form Zeal Onyia's Band, which played jazz and highlife at the Ambassador Hotel in Lagos.

In late 1958, Martins went to the UK, where he obtained a diploma in radio/TV journalism at the Trilsham School of Journalism and Television. Whilst in Britain he worked with American saxophonist Lucky Thompson, and the British percussionist Tommy Jones. Martins then went on to form his own band called Band Africana, which played in a more highlife mode. According to Bender this group included the Nigerian pianist Adam Fiberisima, tenor saxist Babyface Paul Osamade, the Ghanaian bassist George Hammond, percussionist Sol Amarfio and two Jamaicans. When Osamade was killed in a car accident in 1960, his place was taken by the recently arrived Peter King, who had begun his musical career in Ibadan in 1957 with Roy Chicago's Easy-Life Band, before moving to Lagos to join the bands of Victor Olaiya, Agu Norris, E.C. Arinze and Charles Iwegbue.[16] This Nigerian saxophonist subsequently formed his own band in London called the African Messengers, after a 1961 British tour by the Jazz Messengers, an African American band led by Art Blakey that pioneered the modern bebop style of drumming. Peter King's band therefore played bop-jazz, Afro-jazz and a jazzy style of highlife, and in this he was joined by Bayo Martins and the Nigerian trumpeter, Mike Falana.[17]

Peter King, one-time leader of the 1950s African Messengers, for which Bayo Martins played for an Accra show in 2008. (John Collins / BAPMAF)

Martins returned to Nigeria in 1962 and, having brought instruments with him, immediately became the drummer for Zeal Onyia's Koriko (Wolf) Clan Jazz Group that included the saxophonist Chris Ajilo, pianist Wole Bucknor, bassist Ayo Vaughan and percussionist Apollo Aramide.

Although this band played both jazz and highlife, it projected itself primarily as an Afro-jazz band, as by then newly independent Nigerians were seeing highlife as too colonial. As Martins explains:

It was a big turnaround after the 60s. People like myself, and others who were playing European ball room and popular music, suddenly became alienated. Nationalism changed the whole trend. Anything without its ethnic

159

roots was termed colonial mentality. Ballroom dancing completely disappeared, people were not dancing waltzes anymore; nobody danced foxtrots; nobody wanted to dance swing. National pride overtook everything. People wanted something authentic they could identify with as Efik, Hausa, Yoruba or Igbo. Those of us still playing European music just found ourselves a cultural and social outcast. This resulted in the experimentation that came about from the middle 60s – Bassey Ita talked about [it] in his book – and why Highlife as a title had to die.[18]

It was around this same time that Ghanaian Prime Minister Kwame Nkrumah and the CPP unsuccessfully attempted to change the name 'highlife' to 'osibisaaba', the old Fanti name for the coastal guitar form of this music. However, it never took effect as the use of the term 'highlife' was by then widespread in Ghana and beyond.

Around 1962/3 Bayo Martins and Wole Bucknor left Zeal's Afro-jazz group to help set up the Nigerian Navy Band. He also sometimes played trap drums for Fela Kuti's Jazz Quintet (formed before the Koola Lobitos in 1965) and helped co-form the Jazz Preachers in 1964 with Zeal Onyia, Art Alade, Ayo Vaughan and Chris Ajilo. By the time the Nigerian Civil War broke out in 1967 Martins had left the Navy band and was doing some musical journalistic and television work in Lagos. However, as nightlife was paralysed during the war, he jumped at the opportunity to travel with Agu Norris's band to Bulgaria. From there Martins travelled to Germany where he worked with the ethno-jazz band Mombasa led by the African Amercian trombonist Lou Blackburn.

When the civil war ended in 1970 Bayo returned home, where he and Chris Ajilo became two of the important forces behind the Nigerian Music Foundation established in 1971. By the late 1970s Martins was also working as a cultural officer at the University of Lagos. In 1980, he relocated to Hamburg, where he began to write and lecture on African music. In a paper entitled 'The Powers of Drums in the Society' he talks of music being 'the exact miniature of the laws working through the whole universe' and states that 'a society without music is a society without soul and may be regarded as dead.'[19]

The following is what Bayo said about the importance of African drumming, and music in general, in an interview for *African Music* in 1981 entitled 'The Drummer and His Message':

> Drums serve as a means of communication such as calling people to war, to make peace, to praise people, to make them joyful and console them in times of distress ... Above all, however, is the dance through which the individual is led to the discovering of the inner self – the 'I' in all of us. Music is [also] a social instrument or, let's say, a social weapon. Any sociologist will tell you that politicians exploit it for campaigns and indoctrinating political and national propaganda [whilst] advertisers use it to sloganize their products.[20]

During the 1980s Bayo began doing a lot of archival work and constantly travelled between and Nigeria and Germany.[21] He transformed the Nigerian Music Foundation into the Nigerian Music Foundation Archives to provide a database on popular musicians for scholarly, historical and journalistic research.[22] He and his Foundation also organised a series of 'Drum Conventions' that involved collaborative performances and lectures on African drumming. The one I attended was held at the Du Bois Memorial Centre in Accra in 1988, when Martins played with fellow Nigerian Remi Kabaka and the veteran Kofi Ghanaba.[23]

Because of my own archival work on Ghanaian popular music[24] I kept in touch with Bayo Martins until he passed away in Germany in 2003.

Bayo Martins with Ghanaba (in white clay) at the W.E.B. Du Bois
Centre in Accra in July 1981, when they played together at the Focus on
Nigeria event (Yemo Nunu)

The Trumpeter Roy Chicago

Roy Chicago, whose real name is John Akintola Ademuwagun, was born in the town of Ikare on the fringes of Ondo and Edo states and was educated in Sapele, Delta State, in Nigeria. He became a teacher in an Ondo State grammar school and, since he had learnt trumpet and saxophone by this time,[25] he ran the school band and taught trumpet. His students included the young Dele Ojo, who went on to become a well-known juju music performer.

Whilst still a teacher, Roy Chicago was able to do some part-time playing in Ibadan with the band of Hubert Ogunde's theatrical group and the Green Spring Hotel Band. In 1958 Chicago gave up teaching to go into music full-time, and moved to Lagos to join Bobby Benson's Hep Cats. According to Benson Idonije, Chicago 'benefited from the tutelage of Bobby Benson both in terms of learning to play the saxophone and band leadership.'[26]

By 1960, Chicago was ready to go solo and formed his Rhythm Dandies, based at the Abalabi Hotel in Mushin, Lagos. From there, he and his group moved to the Plaza Hotel in Surulere, Lagos, where he finally set up his own nightclub called the Club Chicago. His band provided the same full repertoire of highlifes, jives, Latin music and ballroom dance music as Benson's band – they even had similar clientele that consisted largely of elite Nigerians and foreigners.

A number of musicians passed through Roy Chicago's Rhythm Dandies, including guitarists Mike Enahiro and Alaba Pedro. At one point Chicago's keyboard player was the young Segun Bucknor (cousin of the pianist Wole Bucknor) who later became an early exponent of Afro-soul. Some of Chicago's horns players were the alto/tenor-saxist Etim Udo and the trumpeter Marco Bazz, who could hit prominent high notes; a technique that Chicago himself was also very good at. The singers of Chicago's Rhythm Dandies were Apollo Aramide, Jimi Solanke and the young Tunde Osofisan who became famous as an actor.

By the time of his death in 1989, Roy Chicago had produced almost sixty records. Some of his 1960s hits were 'Bosede', 'Maria' and 'Olojo Nkajo'. Quite a number of his songs had a philosophical or social message, such as 'Aiye Loja', 'Igbehin Lalaya Nnta', 'Asiko Nlo' and 'Tepa Mose'. Chicago was also interested in making his music distinctively Nigerian and so would often orchestrate and record local folk-tunes such as 'Yoyo Gbe', and 'Gbara Mumu'.

Idonije says Chicago's songs helped 'give his highlife the Nigerian and African identity, as opposed to the conventional songs and church-hymn melodies that were bandied around by his predecessors.'[27] Idonije told me about some of these songs:

> Three songs that helped Roy Chicago Nigerianise highlife were 'Iyawo Pankeke', that is condemning the use of a type of round cheap make-up powder or 'pancake' that women rub in their faces. Then there was 'Keregbe Emu', that means a keg of palmwine. And also 'Are Owo Niesa Yoya Gbe', that means we should look well for money, or that money is worth looking for.[28]

Another way Chicago Nigerianised highlife was to become the first dance-band musician to introduce the local dundun pressure drum (or hour-glass drum). The drum, a traditional Nigerian 'talking drum', was usually associated with Yoruba juju guitar bands. An example of Chicago's use of this Yoruba instrument is the song 'Sere Fun Mi, Baby'. This was released by the Phillips Record Company in 1961 and utilised typical Ghanaian highlife chord progressions as well as African American 'blues notes' woven into the trumpet and saxophone's melodies. However, as the Austrian musicologist Gerhard Kubik puts it, 'to give Nigerian highlife a Yoruba authenticity' there is a section of Chicago's song when the melody instruments stop and the percussion takes over, with Apollo Aramide (or 'Dr Apollo') using the Yoruba dundun pressure drums to speak out Yoruba phrases.[29]

Things got very difficult for Roy Chicago during the Nigerian Civil War from 1967 to 1970. Although, like Benson and Olaiya, he was Yoruba and so could continue playing in Lagos, his bandsmen were all drafted into the Nigerian Army and his band collapsed. After the war, dance band highlife in Lagos went into decline whilst juju music rose to ascendancy. It was about this time that I met Roy Chicago. When I visited his house in 1974 he spoke at length to me about the problems he was having running his band and nightclub. Despite some financial help from his old music boss, Bobby Benson, who bought him new equipment, Chicago was never able to revive either his Rhythm Dandies or his nightspot.

1. Benson Idonije, 'Echoes of the Sixties', *Lagos Guardian*, 1 October 2009.
2. Larnyoh was from Takoradi, and had been trained in the Tricky Johnson Palmcourt Band and the Accra-based Delta Dandies, run by the Nigerian Jibril Isa. After leaving the Downbeats, Larnyoh formed his own Star Aces band.
3. Personal communication, Osu Accra, 15 February 1977.
4. Tam Fiofori, 'Zeal Onyia – Trumpet Virtuoso and Music Producer', *Africa Music*, 6 (November/December 1981) pp. 8–11.
5. Benson Idonije, 'Legacy of Bobby Benson of Africa' *Lagos Guardian*, 21 May 2008. Bayo Martins, 'Remembering the Trumpeter Zeal Onyia', *Lagos Guardian*, 2 May 2001. Some of the other members of the Rhythm Aces were Freddy Tate, the trumpeter Apollo Fiberesima, Prince Bruce on vocals and claves, Max Amah (or Armah) on drums, Pete Vanderpuie on double bass, Sunday Eze on maracas and Peter Onyeador on congas.
6. Zeal Onyia had met Lumumba in Ghana in December 1958 when he went to Accra for the All-African People's Conference, a precursor to the Organisation of African Unity.
7. That portion of the tour was financed by Pepsi-Cola.
8. Martins, 'Remembering the Trumpeter Zeal Onyia', 2001.
9. These include Rex Lawson at the Dolphin Hotel; Steve Rhodes, the director of Nigerian Broadcasting Corporation Band; Babyface Paul Osamade's Top Toppers; the Jobafro Aces; Eddy Okonta's Top Aces; and the pianists Fela Sowande, Sammy Akpabot, Sid Morris, Art Alade and Keri Miko.
10. This was when I met Zeal, as I was in Nigeria acting in Fela Kuti's *Black President* film.
11. Akpabot was born in 1932 in Uyo, Akwa-Ibom State, and his career embraced both Nigerian popular music and art music. After folding up his Sextet in 1954 he studied at the London Royal College of Music, then worked for the Nigerian State Broadcasting Corporation until 1962, when he began teaching at the universities of Nsukka and Ibadan. In the 1960s, he composed orchestral pieces, such as the Igbo/Efik folk-opera 'Jaja of Opodo', which drew on local folk resources. However, an earlier piece, 'Nigeriana: An Overture for a Nigerian Ballet', was influenced by highlife.
12. Bayo Martins, 'Tribute to Bobby Benson: The Man and his Music', *Africa Music*, 20 (March/April 1984), p. 11.
13. Idonije, 'Legacy of Bobby Benson', 2008.
14. Wolfgang Bender, 'Bayo Martins: Voice of the Drum' (Lagos: Music Foundation Nigeria, 2004).
15. Martins says this group included the Ghanaian electric guitarist, Longman Akwa, who had been playing with the Shambros Band at the Lido nightclub in Accra' (Bender, 2004).

16. King was in London until 1968, when he returned to Lagos to run The Voice of Africa band. In 1971 he moved back to London to form the Afro-jazz/funk band Shango (which included the Ghanaian bassist Ernie Baidoo) that represented Black Britain during FESTAC '77 in Nigeria. Since the 2000s, King now runs a music college in Nigeria. For more details on him, see Segun Narcet, 'Jazz Scene: Peter King Sax Genius', *African Music*, 2, March/April 1981, pages 16–17.

17. Falana began his career with Godwin Omabuwa's Cassanova Dandies highlife band in Lagos. But he was also interested in modern jazz, and so went to Britain to join Peter King's African Messengers. Falana stayed in the UK and later worked with a number of rock artists in London, like Graham Bond and Ginger Baker.

18. Bayo Martins, interviewed in BENDER, Wolfgang. 2004. 'Bayo Martins: Voice of the Drum', Lagos: Music Foundation Nigeria.

19. Bayo Martins, 'The Powers of Drums in the Society'. A portion of this paper is with the J. Collins/BAPMAF music archives in Accra.

20. Bayo Martins, 'The Drummer and His Message', *African Music*, 3 (May/June 1981), pp. 10–12.

21. This is where I met him in the mid-1980s.

22. This was launched in Lagos in 1996 with the help of Dr Wolfgang Bender of the University of Mainz, the German Foreign Service Cultural Division and the Lagos-based International Centre for the Arts.

23. This was part of a three-day 'Focus on Nigeria' event when the Nigerian High Commissioner in Ghana presented Nigerian cultural material to the archivest of the Du Bois Centre (see Collins, 1988).

24. The Bokoor African Popular Music Archives Foundation, BAPMAF, that I and a group of local highlife musicians set up in Accra in 1990.

25. Benson Idonije, 'Tonight Rains Off Highlife with Roy Chicago's Return', *Lagos Guardian*, 5 February 2003.

26. Idonije, 'Legacy of Bobby Benson', 2008.

27. Ibid.

28. Benson Idonije, personal communication, Accra, November 2009. I spoke to Idonije, after we gave presentations together on highlife history at Ghana's National Theatre for the High Vibes symposium/festival sponsored by the French Embassy, UNESCO and the Ghanaian Ministry of Chieftaincy and Culture.

29. Gerhard Kubik, *Africa and the Blues* (University Press of Mississippi, 1999), p. 156.

10

Victor Olaiya and Chris Ajilo

B andleader Victor Olaiya was a major highlife figure from the 1950s and has been involved in the attempts to revive highlife in recent years. Like Bobby Benson, Olaiya's various bands were a training-ground for a number of musicians including the young Victor Uwaifo, Fela Ransome-Kuti, Dele Ojo, Yinusa Akinnibosun and Rex Lawson. Another leading personality in Nigerian highlife is Chris Ajilo, who worked with Olaiya in an early version of the Cool Cats.

Victor Olaiya, the 'Evil Genius' of Highlife

Victor Owolabi Abimbola Olaiya, the famous Nigerian vocalist, composer and trumpeter, was born on 31 December 1932, in the town of Calabar in Cross River State where his Yoruba parents had settled. His father, Alfred Omolona Olaiya, originated from Lagos and was a church organist, whilst Olaiya's mother, Bathsheba Ayodele Owolabi Motajo, was a folksinger who came from the ancient Yoruba city of Oyo. Olaiya was a pupil of the Roman Catholic Mission Primary School at Owerri in present-day Imo State and his parents' musical inclination helped him get an early musical start. So when he went to the African College in Onitsha in Anambra State in 1946, he became the French-horn player for the school band and then advanced to the B-flat clarinet before eventually graduating to trumpet.[1]

After his secondary education, Olaiya moved to Lagos where he played for several street brass bands such as B. Effiong's band. He then joined the long established Lagos City

Orchestra and Sammy Akpabot's Sextet, before joining Bobby Benson's outfit as a vocalist and trumpeter where he obtained a professional polish. Olaiya could sing fluently in Yoruba, Igbo and Hausa and because of his musical talents Bobby Benson put him in charge of his second band, the Alfa's Carnival Group.[2] It was at this time that Olaiya was first exposed to the big band highlife of E.T. Mensah, when the Tempos made a trip to Lagos in 1951.

Between 1953 and 1954, Olaiya went to Britain to study accountancy. While there, he formed a band called the Cool Cats with fellow Nigerian Chris Ajilo who played saxophone and clarinet and was also studying in the UK at the time. Some of the other members of the Cool Cats were the Nigerian trumpeter 'Consul' Anifowose and the Ghanaian saxophonist and clarinettist Sammy Lartey.

When Olaiya returned to Nigeria in 1954, he became an accountant clerk with the Lagos City Council and formed the Cool Cats Orchestra, retaining the name of the UK group. They were based at the West End Cafe in Lagos. In 1956 Olaiya's Cool Cats was selected to play at the state ball held when Queen Elizabeth II visited Nigeria. In 1959 Olaiya changed the name of the band to the All Stars Orchestra.

Some of the highlife hits of his Cool Cats/All Stars bands were 'Mamude', 'Odale Ore', 'Mofe Muyon', 'Lafia We Lawani', and 'Ko Fo'run'. He also released songs in a Ghanaian mode such as 'Ya Bonsa No. 2', based on the classic Ghanaian highlife 'Yaa Amponsah' and 'Bosue', first popularised by Joe Mensah. Olaiya's recording career was so successful that he was the first to receive a platinum record in Nigeria for the Philips/Polydor/Polygram Company. Indeed, Olaiya became so famous that he became known as 'Dr. Victor Olaiya', the 'Evil Genius of Highlife'.

For a while, Olaiya was an executive of the first Nigerian Union of Musicians (NUM) that had been formed in 1958, and was involved in the NUM demonstration to get a Nigerian band to play at the first Nigerian Independence Ball and Banquet in October 1960. Olaiya's band was enriched at this function by the presence of Zeal Onyia. Despite the success of the NUM, Olaiya and Bobby Benson subsequently split away from this organisation to form a separate music association.

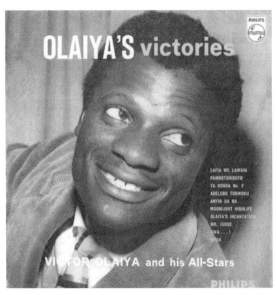

Cover of Victor Olaiya's album, *Olaiya's Victories*, released by Philips

Olaiya's career continued to grow when, in 1963, his All Stars were invited to play at the State Banquet that marked Nigeria's adoption of a republican constitution. The same year Olaiya represented Nigeria at the World Jazz Festival in Prague, Czech Republic, where he was given an honorary doctorate in music. Around this time Olaiya's band was drafted to perform for the Nigerian and other West African troops who were part of the United Nations peace-making mission during the 1960–5

Congolese Civil War. In fact Olaiya's popularity became so great that during Nigeria's civil war of 1967–70 his band was commissioned to play at various war fronts and Olaiya himself was given the rank of an honorary Lieutenant-Colonel in the Nigerian Army.

In the late 1960s, Olaiya's band had begun playing some of their own soul and funk-influenced compositions, like 'I Feel Alright' and 'Mother Popcorn', that appeared on his 1970 album *Victor Olaiya's All Stars Soul International*. According to Michael Veal, when the American soul singer James Brown visited Nigeria in December 1970 he and one of his vocalists, Narva Whitney, recorded some tracks with Victor Olaiya.[3]

Olaiya was a trained accountant and so was able to develop a thriving business in the import and distribution of musical instruments. As a result, by the early seventies he had built his Stadium Hotel Complex, which included the Papingo Nightclub, where he performed, in Surulere, Lagos. The place had interesting mural silhouettes of people dancing and playing instruments. It was there that Olaiya confirmed what E.T. Mensah had earlier told me about the influence of the Tempos band on Olaiya and other Nigerian dance band musicians in the early 1950s. Olaiya also told me that there had been another wave of highlife coming in from Ghana much earlier than E.T. Mensah's dance band variety known as 'konkoma' highlife.[4]

By 1980 Olaiya was running a ten-piece band that he called the International Stars. At the same time, he was attempting to revive dance band highlife, which had gone into decline after the Nigerian Civil War. One part of this strategy was to bring over and collaborate with his mentor, E.T. Mensah. During the Christmas/New Year period of 1983–4, E.T. spent a month with Olaiya playing at the Papingo Club and recording with him at the Polygram studio in Ikeja. The journalist Ndubuisi

Olwechime interviewed Olaiya and E.T. Mensah at their first joint Papingo performance on 24 December 1983 and asked Olaiya about the decline of highlife. Olaiya replied that this was necessary to allow for the development of other African musical forms:

> All forms that emerged are in fact distant off-shoots of highlife. So, in fact, highlife music did not lose its hold, it only transformed into more dynamic tunes.

E.T. Mensah told Olwechime that:

> It is the duty of today's musicians to make an advantageous use of modern techniques of production to give highlife its modern status ... We are trying to promote harmony between both our styles of play, and see whether we can forge some acceptable developments in these styles for highlife lovers.[5]

The result of this Nigerian/Ghanaian highlife collaboration was their joint album *Highlife Giants of Africa*, released in 1984 by Polygram. It included old Olaiya hits like 'Trumpet Highlife', 'Mr. Judge' and 'Omalanke', as well as the Ghanaian songs 'Anyanko Goro', 'Essi Nann' and 'Odofo Nua.'

After this 1984 album, Olaiya continued his highlife revival strategy by going on to release a number of other albums of his old songs for Polydor/Polygram (later called Premier Records in Nigeria). These oldies rereleased in the mid-1980s include 'Ilu Le-O' or 'Country Hard-O', 'Dr Olaiya in the 60s', 'Highlife Reincarnation' and, a little later, 'Three Decades of Highlife'.

Victor Olaiya and E.T. Mensah together on the cover of their 1984
Polygram record album, *Highlife Giants of Africa*

Victor Olaiya has also been involved with the current
highlife revival since the late 1990s that has been going on
in Lagos. These are the various Highlife Elders Forums and
Highlife Parties that have been organised by people like Renate
Albertson, Benson Idonije and Jahman Anikulapo, as well as
Lagos-based organisations such as the Goethe-Institut, O'Jez
Club, Alliance Francaise, the Musical Society of Nigeria
(MUSON) and the Committee for Relevant Art (CORA).
In 2002, Olaiya spoke to the Nigerian journalist Emeka
Nwachukwu concerning the importance of highlife and the
need to maintain it:

> I know that highlife is still on the map of Nigeria, it's the lingua
> franca and there's nothing you can do about that. Every other
> type of music will come and go. Today, pachanga, tomorrow,
> pop. This time it's makossa, next day reggae. Everything soon

dies off as usual. But highlife is the only music in this country that has stood and will continue to stand the test of time. So there is no gainsaying about it, highlife will dominate. If you watch, the up-and-coming artists now go for highlife. And us [veterans] are doing a lot. If we can get more moral support from the media, I think highlife will be placed in its rightful position.[6]

Some of the important musicians who passed through his various bands include trumpeter Rex Lawson who worked with several Lagos highlife bands during the 1950s, including Victor Olaiya's Cool Cats (see Chapter 19). In 1957, after leaving secondary school, the nineteen-year-old Fela Anikulapo-Kuti (then Ransome-Kuti) began working for the Ministry of Commerce in the daytime and singing with Olaiya's Cool Cats in the evenings. A couple of years later, the young Victor Uwaifo spent nine months with Olaiya's band when he was attending Saint Gregory's School in Lagos (see Chapter 11). Other members of the Cool Cats clan were the guitarists Allani Pereira and Yinka Roberts, and the saxophonist Yinusa Akinnibosun.

Yet another Olaiya graduate is Dele Ojo who introduced the highlife guitar style into Yoruba juju music. Ojo moved from his native Ondo State to Lagos in 1959 and joined Olaiya in 1961 as trumpeter, guitarist and singer. In fact Ojo was the second trumpeter for Olaiya's short-lived second band, which collapsed after just two years. Ojo then dropped the trumpet and, in 1963, at twenty-three, formed his own juju-music guitar band called the Star Brothers.[7]

During the 1980s and early 1990s, Olaiya continued playing with his International Stars at his Stadium Club and sometimes toured Nigeria. After this he went into retirement but at the time of writing, he continued to operate and occasionally played at his Stadium Hotel. His son, Bayode, is a trumpeter whilst his grand-daughter Wunmi (Omotayo Olufunke Olaiya) is a UK-based Afrobeat singer.

The Saxophonist Chris Ajilo

As mentioned earlier, Chris Ajilo and Victor Olaiya collaborated on the UK-based Cool Cats band in the early 1950s. Chris Ajilo was born in Lagos in 1930 and left Nigeria in 1946 for Ghana and Senegal, finally ending up in the UK, where he studied engineering in Birmingham. He then opted to study music in London at the Central School of Dance Music where he learnt saxophone and clarinet. He also worked part-time in Birmingham, where the Cool Cats were based. In London, Ajilo played with a lot of West African bands. He was involved with one of the Afro-Cuban combos that Kofi Ghanaba (then known as Guy Warren) formed with fellow West Africans in 1950 to play at parties. Another was the West African Rhythm Brothers set up by vocalist/percussionist Ambrose Campbell and guitarist Brewster Hughes in 1945/6.[8] It consisted of West African and West Indian musicians and played juju, highlifes, swing and West Indian calypsos and mentos. Besides Ajilo other Nigerian members of this band included pianist Adam Fiberesima, bongos player Ade Bashorun,[9] Eddie Edem, Olapido Anjou, Oni Pedro and the percussionist 'Ginger' Folorunso Johnson.

Chris Ajilo returned to Nigeria in 1955, ready to form his own band there. He called his group the Afro Cubanos or Cubanos. Fela Kuti's famous baritone saxophonist, Lekan Animashaun, was one of its members, as was the drummer Bayo Martins, for a while. [10] They were based in Ibadan and played highlifes, jazz, swing and Afro-Cuban music. Ajilo's

Afro-Cubanos went on to have a number of hit records in the 1960s like 'Eko O'Gba' and 'Ariwo'.

UK-based Nigerian musician Ambrose Campbell, with whom Chris Ajilo
sometimes played (*Highlife Today* album cover)

In 1958 Ajilo became executive of the Nigerian Union of Musicians and in 1959 became a founding member of the Nigerian Broadcasting Corporation Band, whose director general was the 33-year-old composer and musicologist Steve Rhodes.[11] Around 1964 Ajilo became involved with the Lagos-based Art Alade's Jazz Preachers, with Zeal Onyia, Ayo Vaughan and Bayo Martins.

In 1971 Chris Ajilo became a member of Bayo Martins' Music Foundation that also included Bobby Benson, Wole Bucknor and Fela Anikulapo-Kuti on its executive board. This foundation operated a music school, based at the Kakadu Club in Yaba, of which Ajilo was the director. In 1979 Ajilo became a music producer for Polygram Records, now known as Premier Records and managed by Toju Ajuiyitchie. Ajilo was also the general manager of the Performing and Mechanical Rights Society of Nigeria until his retirement in 2007.

1. For more on Victor Olaiya, see 'Victor Olaiya: Fifty Years of Ingenious Highlife on Stage', written by Richard Eghaghe, the entertainment correspondent of the *Nigerian Daily Independent*, for the release of the 2009 album *The Best Of Dr. Victor Olaiya*. Released by Premier Records Lagos.
2. Benson Idonije, 'Echoes of the Sixties' *Lagos Guardian*, 1 October 2009.
3. 'Soul or Highlife: Both', *Nigeria Daily Times*, June 1971 referenced by Michael Veal, *Fela* (USA: Temple University Press, 2000), p. 89.
4. It was when I was playing at the Papingo Club in 1974 with the Ghanaian Bunzu Band that I talked to Olaiya and met Dean Dizzy, Segun Narcet and Tony Amadi, the top Nigerian pop-music journalists of the day. As a result, I became the Ghanaian correspondent for Tony Amadi's Lagos-based *Music Express* magazine.
5. Ndubuisi Olwechime, 'Highlife Revival Imminent', *Africa Music*, 21, (May/June 1984), p. 13.
6. Victor Olaiya, interviewed by Emeka Nwachukwu in the *Lagos Guardian*, 9 November 2002.
7. This band had a number of hit records during the 1960s, like 'Bouncing Bona' and 'Christiana Enia Bi Apapro'. The group also toured the UK, and when Ojo left for a prolonged stay in the United States, his popularity was overtaken by the juju stars Ebenezer Obey and Sunny Ade. For more information on Dele Ojo see T. Ajayi Thomas, 1992, pp. 134–7.
8. Both Ambrose Oladipupo Adekoya Campbell and Brewster Hughes (Ade Bashorun) had been members of the Lagos Jolly Boys Orchestra palm wine group in the 1930s, before relocating to London.
9. Previously a member of Ayinde Bakare's pioneering, Lagos-based juju guitar band.
10. Martins says the musicians working with Ajilo's band in 1956/7 were Tony Obs, alto sax; Marco Bass, trumpet; Tex Oluwa, double bass; Landa Sashore, bongos; Candido Ajayi, congas; Victoria Akaeze Peters, maracas, vocals and dance (Bender, 2004).
11. Steve Bankole Omodele Rhodes went on to become programme controller of Western Nigerian Television (WNTV) and during the late sixties and early seventies, ran his Rhodes Sound-Vision Company, which managed artists such as Fela Anikulapo-Kuti, Sonny Okosun, Victor Uwaifo, Pat Finn (of the Hykkers) and the Ghanaian Rolling Beats Dance Troupe. For more information on him see the editorial in *Sun News*, 10 June 2008.

11

Victor Uwaifo: The Nigerian Bini Highlife Maestro

During the 1960s and 1970s, one of the most prolific highlife artists of Nigeria was Victor Uwaifo of Benin City in Edo State (formerly known as Bendel State). During this time he and his Melody Maestros released well over a hundred records, and Uwaifo himself was the first Nigerian to win a Gold Disc award. At the same time he also established a hotel and a nightclub in his home town. Although his full-time musical activities began to decline in the 1980s, Uwaifo went on to set up one of the first privately owned television studios in Nigeria, and later founded a music and arts academy. In the 2000s he was named the Commissioner of Arts and Culture for the Edo State government.

Uwaifo was born into a musical family in 1941 in Benin City. He made his very first guitar, and was first taught the instrument by a local palm wine musician, and later by Dizzy Acquaye, the guitarist for the Tempos, who was visiting Nigeria at the time. Uwaifo left Benin City and went to secondary school at Saint Gregory's in Lagos. In his spare time he joined Victor Olaiya's highlife dance band. This is what Uwaifo told me when I interveiwed him in Benin City in 1975:

I used to see E.T. Mensah and his Tempos play whenever they were in Benin, and the year I lost my father I went to see their guitarist Dizzy Acquaye, to put me through a few chords. I had a guitar book my brother had bought me but I didn't understand the chords; for instead of drawing the full neck of the guitar they only drew three frets. Dizzy helped me. Fortunately at Saint Gregory's we had a music tutor, so I obtained a perfect knowledge of the rudiments of music. So I headed the school band. It was during these school days I spent nine months with Victor Olaiya's All Stars, playing during the holidays and weekends. But the school said I had to choose between them and the All Stars. So I had to leave Olaiya.

In 1962, Uwaifo won a scholarship to the Yaba College of Technology where he focused on his three main interests: studying in the morning, wrestling and athletics in the afternoon and playing with E.C. Arinze's highlife band at the Kakadu Club in the evenings. In 1964 he joined the Nigerian Television Authority as a graphic artist and in 1965 he put together the Melody Maestros, which played his own distinct blend of highlife music based on the Bini folk-art of Edo State.

He rose to fame between 1965 and 1967 when his band released three smash hit singles on the Phonogram/Polygram label. These were 'Sirri-Sirri', 'Guitar Boy/Mammy Water' and 'Joromi', which was so popular that it earned Uwaifo Africa's first Gold Disc Award in 1969. The lyrics of 'Joromi' are based a legendary Bini story about the boy Joromi who climbs a magical palm tree up to hell where, after an eight-hour wrestling match, he vanquished a two-headed giant. He does this with the help of his sister chanting 'Joromi O, Omijoro, Kiri Kesekese, Joromi O'[1] – a key phrase in Uwaifo's song. 'Guitar Boy/Mammy Water' is about how Uwaifo was able to stand his ground in the presence of the West African mermaid or 'Mammy Water', whom he claims he met one late night after a show at Bar Beach on Victoria Island, Lagos. As he explains, he heard a shrill voice calling out, 'guitar boy', and after playing to her for a while, the mermaid floated away; thus the lyrics 'if you see Mammy Water never run away'.[2]

Uwaifo became so famous in Nigeria for his early songs that in 1969 the students of the University of Nigeria, Nsukka, dubbed him 'Sir' Victor Uwaifo.

'Guitar boy' Victor Uwaifo with his famous Siamese twin guitar in the mid-seventies (Victor Uwaifo)

Uwaifo's early songs, like 'Joromi' were based on what he called the 'akwete' beat, which, he explained to me in 1975, had an interesting, non-musical origin as it was created by Uwaifo using colours to represent musical notes:

It was at art school that I discovered colours in sound and sound in colours. I carried out some research in colours and was able to transpose them so that Do, the strongest note, was black; Re was red; Mi was blue; Fa was green; So, white, as it is a neutral color and sound; La was yellow and Ti violet. But the whole change came when I transposed the colours of akwete cloth, the handwoven cloth made in Eastern Nigeria. It is a very beautiful cloth and you will see that different colours recur, creating a moving rhythm of colour. When I interpreted this it gave the 'akwete' sound.[3]

Uwaifo released over one hundred singles and a dozen albums for which he created or utilised a number of rhythmic beats. In the late 1960s there was the 'shadow' and 'mutaba' that combined Edo highlife with the imported twist and soul music. These were followed in the early 1970s by the 'ekassa' and in the mid-1970s by 'sasakossa', both based on traditional Edo music. Here is what Uwaifo told me about ekassa and sasakossa in 1975:

In fact, I wouldn't say I created ekassa, as it was already here as an indigenous dance of Benin [City]. It was a royal dance done during the coronation of a new king and some people thought it an abomination to see it while the king was still alive. I didn't mind them as the first tune was a brilliant hit and others followed. Ekassa incorporates the beat of the tom-tom and agba drums, western wind instruments, two guitars and me singing in the Edo language.[4] After a few years I started to think of something else, so I created 'sasakossa'.

There was a time during the period when the Benin kingdom was overpowered by the British that the Benin massacre took place. It was when the king of England sent explorers to Africa to trade with the King of Benin. But the king had an important festival and said he would not grant the English an audience. But they were stubborn to come and they were intercepted and killed. A few managed to escape to England where they were reinforced and came back for revenge. It was then that Benin was almost completely destroyed and the Oba or king went into hiding.

The king had an orderly named Sasakossa who used to sing in a popular way to warn him that there was danger and it was not safe. He had a peculiar song he used to sing when it was safe to come out of hiding. The song was full of gimmicks. Whenever the white police got information about the hideout they would track the king down, but the orderly or people around would warn him that enemies were around with the song. So that's where I got the rhythm for my latest sound, sasakossa.

Many musicians played with Victor's Melody Maestros, such as the female vocalist Joe Mokwunyei from eastern Nigeria and the Ghanaian guitarist Osei Bonsu Senior. Some of the top highlife musicians of the Benin City area also passed through Uwaifo's band, including Collings Oke, who formed the Odoligue Nobles, as well as Dandy Oboy[5] and Mudogo Osegie, who left Uwaifo in 1971 to form the Musketeers, who played what they called 'bushpower'. Another leading Bini musician who was initiated by the Melody Maestros was the guitarist Sonny Okosun who joined Uwaifo in 1969 and left him in 1972 to create the Afro-rock music he called 'ozzidi' (the name of an Ijaw god), which combined highlife and western rock music. He later released reggae-based songs like 'Papa's Land' and 'Fire in Soweto', which were enormous hits in the late seventies.

Reggae music became so popular in Nigeria during the seventies that Jamaican reggae star Jimmy Cliff toured the country in 1974. As a result, by the late 1970s, Uwaifo began to experiment with this West Indian music in hit releases like 'When the Sun Shines' and 'Five Day a Week Love' which gave Uwaifo his second Gold Award from Polygram.

Victor and his Melody Maestros travelled extensively throughout his early musical career. He toured Nigeria many times, visited other African countries and toured overseas. In 1966 Uwaifo and his band represented Nigeria at the first Black Arts Festival held in Dakar. Between 1966 and 1968 they visited Ghana, Côte d'Ivoire, Togo and Benin. Then, in 1969, they went to the Black Arts Festival in Algeria to represent Nigeria and won a Bronze Medal. The following year saw him and his group in the Middle East and Hong Kong, ending up in Japan for the World Expo '70 where Uwaifo won a Silver Medal. That same year the Melody Maestros visited the USA. In 1971 the band toured Northern Nigeria for a month and then, in 1973 – together with a traditional dance troupe – went on an extended seven-week tour of eastern and western Europe. In the UK segment of this tour they played at the London Roundhouse. Uwaifo commented on the mixed reviews the band got from some British journalists:

> They felt my band shouldn't have been included in a troupe that was basically cultural. They thought my music was too modern and sophisticated than the rest. In fact, some critics tagged my music 'Rock' and some 'Pop'. Unfortunately they failed to see that the foundation of my music was very cultural. I later had the opportunity to answer the press misunderstanding of my music when I was interviewed three times on BBC. I explained that my music is rich in African culture as demonstrated in the beat and lyrics. The fact that I use modern musical instruments to produce my sound has not altered the basic character of

the music; otherwise we might as well argue that a historian should not write ancient history with modern tools like a Parker pen and paper. Nature abhors a vacuum and thus we have had experimentation and evolution of ancient African culture. My music is no exception to this natural phenomenon.[6]

Victor Uwaifo in the Mid-1970s

I first met Victor Uwaifo in Accra in 1975 when he was on a trip to Cape Coast, the home town of his Ghanaian wife, Adelaide.[7] Soon after our meeting I did a recording session with Uwaifo, playing harmonica on the song 'West African Safari' for the *Laugh and Cry* album he released on the Black Bell label. We discussed the idea of my also writing his biography. So he invited me to stay with him in his home town in Benin City during the Christmas/New Year holiday to work on the project and tour with his Melody Maestros band.[8]

Back of the 1975 *Laugh and Cry* album, with pictures of Victor Uwaifo,
John Collins and John Chernoff. (Victor Uwaifo)

In December 1975 I travelled to Benin City from Accra by road and lodged at Uwaifo's Joromi Hotel on the outskirts of town with some of his bandsmen and the Ghanaian guitarist Osei Bonsu Senior. The Joromi Hotel, named after his hit record, was built in 1971 and was full of sculptures and artworks done by Uwaifo himself. The hotel's open-air stage was undergoing extensions at the time and so the first time I saw Uwaifo play was at his newly opened discotheque, Club 400, in the centre of Benin City.

A typical show there would start with the ten-man Melody Maestros warming up with some pop numbers, sung that Christmas by Ghanaian soul music vocalist Picket – now known as 'McGod'. Then Uwaifo would come in wearing spectacular clothes he designed himself. He would dance, sing and play various instruments such as the traditional xylophone, the western flute and the electric organ, which he sometimes played with his chin. But his main instrument was the guitar and he left everyone spellbound with his amazing 'Joromi' solo, especially when he used his double 'Siamese guitar' that he would spin around a pivot on his belt. Uwaifo was accompanied by two 'little people' playing wooden claves and maracas, who moved backward and forward across the stage, darting in-between Uwaifo's legs. One of them, King Pago, told me that during the 1950s he had been with Bobby Benson's Lagos-based dance band. The support band that was also playing at Uwaifo's Club 400 that Christmas was Ignace De Souza's Black Santiagos (more on him in Chapter 13).

I discovered that Uwaifo did not smoke or drink and was a strict disciplinarian with his bandsmen. He was also a restless man, always on the move and looking for things to do. Having been a semi-professional athlete and wrestler he was also physically very strong, and so even after a night's show he would sometimes take me in his sports car to cruise around town and check out the other nightspots. On Sunday mornings, he would take me to Camp David,[9] a drinking spot located in a palm tree plantation that was the haunt of many of the town's 'bigmen'. Here fresh palm wine was tapped from living trees and Nigerian and Ghanaian highlife was played from portable radios hanging from branches.

Some of Victor Uwaifo's Melody Maestros perched on a statue of 'guitarboy' Uwaifo at his Joromi Hotel in Benin City in 1975 (John Collins)

During this trip I toured eastern Nigeria in a minibus with Victor and his group, first crossing the Niger River Bridge that had been partially wrecked during the Nigerian Civil War. The band visited, and played in, Enugu, Onitsha, Aba and surrounding towns. Southeastern Nigeria is musically in the

185

highlife zone, so the ambience of the shows reminded me of my guitar band tours in Ghana. The forms of highlife played by these touring guitar bands were remarkably similar. I also saw townspeople and farmers enjoying unpretentious evening shows together in simple open-air venues that served beer and local drinks to fans seated at small tables surrounding a space for dancing couples.

Victor Uwaifo in More Recent Years

During the late 1970s when he was still developing his sasakossa beat, Uwaifo set up a sixteen-track recording studio in Benin City. In the early 1980s he changed his band's name from the Melody Maestros to Victor Uwaifo and His Titibitis and experimented with local versions of reggae and disco. Then, in the mid-1980s, he established a music academy, an art gallery and Nigeria's first private television studio, called the JTV Studio, where he produced TV programmes and made many commercial music videos for his band and other music groups. In the 1990s he got a master's degree in art at the University of Benin and wrote a book of poems and essays called *Philosophy of Life*, published in 1995 by his own publishing company, Joromi Publications. At the same time he expanded his art gallery into The Legacy Museum and Hall of Fame.

This addition to the Joromi complex included paintings and sculptures done by Uwaifo, costumes designed by him, photos, album covers, newspaper cuttings and other memorabilia connected with Uwaifo's varied and multifaceted career, as well as space for other men and women who had distinguished themselves in various fields. It also includes a room dedicated to the Joromi legend, containing figures of masked demons. Another room is dedicated to the heritage of the Benin Kingdom and yet another, sombre room, is full of statues of African slaves in chains.

In 1997 he became a member of the National Advisory Council of the Performing Musicians Association of Nigeria (PMAN) and a recipient of PMAN's Evergreen Award. In 2000, Uwaifo was appointed Honourable Commissioner for the Ministry of Arts, Culture and Tourism of Edo State and became a member of the Edo State Executive Council.

In August 2003, Uwaifo briefly visited Ghana and teamed up with local highlife musicians to play some of his old hits at Cape Coast for that year's Pan African Historical Theatre Project (PANAFEST). Uwaifo's music has become of interest to world music fans; his music appears on the *Sir Victor Uwaifo Guitar Boy Superstar* and *Nigerian Special: Modern Highlife Afro-Sounds* CDs released by the UK-based Soundways record company in 2005 and 2007 respectively.

---

1. Which means 'Joromi you have conquered the world and you're about to conquer hell.'
2. Victor Uwaifo in *Expo '98: Victor Uwaifo – The Legend* (Nigeria: Joromi Organization, 1998), p.14.
3. John Collins, *Highlife Time* (Accra, Anansesem Press, 1996), p. 203.
4. Uwaifo's 'ekassa' period was 1971–5, during which time he released four albums and some 45 rpm singles of this dance music.
5. Later Dandy Oboy formed the 'Igbo Blues' band called the Jumbos.
6. Victor Uwaifo, *My Life* (Accra: Black Bell Publishing, 1976), p.39.
7. I was introduced to him through John Chernoff, an American musicologist who was also helping produce Uwaifo's music.
8. These interviews were incorporated into the booklet *My Life: The Black Knight of Music Fame.*
9. This spot was named after the US presidential retreat that was often used for cabinet meetings and high-level meetings with foreign dignitaries.

12

Orlando Julius: From Highlife to Afro-Fusion

From the late 1950s, and during the 1960s, a number of Ghanaian and Nigerian highlife artists began developing various styles of 'Afro-fusion' music. For instance, the previously disussed Kofi Ghanaba, Zeal Oniyia and Bayo Martins all experimented with Afro-jazz. Then there were the Ghanaian dance band highlife musicians Teddy Osei, Mac Tonto and Sol Amarfio whose Osibisa supergroup pioneered Afro-rock. And no one can forget Fela Anikulapo-Kuti who pioneered Afrobeat, initially known as Afro-soul. [1]

The stories of both the Osibisa group and Fela's career from jazzy highlife to Afrobeat are well known and well documented. However, the story of Nigerian saxophonist Orlando Julius, who was one of the 1960s pioneers of Afro-soul and made the transition from highlife to Afro-fusion, is not so well known. He later moved to the United States where he collaborated with many artists and was involved with various forms of Afro-jazz and Afro-rock.[2]

Early Days

The famous Nigerian highlife saxophonist Orlando Julius Aremu Olusanya Ekemode was born in Ilesha, Osun State, in western Nigeria. He attended St Peter's Anglican School at Ikole-Ekiti in Ekiti State and played drums and flute in the school band. At the same time he played with the local Mambo Dance Band. Julius's father was a trader and after he died in 1957, Julius left for Ibadan to play as drummer and flautist with various groups in the area.

The young Julius became the percussionist for the Modupe Dance Band led by Ademola Haastrup, also known as 'Jazz Romero', with whom he began to study saxophone. In 1958, he accompanied the Modupe band to Akure-Ekiti, the capital of Ondo State, where Jazz Romero renamed his group the Flamingo Dandies, as they were based at the town's Flamingo Hotel.

Julius then moved back to Ibadan and played with highlife musician Etubom Rex Williams' band at the Mayflower Hotel. He also made frequent trips to Lagos to play with the Nyingifa Band. In 1959 Julius settled down with the Top Aces highlife band, which was based at the Central and Paradise Hotels in Ibadan and led by the former Bobby Benson trumpeter Eddy Okonta. Julius became Okonta's horn arranger and it was as a member of Okonta's Top Aces that he met Louis Armstrong who, on his second African tour, played in Ibadan in October/November 1960.[3]

In late 1960, after the Nigerian independence celebrations and Armstrong's trip, Julius travelled to Ijebu-Ode in Ogun State to work for six months with Y.S. Akinibosum's Right Time Dance Band. After meeting his older 'brother',[4] the juju musician I.K. Dairo, at a gig in Ijebu-Ode, Julius was convinced to return home to Ijesha to join Dairo's ten-piece Morning Star Orchestra. Dairo himself played harmonica, talking drum and accordion. Although Dairo is usually associated with Yoruban juju,[5] it should be noted that he also played highlifes, ashiko and Latin American music. It was whilst involved with I.K.'s dance band that Julius released his first single in 1961, recorded at the Nigerian Broadcasting Corporation's radio station studio in Ibadan. On the A-and-B sides of the record were 'Igbehin A Dara' and 'Jola Ade', and they were released by Alowonle

Records. Julius also co-wrote and arranged some of I.K. Dairo's highlife hits such as 'Salome' and 'Bola Ti To'. Julius remained with Dairo's band until 1963, by which time Dairo was calling it the Blue Spots.

The Blue Spots in the early 1960s, run by I.K. Dairo – a relative of Orlando Julius's (Andy Frankel)

It was in 1963 that Julius was finally able to form the Modern Aces, which became the resident group at the Independence Hotel in Ibadan. It was with this group that he had his first highlife hit record released by the Philips Company in 1963. This was 'Jaguar Nana'. The word 'Jaguar' referred to the luxury British car and was a slang expression used in Ghana and Nigeria to refer to anyone who considered themself up-to-date and sophisticated. The Nigerian writer Cyprian Ekwensi even wrote a book called 'Jagua Nana' in 1961 about an adventurous girl in a big Nigerian city. In 1964, the success of Julius's 'Jaguar Nana' record resulted in several television contracts, such as with the WNTV producer Segun Shofowote and Art Alade's Lagos Channel 10 'Bar Beach' programme.

Julius's Modern Aces played highlifes and ballroom numbers while beginning to experiment with a fusion of highlife and jazz. Its members included vocalist Jimi Solanke, trumpeter Eddie Fayehun and drummer Moses Akanbi. Jimi Solanke was an Ibadan-based singer and actor who also occasionally sang in Lagos with Art Alade's Jazz Preachers and Roy Chicago's Rhythm Dandies. Eddie Fayehun later joined Fela Kuti's Africa 70, whilst Moses Akanbi joined Sunny Ade's African Beats in 1967 and helped introduce an Afrobeat influence to this juju band. Whilst playing at the Independence Hotel in Ibadan, Julius's band would play on the same stage as highlife musicians who were on tour like Rex Lawson, the Paramount Eight from Ghana, and Fela Kuti, who was then running his Koolo Lobitos band.

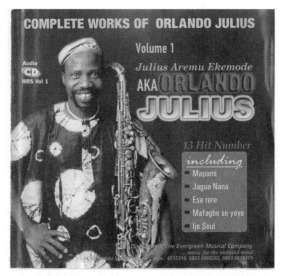

CD cover for the *Complete Works of Orlando Julius*, Volume 1 released by the Evergreen Record Company, Lagos

By 1966 American soul music was beginning to become popular and this began to influence Julius's music. At the Independence Hotel Julius began to rub shoulders with a number of younger Nigerian artists who, by the late sixties, were experimenting with highlife combined with soul and funk music. One was the previously mentioned Fela, and some others were the former Bobby Benson saxophonist Eric 'Showboy' Akaeze, Bola Johnson of the Easy Life Top Beats and Tunji Oyelana of the Benders Band. That year, Julius's Modern Aces released the album *Super AfroSoul*.

As a result of the success of this album, Julius changed the name of his Modern Aces to the Afro-Sounders in 1967 and, like fellow Nigerians Fela Anikulapo-Kuti and Segun Bucknor, he began to pioneer what was later called 'Afrobeat'. In 1967, the Afro-Sounders released 'Topless' and 'Ijo Soul Ololufe', followed between 1968 and 1970 with 'Psychedelic Afro Shop' and 'James Brown Ride On'. Julius even met James Brown and his bassist Bootsie Collins when Brown's band, the J.B.'s, visited Nigeria in December 1970. On this trip Julius was able to give James Brown a copy of his soulish Afro-Sounders album.

By 1972, Julius was beginning to make trips to Europe and had relocated his Afro-Sounders band to Lagos spots like Roy Chicago's Club Chicago in Surulere, the Gondola Nightclub and Bata Koto. In 1974 he collaborated with the well-known Nigerian singer and TV personality Dora Ifudu on her two albums *Disco Highlife* and *Children of the World*.

Later that year, Julius relocated to the United States, where he largely moved out of the highlife arena into Afro-jazz and Afro-rock. He settled briefly in New York and then moved to Washington DC where he formed the Umoja band with fellow Nigerian Gboyega Adelaja (or Adaloja), who played keyboards, and the Ghanaian guitarist Stanley Todd. Other members of

Umoja included Frank Todd on trap-drums, percussionists Harry Opoku and Okyerema Asante, and two of Kofi Ghanaba's sons: Glen Warren and 'Odinga' Guy Warren Junior. In 1975, Umoja made the classic Afro-rock album *The Boy's Doin' It*[6] with the South African trumpeter Hugh Masekela.[7] The album's hit song 'Ashiko' was actually written by Julius, who appears in the sleeve notes under the name O.J. Ekomode. Umoja was very successful and played at shows in Los Angeles and New York alongside Sarah Vaughan, Herbie Hancock, Isaac Hayes and Duke Ellington.

Dora Ifudu, with whom Orlando Julius worked (*Africa Music*, 7, 1982)

After running his Umoja band for a year or so, Julius spent two years playing and recording with Hugh Masekela's Ojah band. Then in 1977 in Washington DC, Julius formed the band *Ashiko*, which relocated to the San Francisco Bay area of California in 1978. There Julius took courses at the Berkeley Film Institute and the Lanley College of Photography and Television. It was also in 1978 that Julius met his singer–dancer wife, Latoya Aduke, through the veteran Nigerian musician Ambrose Campbell. As mentioned in a previous chapter, Campbell had been the leader of the London-based West African Rhythm Brothers, until 1972 when he settled in Los Angeles for some years.

Around this time Julius worked on the music for and appeared in the 1979 mini-series *Roots: The Next Generation*; a sequel to the 1977 *Roots*, which was based on Alex Haley's 1976 book of that name. The cast included several other Nigerians such as Shamsi Sarumi who was one of Ambrose Campbell's artists; the percussionist Gaspar Lawal, who had worked with the British Caribbean singer Joan Armatrading in the mid-1970s and the choreographer Peter Badejo. Whilst in California Julius also played on two music videos: one with his 'brother' I.K. Dairo and the other with the pioneer of Latin-rock fusion, Carlos Santana.

In 1984, Julius and his wife decided to go back to Nigeria, where he recorded his *Dance Afro Beat* album at the EMI studio in Lagos. But the couple did not remain long in Nigeria due to the economic problems of the period. The repressive military government, the collapse of the naira currency, spiraling petrol prices and a musical 'brain drain' of talented artists were forcing major recording companies to close down.[8]

In a 2003 interview Julius said:

Military regimes compelled people to take flight from their oppressive environment. Nightclubs were closed to business. Ban of imports of goods also affected musical instruments. Bilateral relationships with other countries were so badly affected that only a privileged few among musicians could promote their music outside Nigeria.[9]

As a result of these difficulties, Julius returned to the United States in 1987 and formed O.J. Ekemode and His Nigerian All Stars. Over a period of ten years his group went on many American tours. For instance, they played at the New Orleans Jazz Festival in 1989, and performed in 1994 for the opening ceremony of the Disney film *The Lion King*.

Julius and his wife finally returned to Lagos in 1998. He quickly regrouped the Nigerian All Stars and set up an analog recording studio in Surulere to record live performances by traditional drummers and local gospel artists, and also provide soundtracks for Nollywood movies. At his studio he recorded many highlife musicians such as the palm wine guitarist Fatai Rolling Dollar, the guitarist Alaba Pedro and actor–singer Tunde Osofisan; the latter two having been members of Roy Chicago's sixties highlife band.

In 2001, Julius became involved with the Nigerian Musician's Forum and began working hard to revive highlife music. As a result he played at some of the Highlife Elders' Forums initiated from the late 1990s by the French and German foreign cultural missions in Nigeria, and local organisations such as the O'jez Entertainment Company, the Musical Society of Nigeria (MUSON) and the Committee for Relevant Art (CORA).

Around 2003, Julius moved again, this time to Ghana, making his musical debut at PANAFEST, a major Ghanaian event held every two years in Cape Coast. He also became involved in the local jazz scene and played at the 2004 and 2005 Jazz Festivals held at the W.E.B. Du Bois Centre in Accra. Julius and his wife, Latoya, also established a recording studio in Accra but later returned to Nigeria. In August 2011, he celebrated fifty years on stage at an event held at the Lagos Airport Hotel's Oranmiyan Hall.

---

1.   Another Nigerian Afro soul pioneer was Segun Bucknor (Collins, 1985).
2.   For more details on him, see his self-published 2002 brochure *Orlando: The Legendary Orlando Julius Ekemode*, edited by his wife Latoya Gill-El (Aduke).
3.   This was part of Armstrong and his All Stars' three-month 1960–1 African tour that began in October/November, with the Ghana/Nigeria segment financed by Pepsi-Cola.
4.   Although Julius calls I.K. his 'brother' he was in fact an older cousin who was born in 1930.
5.   The Blue Spots formed in 1961 and became the top Nigerian juju band as, with its inclusion of dance band instruments, it helped modernise juju music. I.K. Dairo made many foreign tours and released forty albums. In fact, he was so successful that he and the apala musician Haruna Ishola formed their own Star Record Label in the mid-sixties. In 1963 Dairo received a Member of the British Empire award for his musical contribution to the British Commonwealth.
6.   Released in 1975 by Casablanca Records (NBLP 7071).
7.   Okyerema Asante and the Todd Brothers had previously toured the US in 1974/5 with Hugh Masekela as members of Faisal Helwani's Accra-based Hedzoleh Afro-rock band.
8.   For instance, EMI (established in Nigeria in 1964 and run by Mike Wells) relocated to Abidjan in Côte d'Ivoire, whilst SONY-CBS moved to South Africa.
9.   Orlando Julius in Jean-Christophe Servant, *Which Way Nigeria?* (Denmark: Freemuse Publications, 2003), p. 35).

13

Ignace De Souza of Benin

The career of the dance band trumpeter and highlife composer Ignace De Souza began in his home country, Benin, but he also played in Ghana, Nigeria and Togo. His Black Santiagos played highlife and was the first dance band to play the Afro-Cuban-influenced Congo jazz (soukous) in Ghana. Both Ghanaian highlife dance bands and guitar bands were influenced by the Congolese double-string guitar-solo technique and by its dance rhythms, partially derived from Afro-Cuban dances like the son, rumba, cha-cha, mambo, pachanga and bolero. De Souza's live shows in Accra between 1964 and 1970 enhanced the influence of this central African popular music.

Ignace De Souza and the Shambros band in Accra, 1962. De Souza is fourth from the left, holding a trumpet. (BAPMAF)

The Early Popular Music of Francophone Central Africa, Benin and Togo

The origin of Congolese urban popular music can be traced back to 1908 after the Congo, then called the Belgian Congo (now the Democratic Republic of the Congo, or DRC), was confiscated from the Belgian King Leopold II by the government of Belgium. The Belgian government began developing the railway and mining industry of the colony and it was this first generation of Congolese urban workers, miners and railwaymen who developed and spread the DRC's earliest recognised local popular music style – maringa.

Maringa combined western and traditional musical elements and instruments and was also affected by the Africanised guitar music of the thousands of English-speaking West African 'coastmen' who had been operating as clerks and artisans on the Congo River and its port at Matadi since the late nineteenth century. According to the Congolese musicologist Kazadi wa Mukuna (1992), maringa was a bar room dance music that evolved around 1914 in the coastal areas and, by the 1920s, had spread as far inland as the Shaba mining camps of eastern Congo. It was played on local frame drums and 'likembe' thumb pianos, with western accordions and guitars being added later. It was sung in Lingala, the evolving trans-ethnic trade language of central Africa.

Early pioneers of this music were the sailor-musicians Dondo Daniels and Antoine Wendo, who had learned the African two-finger guitar-plucking technique from West African sailors. Their guitar style reached the Swahili-speaking eastern Congo in the 1940s where it was taken up by the likes of Jean Bosco Mwenda and Losta Abelo.

During the Second World War the anti-Nazi 'Free French Forces' of General De Gaulle were based in the French colony of Congo-Brazzaville, the DRC's immediate neighbour. There, American soldiers introduced jazz and, for wartime propaganda purposes, built the most powerful radio transmitter in sub-Saharan Africa. After the war, local maringa was blended with traditional Congolese music, Latin and Afro-Cuban dance music (enjoyed by the French and Belgian colonialists), and American jazz, with its prominent horn-section and brassy sound. By the early 1950s this resulted in 'Congo music' or 'Congo jazz', also known later as kara-kara or soukous. This locally blended dance band style was popular in both the Congos and was sung in Lingala rather than Spanish or French.

This urban dance music was pioneered in Kinshasa by Antoine Wendo, Le Grand Kallé and his African Jazz band, Luambo Makiadi Franco and his O.K. Jazz, Dr. Nico and Tabu Ley Rochereau, and in neighbouring Congo-Brazzaville by the Orchestre Les Bantous de la Capitale. Congo jazz was disseminated into every corner of the African continent via records and the powerful wartime transmitter of Radio Congo-Brazzaville inherited from the Americans. However, it became particularly popular in French-speaking African colonies, including Togo and Benin.

During the 1950s both Benin (former Dahomey) and the neighbouring French colony of Togo had few prestigious dance orchestras. They played western quicksteps and waltzes, Latin American sambas and tangos as well as Afro-Cuban music. By the 1960s this had changed as bands that included Congo jazz and the Ghanaian highlifes in their dance repertoires began to emerge. These included the Jonas Pedro Dance Band and Elrigo and his Los Commandos from Benin, as well as the Los Muchachos and the Melo Togo Dance Orchestra of neighbouring Togo.[1] The very first of the Beninese dance bands was Alfa Jazz, which was formed in 1953 in Cotonou and played western and Latin ballroom music, Afro-Cuban music and an occasional highlife. It was in this dance band that the young Ignace De Souza obtained his musical training.

The Story of Ignace De Souza

When Ignace De Souza was a youngster, the only dance bands in Benin were run by the police and the army. However, E.T. Mensah's Tempos started to become popular in the 1950s and, as De Souza told me in 1975, Alfa Jazz was the first private dance band in Benin and consisted of ten professional musicians:

> When I was young I learned music in the cultural way [the traditional music of the Fon people]. Then one morning in 1953 we went to the place that someone had opened, as he was wanting to form a band. He had brought instruments and asked me what type I wanted to play. I saw many instruments and there were two trumpets and I said I would like one because I saw only three valves and thought it would be simple to play. They laughed and gave me an alto sax and showed me how to play it. The band was called Alfa Jazz, and the man told us after everything was going on we would be paid a salary.
>
> We had a tenor player from Paris. He worked at the bank and every day he came in to teach us the theoretical part of the music and played with our group on Saturdays. Later on, the manager brought in two musicians from Nigeria. One was Babyface Paul [Osamade] on tenor sax and the other, Zeal Onyia, on trumpet. When Paul came he was pushing me on the sax, but when Zeal came I enjoyed the way he played better, so I switched to trumpet. So Zeal started teaching me the trumpet and I abandoned the sax. Since then I've concentrated on the trumpet. We played

dance music, like quicksteps, highlifes and boleros. At that time E.T. Mensah was reigning so we used to do some of his songs.[2]

It was in 1955 that De Souza decided to go to Ghana, and he explains how this happened:

After everything was going nicely with the Alfa Jazz, the manager stopped paying us, so everybody had to find his way and I chose to go to Ghana in 1955. There I joined a band called the Rhythm Aces [led by the ex-Tempos saxophonist Spike Anyankor]. Zeal and Paul Babyface had left Cotonou to join the Rhythm Aces before me, but by the time I arrived they had left for Lagos. I played in the Rhythm Aces until 1956 when I went to the Lido Nightclub [in Accra] playing in a band called the Shambros, run by the Shahim Brothers, who were Lebanese. These Lebanese people were making a hell of a lot of money and at the end of every month they wouldn't pay us. All the time we were pocketless.

I advised my musicians that we should start a bank account so that after one or two years we should have enough money to buy our own instruments, because these people were making fools of us. The secret leaked out and they stopped me playing for three months. But when people saw my absence, the band didn't go too well, because during those days the French music [i.e. Latin and Afro-Cuban music] was making money. So the brothers brought me back and I told them that if they wanted me to work, number one: I would like to be paid more than the £9 a month I had been earning, and I would always like to have my pay at the end of the month. Number two: as there was no days off, I would like the band to have a rest every week on Mondays. So we signed the contract and I started getting £15 a month and I always kept £10 and saved it.[3]

De Souza had been quietly building up a stock of his own instruments and so in 1964 he was able to form his famous Black Santiagos band that was 'outdoored' at the Metropole, playing side by side with the Ramblers. The Black Santiagos was the first band to introduce live Congo jazz to Ghana and travelled all over the country. In 1965, it became the resident band at the Ringway Hotel in Accra,[4] playing alongside Uhuru, the Ramblers, Geraldo Pino's Heartbeats band of Sierra Leone (in 1966) and Fela Kuti's Koola Lobitos (in 1968). I asked De Souza how he was able to form the Black Santiagos:

In 1961 I composed the cha-cha number 'Paulina' and on the other side the highlife number 'Patience is Best'. The record became a hit and I used the Shambros in the recording but changed the name to the Melody Aces. I had the contract with Decca, and after the recording I paid the boys and kept what remained. I was lucky the record was a success and I made £700 in royalties. So I persuaded the man from Decca to sell me a set of instruments instead of paying me the money. I bought two tenor saxophones, one alto, one trumpet, one guitar and I already had the drums and the other instruments. The man from Decca balanced me the rest, which was £350. I even bought materials for uniforms for whenever I would need it. I kept the instruments under my bed because I didn't want anyone to see them.

By 1964 all my instruments were complete and I was finding a way to get out of the Shambros, when there was trouble between the proprietor and the Minister of the Interior. The Lido was locked up and I had to run to the TUC [Trade Union Congress] where I made a report and we fought it out and they paid all that was due. I got a reasonable amount and went back to Cotonou and had my passport done. When I was there I thought of what sort of music I should introduce in Ghana, because at that time dance bands like the Ramblers, the Armed Forces Band and the Black Beats were in top form. At that time Ampadu [later the leader of the African Brothers guitar band] was working under me during the Lido times. Everyone used to come to me as I taught the theoretical part of music. When I thought about which music to introduce, I knew that there was nothing like Congo music in Ghana, so I brought a bass player from Dahomey and went to Togoland to join with two boys who sang Congo music. I also brought many Congo records with me and we learnt them nicely in Accra.

Ignace De Souza had to leave Ghana in 1970 because of the Aliens Order,[5] as did some of his other musicians who were also from other African countries like Nigeria, Togo, Benin and the DRC. He returned to Cotonou, the capital of Benin, but later, due to problems like nightly curfews,[6] he and the Black Santiagos began doing extensive West African tours, particularly of Nigeria.

In 1976 they backed the Cameroonian makossa music star Sam Fan Thomas in his album *Funky New Bell,* and in the late 1970s they collaborated on albums like *Do Dagbe We* with Honoré Avolonto, one of Benin's most prolific composers. De Souza also lent a helping hand to talented musicians. For instance, he was so impressed by the Ghanaian borborbor highlife musician Abebe (Jonathan Kakraba) who visited

Cotonou in 1978 that he employed him in his group and helped him find a producer for his first solo album *Mawu Ana*.[7]

As there was not enough work for a band in the relatively small country of Benin, De Souza decided to relocate his group. In the mid-1980s he moved permanently to Lagos, though he sometimes worked with visiting singers. For instance, in 1988 De Souza played trumpet for the first LP of the Ghanaian singer Pozo Hayes entitled 'Looking Over There'. Sadly, De Souza died in a car crash in 1988 whilst on one of his many tours.

Album cover of Honoré Avolonto with Ignace De Souza (centre, with trumpet) and his Black Santiagos, by then based in Cotonou, the capital of Benin. (Satel company label)

During De Souza's recording career he released highlifes,[8] pop songs, Afro-Cuban cha-chas,[9] Congo–jazz–style songs[10] and Afrobeat,[11] all sung in a variety of languages. These included the Ghanaian Akan dialects of Fanti and Twi, the Ga language of Accra, the Yoruba language of western Nigeria, his native Fon language, the Ewe language of Ghana and Togo, as well as pidgin English. Despite De Souza's premature death, some of his top Black Santiagos hits became available on the international world-music market. John Storm Roberts' American-based Original Music Company[12] released two CDs in the early 1990s and more recently the German Analog Africa and British Soundway companies released some compilation albums featuring his hits.[13]

1.   Togo also boasted the singer Bella Bellow, who represented her country at the First World Festival of Negro Arts, held in Dakar, Senegal in 1966. From 1969, with her big record hit 'Rockia', until her death in 1973 she released many Ewe highlifes, pop tunes and folk-oriented compositions.

2.   Ignace De Souza, personal communication, December 1975. I met him in Benin City, Edo State, when the Black Santiagos were playing at Victor Uwaifo's Club 400. Also see *Highlife Time* (1996) by John Collins, p. 64.

3.   John Collins, *Highlife Time* (Accra, Anansesem Press, 1996), p. 65.

4.   This hotel on the Ring Road in Accra was owned by the lawyer Edward Akufo-Addo, one of the 'big six' who fought for Ghana's independence and went on to become president of Ghana's Second Republic between 1970 and 1972.

5.   This was the infamous 'Aliens Compliance Order' of 1969, when Prime Minister Kofi Busia and his Progress Party government of Ghana's Second Republic suddenly, and with only two weeks notice, expelled hundreds of thousands of Nigerians, Burkinabes, Liberians and other non-Ghanaian Africans, some of whom had been living in Ghana for generations.

6.   In 1972, Major Mathieu Kerekou came to power in Benin and established a Marxist–Leninist regime there.

7.   Abebe went on to release about twenty-five albums of Ewe highlifes, agbadzas, borborbors, reggae and funk.

8.   Like 'Suru lo Dara', 'Anyenko', 'Augustina', 'Papa Kou Maman', 'Adan Egbomi' and 'Monkey No Fine'.

9.   Like 'Paulina'.

10. Such as 'Caroline Bateau' and 'Mayape'.

11. For instance, 'Ole' and 'Bani Wo Dzo'.

12. These are *Giants of Dance Band Highlife* (OMCD 011) and *The Great Unknowns: Ignace De Souza* (OMCD 026).

13. Their respective *Legends of Benin* (2009) and *Nigeria Afrobeat Special* (2010) compilations.

14

King Bruce and The Black Beats

King Bruce belongs to the generation of Ghanaian musicians/composers who were influenced by both traditional Ghanaian music and the swing music of the Allied forces in Ghana during the Second World War, and went on to help create the classic highlife dance band style of the 1950s. His career spans the tail end of the dance orchestra era through to the classic 1950s/1960s dance band highlife period and right into the pop music period of the sixties and after. He was not only a musician and composer but also a music promoter, music union activist and recording studio manager. In short, he was a key figure in the development of Ghana's popular music.

King Bruce was a Ga born in Jamestown, Accra, in 1922 and his varied musical experiences started early. His mother belonged to a traditional women's singing group called Etsi Penfo. His eldest brother, Kpakpo Thompson, taught him piano. Another brother, Eddie Bruce, played palm wine guitar styles like 'fireman' and 'dagomba wire' with a group of seamen called Canteen. At the same time – and much against his parent's wishes – King was a keen follower of local street music such as Ga drum dances and brass band parades. Here he talks about the Accra marching bands:[1]

The management of the Palladium Cinema near my home, one of the oldest cinemas in town, operated a marching band and in the old days, to get people to attend the nightly film shows, this band would start at the Sea-View Hotel, Jamestown. The band consisted of a bass drum (held horizontally by two people whilst a third person did the actual drumming), a side drummer, a pati [local copy of a military side drum] drummer, one or two flute players and steel claves players. They would start drumming at the Sea-View from about 6:30 p.m. and march steadily from there right up to the Palladium by eight o'clock, making 'campaign' and picking up followers all the way. This band grew in size over the years. Occasionally we even had a full brass section, called a Kru band, because many of the instrumentalists were Kru sailors and stevedores from Liberia.

King also comments on the numerous Accra dance styles in the 1930s and 1950s that evolved as a combination of foreign music and local Ga recreational music:

People sang and drummed, then a particular song would become popular and give the whole thing a name. For instance, the [1930s] marching music, when it wasn't for marching, we called 'adaha'. This was not a brass band, but a drumming group which included a pati drum, sometimes a big bass drum, plus congas [local hand drums], jingles [triangles], cowbells and voices – but no horns or wind instruments.[2] Then in the 1930s and 1940s, there was a dance called 'borwer', which had strong Kru connections, and another called 'tsiboder'. Another dance was called 'soshi owo nli', which means to 'crouch' or 'bend down'. Yet another was 'koyin', which means 'to pick up the mind' or 'think about it'. Others were 'ayika', 'G-ram' and 'kenka'.[3] Much later there was a dance called 'something'. And in the 1950s there was a dance called 'kolomashie', the 'mashie' part meaning, 'it's on top' or 'outstanding'.

All these drumming and singing groups weren't like tribal or fetish music, they were more modern. But my parents didn't like them and I often used to slip away and watch these groups. Usually by the time I came back, someone had always reported to my father that they had seen his son on the street dancing, and I would never hear the end of it. I suppose this was partly the reason I was shipped to boarding school in Achimota.

At the prestigious Achimota College, King continued to be inspired by music, particularly by some of the teachers who taught there. These included Philip Gbeho who composed Ghana's national anthem. Another was Doctor Ephraim Amu – as King explains:

Ephraim Amu was my housemaster as well as my music teacher and taught us his Twi and Ewe songs. He had come to Achimota after he lost his appointment as a teacher at the Akropong Training College because of his strong African tendencies. He didn't believe in the idea of going to classes or church in Western-style suits, but always wore traditional kente cloth or batakari. He had these strong feelings about African culture as far back as the 1930s and was welcomed at Achimota, as the founders of the school – Guggisberg, Fraser, and Aggrey – were strongly interested in promoting African ways.

It was at the end of his school days at Achimota that King developed a taste for swing and dance-band music. King reflects on this period:

These were the war years and we had British and American

army units stationed here. They had bands for their entertainment and so ballroom music progressed very much. The airport was virtually taken over by the Americans and one wing of Achimota College itself was taken over by the British resident minister, who was taking care of the British war effort here. This was the time of musicians like Glenn Miller, Benny Goodman, and Artie Shaw, so by the time I left Achimota I had a definite liking for jazz and swing.

King did not actually start playing in a dance band, however, until he had spent a couple of years in England studying to be a civil servant with the Posts and Telegraphs. There he learnt to play the trumpet and came into contact with famous jazz artists, like the British 'trad jazz' revivalist Humphrey Lyttelton and the American trumpeter Jimmy McPartland.

On returning to Accra in 1950, he hung around for a while with top musicians like Adolf Doku, E.T. Mensah, Kofi Ghanaba, Joe Kelly, and Pop Hughes. When King felt he was ready to go on stage with his trumpet he joined Teacher Lamptey's Accra Orchestra:

My first real band was the Accra Orchestra; as a matter of fact, I did play claves for E.T. one time when the Tempos played at Burma camp. What happened was that soon after being with E.T. Mensah I met Tommy Grippman. He had been a playmate of mine before, as we lived in more or less the same area of town. Then, he wasn't into music, but when I came back from the UK I discovered that he was one of the leading trombone players with the Accra Orchestra run by Teacher Lamptey. I got invited to join both the Accra Rhythmic Orchestra run by E.T.'s elder brother Mr Yebuah Mensah, and the Accra Orchestra.

But I had made the decision to join the Accra Orchestra. I joined them somewhere in the middle of 1950, and one thing I liked about them at the time was they were playing from written music. It was standard strict-tempo ballroom and jazz numbers using stock arrangements imported from England. But I must say I owe my real progress to personal coaching from Mr Tommy Grippman.

The Accra Orchestra played at prestigious Accra venues like the Accra Town Hall, the Rodger Club, Madison Square Gardens and the European Club. Besides imported foxtrots rumbas, jazz, swing and mambos, this dance orchestra also played highlifes like 'Everybody Likes Saturday Night', 'Aye' (Witch), 'Meele Ni Yaa E' (A Passing Sailing Ship) and 'Sekondi Market'.

King stayed with this group until 1951, and then in April/May 1952 he and Saka Acquaye formed the Black Beats band. This is what King says about coming up with the band's name:

> One evening when we were coming home from rehearsals Saka asked me what name we were going to use. Without hesitation I said Black Beats. The reason was that Doctor Amu at Achimota had impressed on us the necessity for doing things African. At the same time, as a group we were very much enamoured with jazz, swing, and music with a beat. So we were all interested in playing good dance band music, but keen on giving everything a recognisable African beat.

King was on trumpet, Saka on tenor sax, Jerry Hansen on alto sax, Frank Kwamena Croffie on double bass, Billy Sam on guitar, George Annor on drums and Adoquaye Acquaye (Saka's younger brother) on congas. The band's two lead singers or

'Black Birds' were Mike Lewis Wadawa and Frank Atoo Barnes.

The Black Beats in 1953, just after Saka Acquaye had left. King Bruce
is on the left (with trumpet); next to him, on sax, is Jerry Hansen.
Acquaye's brother Adoquaye is holding the African drum on the right.
(King Bruce)

Unlike the other Ghanaian dance bands, the Black Beats'
vocalists, the 'Black Birds', dominated the instrumental line-up,
and in this they were influenced by the currently popular
'jump' music of African American alto-saxophonist, pianist
and singer Louis Jordan, which was a fusion of swing, blues and
boogie-woogie.[4] Jordon's emphasis on vocals was much to King
Bruce's liking, as he discusses below:

> When we started up, it was unheard of for a person who
> had not distinguished himself as an instrumentalist to
> think of forming or leading a band. Now all the boys in
> our group were beginners who hadn't really mastered their
> instruments, and those already in the field didn't think
> much of us. However, this was the time when groups like
> that of the American Louis Jordan were very popular here
> with the stress on singing. Before our time, a band would

play sometimes for half an hour without a singer because they were playing mostly stock arrangements. We stressed close harmony singing and it went down particularly well with the young people. So a group that didn't have skilled instrumentalists, like our early Black Beats, could very successfully use Jordan's music.

Besides 'jump' music another musical influence on King Bruce came from two UK-based trumpeters. One was the Trinidadian musician Leslie Hutchinson,[5] who played in Lord Kitchener's Calypso All Stars Band in the late 1940s. The other was the West Indian trumpeter Ken 'Snakehips' Johnson, a Guyanese dance band leader who, in the late 1930s, teamed up with the Jamaican trumpeter Leslie Thompson to form the Emperors of Jazz, which played swing and calypso in London.

By June 1953 the Black Beats co-founder, Saka Acquaye, left to the United States for further studies and it was then that the Black Beats began to release a string of highlife hits on single 78 rpm shellac discs for British companies like HMV, Decca and the French Senofone Company.[6] According to Flemming Harrev,[7] between 1953 and 1972 the Black Beats released about fifty singles and ten albums with these companies as well as the Philips Records company.

Many of the top hits were King Bruce's own compositions such as the highlifes 'Teemon Sane' (A Confidential Matter), 'Laimomo' (Old Lover), 'Nkuse Mbaa Dong' (I'll Never Return), 'Nomo Noko' (A Thing of Joy), 'Srotoi Ye Mli' (Distinctions) and 'Telephone Lobi' (Telephone Love). As King composed in the Ga language of Accra and he wanted to broaden the market of his records, he included Akan highlife on the flip sides of discs he released. Some examples of these were 'Agoogyi' (Money) composed by Oscarmore Ofori, 'Dear Si

Abotar' (Dear be Patient) by Kwadwo Donkoh, and 'Wosompa Nti' (Your Helpfulness) by Ani Johnson.

The Black Beats also made extensive tours of Ghana, played in Togo and made one Nigerian trip to Lagos and Ibadan. The band also released some Nigerian highlifes and employed Nigerian musicians. For instance, for their 1954 Senofone release 'Tsutsu Blema Beneke' (The Old Days Were Not Like This) based on an old Ga song, King Bruce employed the Nigerian clarinettist and sax player Jibril Isa and some other Nigerian musicians who were with Isa's Accra-based Delta Dandies group. Then, around 1960, the Black Beats collaborated with two Nigerian singers called Bassey and Chuks and released four Nigerian highlifes with them on the Decca West Africa label. These were the Yoruba highlifes 'Fe Ron Re' and 'Dwo Ko Ni Fe' (which were about God), the Efik highlife 'Abasi Do', and a Hausa song called 'Bu Duru Wana'.[8] According to King Bruce, Chuks later died in Ghana whilst Bassey went back to Nigeria.

Besides working as a civil servant and running a band, King Bruce also had time to become involved with the various early Ghanaian music unions. Most important was the Ghana Musicians Union that was formed in 1961 and included E.T. Mensah, Joe Kelly, Tommy Grippman, Kofi Ghanaba, Saka Acquaye, Philip Gbeho and Bruce himself as its executives.

In 1961, disaster struck the Black Beats when its alto saxophonist, Jerry Hansen, and nine other musicians left King Bruce to form the Ramblers dance band. Nevertheless, within a few months he had reorganised his 'second-generation' Black Beats and even got them into a studio to record Decca hits like 'Se Nea Woti Ara' (I Love You Just As You Are) and 'Nkase Din' (I Am Quietly Poised).

During the whole period when King was running the Black Beats he was slowly working his way up the civil service ladder, but getting a lot of criticism from his superiors for playing on stage. In 1967 he got an ultimatum from the Administrative Civil Service that unless he quit playing in public he would not be promoted to a senior post. As a result he stopped playing in 1968 and, as he told me, 'I was very much annoyed because I had always believed that it was the actual playing in a band that sharpens your faculties and brings new ideas'.

As a result of this ban on him playing in public King Bruce was forced to hand over the Black Beats to one of his musicians, the young guitarist and keyboard player Sammy Odoh who had joined the group in 1964. In short, Bruce became the manager of the band. This in turn resulted in him going on to manage six other bands that played highlife and pop music: the Barbecues, Barons, Bonafides, Barristers, Boulders and 'B' Soyaaya. These bands, together with the Black Beats, subsequently became known as the 'B.B.' bands.

At the time I was interviewing King Bruce in 1987–8 he was down to just two of his B.B. bands, the Black Beats and the Barristers. He was working with the Copyright Administration, MUSIGA and its associated Greater Accra Musicians Welfare Association. Furthermore, he was on the Advisory Committee of the Greater Accra Regional Cultural Centre and in 1988 received an award from the Entertainment Critics and Reviewers Association of Ghana (ECRAG) for his 'immense contribution to the development of Ghanaian arts and culture in the field of highlife music'.

It was in 1987 that he came to my Bokoor Studio in Accra to do a number of recordings. First he did a composition for Felix Houphouët-Boigny (President of Côte d'Ivoire) on his eighty-fifth birthday. Then, in December of that year, King Bruce did four more of his compositions at my studio. Two of them, 'Esheo Heko' (There Comes a Time) and 'Onyiemo Feo

Mi Feo' (You Walk Attractively), date back to 1972. The other two were recent compositions of his: namely 'Ekole' (Perhaps) and 'Tsutsu Tsosemo' (Old Time Training).[9]

The Muscians Union of Ghana (MUSIGA) interim executive in 1979, with King Bruce seated third from left. John Collins is standing behind him, and Sammy Odoh is seated on the extreme right. In the back row, left to right, are Sidiku Buari, Koo Nimo, Faisal Helwani, Blay Ambolley, Joe Eyison and Kwaa Mensah. In the front row, left to right, are Osei Tutu, Ani Johnson and C.K. Mann. (MUSIGA)

From 1989 to 1991 King Bruce was the manager of the sixteen-track Essiebons/Phonogram Elephant Walk recording studio in Kaneshie, Accra. Then in 1990 he helped set up the Bokoor African Popular Music Archives Foundation (BAPMAF). King helped to sort out some of the initial documentation for the archive with the Department of Social Welfare and later donated materials. He also became involved with some of the archive's projects, such as the joint BAPMAF/Goethe-Institut Highlife Month in 1996.

In 1995, with the help of his son Eddie, King launched a very successful double-cassette album of old Black Beats songs entitled *Original Highlife Golden Classics*. The album was also released in London on CD by the Retroafrik label.

King Bruce died in September 1997 and many bands played

at his wake at the Arts Council in Accra.[10] In 2007, ten years after his death, his son Eddie Bruce released *Golden Highlife Classics*, Volume 2. A biography titled *The Making of a Highlife Legend: King Bruce and the Black Beats* is set to be published in Ghana in 2016.[11]

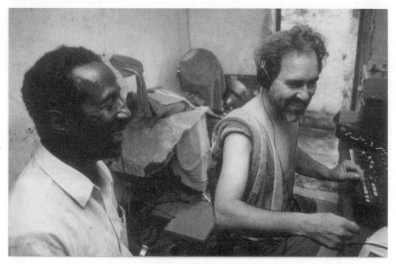

King Bruce recording at John Collins' Bokoor studio in Accra in 1987.
(Flemming Harrev)

---

1. Bruce's quotes in this chapter are from a series of interviews I did with him at his house in Accra in 1987–8 for a book we were planning. This followed a conference of the International Association for the Study of Popular Music (IASPM) in 1987, with which both King and I were involved. The Danish IASPM delegate Flemming Harrev supplied some editorial and discographical input.
2. This was a Ga version of Akan konkoma, a marching and dance music influenced by brass band music but using local rather than imported instruments. Also see Chapter 1.
3. Kenka or kainka is another name for early indigenised Ghanaian brass band music of the Fantis, Ga, Krobos and Ewe. Amongst the Ewe today, kainka is also the name of a local recreational music.
4. Louis Jordon's Tympany Five (later Seven) was formed in 1938 and had many American hits in the 1940s and early 1950s like 'Caladonia', 'You Broke Your Promise' and 'Saturday Fish Fry'. His music was introduced to Ghana through wartime V-Disc records for American forces, and also Decca's Sepia Series Records.
5. This famous calypsonian was amongst the first five thousand or so post-war West Indians who immigrated to Britain in 1948 where he subsequently formed a band that

released many records. In 1957 he and A. Roberts released the record 'The Birth of Ghana' (Melodisc 1390) celebrating the country's independence.

6. HMV/Zonophone had been recording West African materials (its JZ series) from the late 1920s and 1930s. Senofone (a subsidiary of the French CFAO trading company) began operating a recording studio in Ghana in the 1950s out of a converted cocoa storage shed in Nsawam. Decca opened its first West African recording studio in Accra in 1947 when it began its famous West African (WA) Series that was pressing fifty thousand records a year.

7. This Danish researcher and journalist helped with the editing and the discographical section of the King Bruce biography that I was working on in 1987–8.

8. These four songs appear on Decca WA 953 and GWA 4020.

9. This last song was later released on the NAXOS *Electric Highlife* compilation CD in 2002.

10. This included the Local Dimension highlife band that I co-run with Aaron Bebe Sukura.

11. This is a book I co-authored with King Bruce in the late 1980s forthcoming from Smartline Publications, Accra 2016.

15

Saka Acquaye: The Ghanaian Musician and Artist

Saka Acquaye is a well-known Ghanaian saxophonist, sculptor and dramatist who, from the 1940s to the early 1950s, played with and ran a number of highlife dance bands. The first band he was with was Joe Lamptey's Accra Orchestra and he played briefly with E.T. Mensah's Tempos. As mentioned in the previous chapter, he helped King Bruce set up the Black Beats in 1952, then went on to run several bands in the United States and Ghana.

Saka Acquaye was born in 1923. His father, John Acquayefio, was a musician who played the concertina. He would play hymns, highlifes, traditional Ga songs, and tunes he had learnt from his travels as a carpenter in Nigeria and the Congo. This is what Saka told me about his musical recollections as a child:

> On Saturdays they had flutes and this big bass drum at the Light House [in Jamestown, Accra]. As a little boy some of us who got there early enough, they would give the drum to us to hold at the sides, and we would play it all away along the road to the Palladium Cinema, which we got to by eight o'clock when it was almost ready to start the film. The daily shows on Mondays to Fridays was what were called 'small films', but Saturdays were for 'big film', like Charlie Chaplin and *Madagascar Madness*. I didn't have money, so sometimes by helping hold the drum I was able to get into the entrance. What we call the 'kolomashie' and 'okpeyi' music was played by these sorts of [street] bands.[1]

Saka Acquaye went to the Government Boys School in Kinbu, Accra, and joined their brass band, playing flute and then becoming assistant leader. He then took the Achimota Teachers Training Course and after finishing in 1946, he taught at the Government Junior School in Adabraka. It was then that he joined the Accra Orchestra, which as Saka explains, was led by Teacher Joe Lamptey:

> He was a teacher, a goal-keeper and music director, and he taught at the Government Boys School near the Public Works Department in Ussher Town. His was a full orchestra with three saxophones, two alto[s] and one tenor, and a couple of trombones. I'm not sure if there was a guitar. There was also double bass, but no violins. I got on well with the saxophone and King Bruce was there, but I didn't know him then. In my case it took me less than one year to get ready with them. We copied some of the western sounds and popular songs from abroad and that's what Teacher Lamptey helped me with.

After further studies at Achimota and then teaching at St Augustine's Training College in Cape Coast around 1950, Saka decided to form his own band. As he explains, this transmuted into the Black Beats:

> In Accra, as I was then working for the Kingsway Store on High Street, I formed a band that rehearsed at Farisco House in Adabraka and the owner of the instruments played the clarinet and I played the tenor sax. Jerry Hansen was playing the alto sax and he was a funny guy. As I mentioned, I was working at Kingsway and Jerry Hansen was working nearby, and if I didn't stand outside of the gate early before

he came out, he would run away. When he saw me waiting he couldn't run away. And then we got King Bruce who had started trumpet from Britain. Because King Bruce had a car he helped us a lot travelling around and we began rehearsing at his house in Korle Woko. His sound was not very firm or convincing – but gradually improved. However his compositions were pretty good. He was more of a poet. We asked ourselves what name. I am not sure if it were me or him [but] I think it must have been King Bruce more so than me. We were looking for the kind of name that would suit us, as we were looking for an African expression. When I left in 1953 he took over. He had wonderful ideas and they sent me one of his records and I was highly impressed by the sound.

Saka Acquaye left for the United States in 1953 to do further studies, and whilst in Philadelphia studying fine arts,[2] he also taught African dance. He formed his African Ensemble band, which released records and played at a reception at Carnegie Hall for Ghanaian President Kwame Nkrumah who was on an American visit. Below, he talks about his African Ensemble:

When I got to America the bongos had become very popular throughout the world and I met a group of African American drummers who had never met an African. So we started a band and they were very hard-working and I taught them traditional music, not highlife. One of them was called Garvin Masseaux and another Bobby Crowder who later came to Ghana. We started with drummers and we later expanded into an orchestra called the African Ensemble. This man picked bass, this man picked vibes and this one guitar. It was a tremendous orchestra and we recorded an album called *Gold Coast Saturday Night*.[3]

Saka returned to Ghana in 1959, invited by Nkrumah to become an Exhibitions Officer in the Ghana Information Department. He also formed the African Tones highlife dance band and dance group with which he toured Russia in 1961:

The African Tones was a full sixteen-piece dance band that took me a year to set up. We made our debut for the Nkrumah Trust Fund and after that I set up a dance troupe of boys and girls with the band backing it. And [in 1965] I wrote a dance-play called *Obadzeng Goes to Town*. It was sponsored by Coca-Cola and we performed it for three weeks at a cinema near the Post Office. Immediately we finished Nkrumah sent for me and wanted a command performance. He was so impressed that he said he was taking it to the Soviet Union. So in 1961 we went for six weeks. They gave us a plane all to ourselves as the group was big. The leader was the trumpeter Amartey Laryea, and then we had Nii Oscar Tei. My point was to refine and lift things up, as some highlifes are raw.

The African Tones broke up in 1963 as Saka Acquaye diverted away from dance band music into administrative cultural work and writing plays and folk operas such as *The Lost Fisherman*. As he explains, he also became increasingly keen to travel abroad to do further studies in drama:

Madam Du Bois[4] was in charge of the construction of [the government] television [station] and I met her one night at a cocktail. She told me that I had been ear-marked to head the arts section of the television [station] when it was ready. But she said she had heard that I was planning to go back to the States. I said 'oh yes' but just for a short while to study folk opera. Then one Monday morning there was a call from Nkrumah's office that I should go and see him at 12 o'clock. When I got there he told me that I was going to be the guy for theatre. I don't know what Nkrumah had been told, but he was annoyed that I was leaving the country. He said he didn't want me to go and what help did I need from him to stay. I said the best help would be to let me go, and he burst out laughing as I explained to him that I had failed to produce this folk opera thing in the way I wanted. I gave him the background on it and told him if we could do it properly the country would move forward. He was looking at me with eyes wide open. He picked the telephone and called [his secretaries] and told them to let me go. So I went to the States in 1964.

Scene from Saka Acquaye's folk opera *The Lost Fisherman* (DRUM, November 1963)

In fact it was a Fulbright scholarship that enabled Saka Acquaye to return to America in 1964 where he spent two years at UCLA studying opera and theatre. He also reformed his African Ensemble and recorded a number of albums on the Elektra, Nonesuch and Reocord labels. The Nonesuch recording called *Saka Acquaye: Highlife and Other Popular Music* was released in 1969.[5] According to its sleeve notes Saka Acquaye played drums, flute and tenor saxophone. The album explored a fusion of highlife and free jazz. Some of the other musicians included were Robert 'Bobby' Crowder and Garvin Masseaux, as well as the free-jazz saxophonist Charles Earland and the Ghanaian drummer Joseph Acquaye.

In 1968 (two years after Nkrumah was overthrown) Saka returned to Ghana. He was immediately appointed as head of the Ghana Arts Council and stayed in this post until 1972. He produced his musical play, *The Lost Fisherman*, in this period and initiated the popular Saturday matinee 'Anansekrom' programmes.

He also helped promote the famous Wulomei band set up by Nii Ashitey in 1972. This band, which combined highlife guitar with local flutes and percussion instruments, spearheaded the numerous 'Ga cultural' groups that proliferated in the Greater Accra area from the 1970s. Saka helped produce some of their first recordings, like 'Walatu Walasa' and 'Wulomei in Drum Conference'. As director of the Ghana Art Council, Saka Acquaye was also the principal local organiser of the Soul to Soul concert held at Independence Square (then called Black Star Square) in 1971. The concert brought many top American acts to Ghana, like Wilson Pickett, Roberta Flack, Ike and Tina Turner, The Voices of East Harlem, Les McCann, Eddie Harris and Carlos Santana.

Saka Acquaye died at 83 in 2007. Besides his musical

legacy, his enduring sculptural works are still visible in Greater Accra: for instance, the J.B. Danquah monument at Danquah Circle and the horn-playing figures at the entrance of the old African Studies building and School of Performing Arts at the University of Ghana at Legon.

1. Saka Acquaye, personal communication, 14 March 2004. This took place at Acquaye's house in Accra. Also present were the American film-maker John Dansey and Saka Acquaye's daughter, Aku Sika, who was continually popping in and out to check on her father during the interview, as by then he was completely blind.
2. According to the obituary on Acquaye written by James Gibbs (2007), Saka studied art, sculpture and industrial design at the Pennsylvania Academy of Fine Arts in Philadelphia, USA (1953–6), and then advertising and public relations at the Charles Morris Price School (1957–9).
3. This album was recorded by Saka Acquaye and His African Ensemble from Ghana and was released in the USA around 1959 by Elektra (ELK 167).
4. She was the wife of the African American thinker W.E.B. Du Bois who, in 1961, had been invited to settle in Ghana by Nkrumah to head the Encyclopaedia Africana project.
5. On the American Nonesuch label no. 72026. In 2002 Nonesuch released it on CD.

16

Jerry Hansen and the Ramblers International Band

A s mentioned in the previous chapters on King Bruce and Saka Acquaye, the Ghanaian highlife saxophonist Jerry Hansen was one of the original members of the Black Beats, before moving on in 1961 to form the top highlife dance band, the Ramblers International. In the 1960s and 1970s this band released some of Ghana's most well loved highlife tunes and travelled extensively throughout East and West Africa, as well as the UK.

Jerry Hansen (extreme left, with saxophone) in 1957 at Broadcasting House Studio One whilst still with the Black Beats (BAPMAF via King Bruce)

John William 'Jerry' Hansen was born in Bekwae in southern Ghana on 23 February 1927, the third of five children of an Ashanti mother and a Ga father. His mother, Maami

Senkyire, was a farmer in Bekwae, but Hansen was mainly raised by his father, Johnny Hansen, who was a pharmacist in Koforidua and then Accra. Before leaving for Koforidua, the young Hansen attended the primary school at the Seventh Day Adventists church in Bekwae where he was much impressed by his teacher Mr. Stokes, who played the piano-accordion. In 1938, Hansen went to a Methodist Elementary School in Koforidua and then went to Osu in Accra. In 1941, he obtained admission to Achimota College where he was taught to play and read music. Hansen also joined the Achimota School choir. He completed his secondary schooling at the Accra Academy in 1947 and the following year he joined the staff of the United African Company (UAC),[1] which at the time was one of the few retailers selling musical instruments in Accra.[2]

Jerry Hansen and the Ramblers, 1960s (Isaac Bruce Vanderpuie)

During his schoolboy years Hansen would attend shows put on by the guitarist and concert party actor Kwaa Mensah, and dance sessions held by Teacher Lamptey's Accra Orchestra and Yebuah Mensah's Accra Rhythmic Orchestra. During the Second World War years the young Hansen also became attracted to the American-swing big band style of jazz introduced by Allied troops stationed in Ghana. At this time American military bands that visited Accra sometimes played the music of Benny Goodman, Tommy Dorsey, Louis Armstrong and Duke Ellington.

Swing jazz was also introduced to Ghana through the American V-disc 78 rpm records that were meant for the Allied troops, many of which found their way into the hands of schoolboys like Hansen. It was through these records that the young Hansen got to know the music of the trumpeters Cootie Williams and Cat Anderson, and saxophonists Ben Webster (tenor) and Johnny Hodges (alto). The impact of wartime Amercian jazz was augmented by American films of Glenn Miller and Duke Ellington. These short music clips, or 'shorts', acted as fillers before the feature films at Accra cinemas and were screened at the free shows put on by American troops at the military camp in Cantonments. Hansen was particularly fascinated by both the records and 'shorts' of Duke Ellington, as can be gathered from what he told Ampofo Seth Anim in 2009:

Of all of them at that time, Duke Ellington was the greatest jazz musician because for over 35 years his band was the best jazz band in the world. Most of my [later] arrangements were done in the style of Ellington.[3]

Indeed, years later, Hansen actually met this famous African Amercian jazz musician who he so admired when they both played at a Black Arts Festival in Dakar, Senegal.

The Allied Forces' presence in Ghana ended with the close of the war in 1945 and in the late 1940s Hansen began taking lessons on the saxophone from from E.T. Mensah, whose Tempos band had itself been shaped by wartime jazz. Hansen would go to E.T.'s American Drug Store, which he was using for rehearsals. Then, in 1950, Hansen joined Teacher Joe Lamptey's Accra Orchestra, initially as a packer, then as a drummer and finally as a trombonist when he became inspired by local players of this instrument like Tommy Grippman and Moi Buckman.

Hansen moved on to the saxophone after he was given his own instrument by a senior colleague at the UAC. According to Ampofo Seth Anim, Saka Acquaye and Oko Square (or Squire), who were also members of the Accra Orchestra at this time, coached Hansen on the instrument.[4] During his time with the Accra Orchestra, Hansen joined Moi Buckman to set up a short-lived group called the Dark Stars in which Hansen sang Mills Brothers numbers, Negro spirituals and other popular American songs that the two of them had heard at the free wartime shows given by the American soldiers.

When the Accra Orchestra broke up in 1952, Hansen moved to the Black Beats. The band had just been established by King Bruce and Saka Acquaye and was rehearsing at Farisco House in Adabraka and at King Bruce's house in Korle Woko. At this time the Black Beats became the resident group of the Weekend-in-Havana and was sponsored by the Amstel Company. Hansen played alto sax for the twelve-piece band and sometimes sang popular tunes by African American close-harmony groups like the Ink Spots and Mills Brothers.

When Saka Acquaye left the Black Beats, Hansen took over on the tenor sax. This is what Hansen said about King Bruce and the Black Beats in a 2006 interview by Will Magid:

> King was a lovely man and we were great friends. He did not take any leading role [as a solo trumpeter] but he was a crack composer. Most of his songs can still be rated with the best. The standard of education was much higher than other bands. It was a band with respect. You had other bands with illiterate trumpeters and saxophonists arguing their way through dance after dance. The Black Beats were serious and there was no room for seeing women or anything. Without practice you can never be a good band. Even during electrical shortages, I would go and buy candles and we would still practice. We would normally rehearse three or four times a week, but there were times when we couldn't even practice once a week because we were in demand. This is when musicians go rotten. When people are in demand they think they will be in demand forever. But when you don't practice things will overtake you.[5]

By this time the Black Beats was the resident band at the Metropole Club in Accra and they made recordings for HMV, in Nsawam, and Decca, whose studio was located near Ridge Hospital in Accra. The band also made extensive tours of Ghana, played in Togo and made one Nigerian trip to Lagos and Ibadan. By the late 1950s, whenever King Bruce was away on leave, Hansen took over as the band's director.

In 1961, Hansen and a group of musicians left the Black Beats to form the Ramblers International highlife big band, helped by Habib Zakar, the Lebanese owner of the Metropole

Club. According Ampofo Seth Anim, Hansen chose the name Ramblers because, when he had been a member of the Black Beats, the UAC had sent him on a one-year scholarship to Stuttgart, Germany, where he heard and made friends with a band composed of medical doctors and teachers called the Ramblers.[6]

Original members of the Ramblers in 1962, just prior to travelling to Gambia. Jerry Hansen is standing in a white shirt, in the middle (Peter Marfo of the Hansen family)

Hansen's Ghanaian Ramblers included Eddie Soga on bass guitar,[7] Felix Amenuda on tenor sax, Eddie Owu (or Owoo) on drums, the vocalists Joe Atiso and Pat Akrong, and guitarist Frank Kwamena Croffie. The latter was a specialist in the 'double strings' technique, which involved playing the third and sixth of the scale on two strings, a feature often found in Cuban and Congolese popular music. Other members included Kwesi Forson and Aryee Hammond. The Ramblers mostly played at the Metropole, the Star Hotel, the Lido and the Ambassador Hotel in Accra. When Queen Elizabeth II and Prince Phillip visited Ghana in 1961,[8] the Ramblers were on hand to entertain them. By this time Ghana had become became a republic with Dr Kwame Nkrumah as its first president, but it was still a member of the British Commonwealth.

In the mid-1960s, Hansen's Ramblers International travelled to Gambia, Sierra Leone and Togo. Their first two trips were of a political nature, however. In 1962 Nkrumah asked the Ramblers to go to Gambia to support election rallies in favour of the CPP's preferred presidential candidate, Bala Garba Jahumpa, who was competing against Dawda Kairaba Jawara.[9] That same year, there was another presidential-command performance and as Hansen told Will Magid:

Siaka Stevens[10] was running for presidency in Sierra Leone that was heading for its first general elections [in May 1962]. We in Ghana were supposed to be supportive of Siaka Stevens, and against his opponent Milton Margai. We were to go to Sierra Leone for a month, organizing dances at rallies to help defeat Milton Margai[11]. After a week I wrote to the [Nkrumah's] Bureau of African Affairs telling them that as far as I was concerned Siaka Stevens had already lost the elections as he wasn't organized at all. As a result I nearly fell out of grace with him [Nkrumah]. When the votes came in my words came through, Milton Margai won the elections. [12]

The Ramblers released twenty long-play albums and well over a hundred singles. Some of their albums were *Dance with the Ramblers*, *West African Highlife Scene*, and *Doing Our Own Thing*. Some of Hansen's most famous songs, mainly released on the Decca label, were 'Work and Happiness', 'Ama Bonsu', 'Okonini Abankaba', 'Egyanka Dabre' and 'Yiadom Boakye'. However, some of the Ramblers songs were not written by Hansen himself, but by other well-known highlife composers like Joe Eyison who composed 'Auntie Christie' and 'Ewuraba Artificial', and Kofi Ani Johnson who wrote 'Woma Wonko' and 'Akokonini Abankwaa Wu'.

The UAC had sent Hansen to Stuttgart, Germany, in the late 1950s where he had trained in camera and microscope optical mechanics and in 1965 Hansen set up his own shop in Accra repairing optical equipment like cameras. Hansen had gained retail experience working as assistant manager for the company from 1948–65 and through his business acumen he became the Ghana representative for the British Henri Selma musical instrument company and his shop also began to sell musical equipment.

From 1967 the Ramblers International began visiting the UK. Their first trip there was arranged by Ghana's foreign minister, Victor Owusu. On this occasion, the band played at such places as the Battersea Town Hall in London and the Manchester Empire Rooms. They also performed for BBC radio, the first live Ghanaian band to do so since the Gold Coast Police Band visited the UK in 1948. It was on their second London trip in 1968 that the Ramblers recorded their first stereo record album for Decca called the *Sounds of the Ramblers*. Then in 1972 they made an East African trip in connection with the All-Africa Trade Fair in Nairobi, Kenya, during which they played for Kenya's President Jomo Kenyatta. They also played at the University of Kampala in Uganda. In 1973 the Ramblers teamed up with Professor Albert Mawere Opoku and the Ghana University Dance Ensemble for a two-and-a-half month US tour. This is what Hansen told the Ghanaian music journalist

Eric K. Ashie II in 1981 concerning the Ramblers various trips abroad:

> Believe me, I am the most travelled band in Africa today. I started travelling from 1961 outside Africa and I've seen no less than eighteen African countries including Nigeria, Uganda, Kenya, Gambia, Senegal, Togo, Liberia, Somalia, and Sierra Leone. The audience reaction to my music has all along been very encouraging and I can say that this has led to my being invited to play for so many African Heads of States during State functions. I played for Idi Amin, the late President [William R.] Tolbert, Jomo Kenyatta, Sir Milton Margai, President Eyadema, [Dawda Kairaba] Jawara[13] and a host of them. And I was the first band from West Africa to visit Britain on a tour. [14]

In 1975, Hansen was elected president of the newly-formed Musicians Union of Ghana (MUSIGA). This is what Hansen told Will Magid about music unions in Ghana:

> We the musicians were operating as freelancers and were never given ample payments and, as a result, suffered. We didn't have control of our own royalties and we didn't have any form of retirement. It was a problem, especially for the government-employed musicians who should have been taken care of.[15]

However, this was not the country's first union. The Ghana Musicians Union was formed in 1961, the year that Hansen began to make international tours with his Ramblers, and Hansen was an executive member of this union. It was affiliated with Nkrumah's CPP political party through the Trade Union

Congress. The poor conditions at the time resulted in the musicians in the union going on strike, as Hansen explains:

> After one year of being on strike we went to the conference table. I told those there that we wanted the type of royalty contract that Bing Crosby could get. We got better deals worked out, but none of us were ever as rich as Bing Crosby. But [this union] had a very dangerous flirtation with the CPP government, as back then it was a rather socialist thing. We were given offices, but the party controlled everything. We thought the musicians union should be a separate professional unit to fight for the cause of musicians and nothing else.[16]

Indeed it was precisely because of the close links between this union and the CPP government that it was was dissolved immediately after the anti-Nkrumah coup of 1966. As a result there was no music union in Ghana until MUSIGA was formed in 1975.

The succession of military governments of the late 1970s and 1980s were a difficult time for the Ramblers, as it was for many Ghanaian musicians. Hansen found it was becoming increasingly hard to get import licenses to stock his shop in Accra. In 1984 Hansen left Ghana for Washington DC, where he stayed and worked as a security guard for seventeen years. Whilst in the United States, Hansen recieved a number of awards for his contribution to Ghanaian highlife music including awards from the Brong Ahafo Association in the US and the Adisadel Old Boys' Association (North America). He also received awards from Ghanaian agencies such as the Certificate of Merit from the Rex-Images Foundation of Ghana in 1990. However, even this honour did not induce Hansen to return home, due to the continuing economic plight of musicans in Ghana at the time. This is what Hansen said about the state of Ghanaian music at the time when he was interviewed in 2007 by the journalist Jonathan Gmanyami:

> In Ghana where there is music, there is frustration. Musicians barely have enough to clothe themselves and as such can't live peaceful lives. You meet most musicians and they are found lean and just trying to survive. Well, to me this is not peace .... Sadly however, those who have enough to eat and wear are those who take the poor musicians' recordings to the market to mass produce them and make millions of cedis.[17]

Nevertheless, the Ghanaian economy began to pick up in the 1990s, particularly after the return to democracy in 1992, and Hansen returned home in 2001. He was able to revive the Ramblers, though he had to call in some of his old musicians as well as some of his musically-inclined children. The new fifteen-piece Ramblers was first led by Felix Amenuda, but after Amenuda's death in 2004, Hansen reorganised the band with a new batch of young musicians led by his nephew Peter Marfo[18] and Felix Amenuda's son, Yaw. Two of Hansen's children with his wife Rosemary, Jojo and Jerry Junior, also joined the new Ramblers as vocalists.[19]

After returning home form the United States in 2001 Hansen received more awards. One was the Living Legend Award in 2004 from Ghana's National Theatre, and another was the Lifetime Award he was given during the African American History/Heritage Month in 2005 organised by the US Embassy's Public Affairs Section and BAPMAF. The same year Sunshine Arts and Music gave him the Kanrewa Award. In 2007, two of the Ramblers songs, 'Ama Bonsu' and 'Auntie Christie', were selected for the Ghana Telecom/One Touch company's promotional CD *The Best of Ghanaian Highlife Music* made to commemorate Ghana's fiftieth year of independence. During this period of national celebration Hansen also received a Music Merit Award from the Ghana@50 Secretariat. Then, in 2008, Hansen was given the prestigious Ghanaian ACRAG Award and the same year became a Patron of the Ghana Musicians Union.

In 2010, Femi Esho's Lagos-based Evergreen Musical Company released seventeen old Ramblers hits on CD.[20] This release was part of a series of CDs of old Nigerian and Ghanaian highlife music repackaged for the celebrations surrounding the fiftieth anniversary of Nigerian independence. Hansen's New Ramblers band was still going strong when Hansen passed away on 7 April 2012. Due to his huge contribution to Ghanaian highlife music there was a huge wake at the MUSIGA headquarters in Accra a week later, at which many Ghanaian bands performed.

1. An old British trading company formed in 1919. In 1992 it merged with Unilever.
2. Two others were the Argentinean-owned Chebibs at Post Office Square and a shop on what is now Kwame Nkrumah Avenue, owned by Benko Safo from Koforidua.
3. Jerry Hansen, interviewed by Ampofo Seth Anim, 2009. Anim was one of my undergraduate students from the Process of Art course at the music department of the University of Ghana.
4. Ibid.
5. Jerry Hansen, interviewed by Will Magid, 2006, for a term paper. Magid was an international student from the US who took one of my African popular music courses in the music department at the University of Ghana.
6. Ampofo Seth Anim, student paper 2009.
7. Soga was also a dentist.
8. This 9–20 November trip was to make up for the royal couple's 1959 visit that had to be postponed due to the Queen being pregnant with the future Prince Andrew.
9. Jawara actually won Gambia's 1962 elections. Incidentally, he was educated at Ghana's prestigious Achimota School.

10. Later in 1967, Siaka Probyn Stevens (1905–1988) became the third prime minister of Sierra Leone and, in 1971, its first president.

11. Sir Milton Augustus Strieby Margai (1895–1964) became Sierra Leone's first prime minister in 1962.

12. Will Magid, student paper, 2006

13. As mentioned earlier, Margai and Jawara were Sierra Leonean and Gambian politicians. Idi Amin was the 1970s Ugandan president; William Tolbert the Liberian president in 1971–80; Jomo Kenyatta was the Kenyan president, 1964–1978; Gnassingbé Eyadéma was the Togolese president in 1967–2005.

14. Eric K. Ashie II, 'Why Ghana Ramblers are Consistent', *African Music*, 5 (September/October 1981), p. 32

15. Jerry Hansen, interviewed by Will Magid, student paper, 2006.

16. Ibid.

17. Jerry Hansen, interviewed by Jonathan Gmanyami, *Ghanaian Spectator*, 3 March 2007, p. 18.

18. A fine trumpeter and one of my University of Ghana music department students.

19. Hansen's daughter, Mildred, is a singer with the Triple M hiplife group, one of the few female rap groups in Ghana.

20. Entitled *Highlife Hits from the 1950s & 1960s*, Vol. 2.

Broadway, Uhuru and Ebo Taylor

The important Broadway dance band, and the Uhuru band that evolved out of it, expanded the eight to eleven-piece size of the Tempos and Black Beats to a big band format by including large horn sections. Moreover, Broadway and Uhuru became closely associated with Nkrumah and some of the CPP ministers. Indeed, Uhuru became recognised as a national band. One important musician who passed through both these bands was the guitarist Ebo Taylor, who helped introduce advanced jazz chords to many highlife bands. He also helped to blend highlife with funk in the 1970s.

The Broadway Band

The Broadway dance band was established in 1958 as the resident band of the Zenith Hotel in the twin towns of Takoradi-Sekondi in Ghana's Western Region. They played everything from ballroom numbers to the big band jazz of Glenn Miller, the bebop of Charlie Parker and local highlife. The band's proprietor was J.K. Agyepong who owned the Prempeh and Gyandu Cinemas. The band had five saxophones, five trumpets, three or four trombones, a double bass, a rhythm guitar, a set of trap drums and percussion. It was led by the Nigerian Sammy Obot, who had originally been the trumpeter for Lord Eddyson's Starlite Melody Orchestra in Port Harcourt, Nigeria.

The Nigerian trumpeter Sammy Obot, from an album released in 1985 by Sagata Records Nigeria. Much earlier, he was the leader of the Ghanaian Broadway band.

Broadway included top local artists like the percussionist Darko Adams 'Potato', bassist Slim 'Bright' Amoaku, trumpeter Teddy Kpakpo Addo, Duke Duker, the ex-Tempos guitarist and drummers Bebop Aggrey and Tom Tom Addo. Broadway also, at different times, featured singers Joss Aikins and Joe Mensah. One of the band's saxophonists was George Kojo Amissah (or Emissah) who joined in 1961, as did the guitarists C.K. Mann and Ebo Taylor. The guitarist Stan Plange joined in 1963.

Some popular Broadway songs on the Decca label were 'Mankasa', 'Odo Bra', 'Meido Wo', and 'Ashewo'. Although not a member of Broadway, Oscarmore Ofori, who is discussed more fully in the next chapter, wrote a number of compositions for the band such as 'Nkae' ('Remember' those who died for independence) and 'Edusei Okamafo', in praise of the 1959 CPP minister of interior.

In early 1963, the Broadway band, together with the local highlife guitar band artists Kwabena Onyina, Dr K. Gyasi, E.K. Nyame and 'Kakaiku' Kweku Moses Oppong, and the concert-party comedians Bob Cole and 'Sampson', accompanied President Nkrumah on a six-week state visit to Mali, Tunisia, Poland and the Soviet Union. The trip was organised to inaugurate Ghana Airways' first flight to Moscow in March 1963, one year after Nkrumah had been awarded the Lenin Peace Prize. Whilst in Moscow, Broadway and the other Ghanaian artists performed on television and at hotels and universities.

That year, Kwame Nkrumah began to encourage a number of highlife dance bands to undergo a three-month-long training course in traditional drumming and dancing at the Arts Council of Ghana to enhance their overall delivery of African rhythms and percussion. George Lee's Messengers band, which had been based at the Ambassador State Hotel, was the first to undertake the course. They were then promptly sent on a state-sponsored tour of West Germany. Other bands including Broadway, the Farmers Council Band, the Brigade Band and the Globemasters followed. According to a November 1963 edition of *DRUM* magazine, Broadway caused:

> a sensation at the Press Club in Accra when, after playing highlife for a while, it plunged straight into an *agbadza* [a local drum-dance of the Volta Region]. The Ewe pressmen present couldn't resist and danced and danced. It was great to see this so traditional dance being performed by such an ultra-modern crowd.[1]

During its 1958–63 heyday, Broadway played regularly at the Flagstaff House to entertain Nkrumah and his visitors as, according to Stan Plange, it was regarded as a 'national' band. However, after the Arts Council course, problems began to arise and the Broadway band had to change its name.

Broadway's Stan Plange on xylophone, and drummer Darko Adams
'Potato' training on traditional instruments at the Ghana Arts Council,
Accra, 1963 (Oppong)

The band's owner, Mr Agyepong, refused to pay the bandsmen for the three-month Arts Council training period, and so the musicians resigned en masse. As a result, there was a tussle over the legal ownership of the band's name. This is what Stan Plange told me about the matter:

What happened was that we [Broadway] came down to Accra for the Arts Centre course in traditional drumming and dancing. We stayed for three months and were housed at the Puppet Theatre near the Drama Studio. Our group, George Lee's Messengers and the Farmers Council Band took advantage of the course. It was free for musicians. When we returned, there was some trouble about our salary so we decided that we would work with the management on a percentage basis. But the percentage they wanted was too much, taking into account the old state of the instruments. So we left and within two months we got E.K. Dadson and Krobo Edusei [two CPP ministers] to buy us instruments: in those days the whole set cost £1,600. Later Dadson paid back Krobo Edusei his share, so the band became Dadson's property. We continued to use the name Broadway as the manager of the Zenith hadn't registered it; in fact, we registered it. However, Edusei took us to court saying that the name belonged to him and he sued us for £26,000 for the thirteen of us. He lost, but kept the name and was awarded £75 for costs. So we chose the name Uhuru.[2] This was in 1964 [actually late 1963].[3]

The Uhuru Band

After the Broadway band changed its name to Uhuru, Sammy Obot remained the leader. However, in 1965, he returned to Nigeria and the 28-year-old guitarist Stan Plange took over as director of the band.

Stan Plange's career began in Accra in 1957 when he joined the Downbeats, led by the Nigerian trumpeter Chief Bill Friday. Stan then played briefly with Ray Ellis's Comets and Eddie Quansah's Stargazers before rejoining the Downbeats in Lagos in 1958. It was whilst there that Plange became an executive of the Nigerian Union of Musicians and was involved in the 1960 march demanding the use of local highlife musicians for the Nigerian Independence Ball. Plange also played with the Nigerian Broadcasting Corporation's dance band and began his lifelong friendship with Fela Anikulapo-Kuti. He left the Downbeats around 1962 and returned to Ghana to play, first for the reformed Stargazers, then for the Broadway and Uhuru bands.

Uhuru had an eleven-piece horn frontline and its musicians included many of those from the earlier Broadway. Newer members were the percussionists/drummers Rim Kwaku Obeng and Max Hammond, the saxophonists Ebo Dadson and Lofty (or Loughty) Lasisi Amao, and the trumpeter Mac Tontoh. The group still featured Joe Mensah as a vocalist, but other singers were Eddie Ntreh, Pat Thomas and the Krobo singer Charlotte Dada. It was with Uhuru, under the recording name Big Beats, that Joe Mensah made his famous 1963 'Uhuru Special/Bosoe' song in Lagos.

It is impractical to list all the big recording hits for Philips and Decca that Uhuru released. In 1964, the band, produced by E.K. Dadson and with singer Joe Mensah, released 'Kojo Botsio' that praised this CPP minister of state. In 1964–5 the Ghanaian diplomat and music producer Kwadwo Donkoh wrote songs for Uhuru like 'Time for Highlife', 'Go Slow', 'Wobeku Me', 'Wobetumi No' and 'No Parking'. Another was 'Skin Pain' by E.C. Arinze, previously released by Decca in Nigeria in 1960/1. Arinze had obtained the song from Kwadwo Donkoh, who was a young diplomat in Lagos and often visited the Kakadu Club where Arinze's band was based. Some other top Uhuru hits of the late sixties and early seventies, released as singles or on LP, include 'Odo Handkerchief', 'Kanova', 'Wofa Nunuo', 'Picadilly', 'Konkoma Medley', and 'Onyame Bekyere'.

After the 1966 coup that overthrew the Nkrumah regime, the band lost all its official engagements. However, the group continued to play at private programmes. That year, they toured Ghana with Chubby Checker, the African American 'King of Twist', and the following year they backed him again for his Nigerian tour.

The group also travelled throughout Africa, the Near East, and Europe. In 1968, music promoter Faisal Helwani promoted a six-week tour sponsored by East Africa Airways that included Uhuru, the Rolling Beats dance troupe and the drummer Kofi Ghanaba. In 1970, Uhuru went to London to record an album for Decca.

During the late sixties Uhuru made a big impact on the young Fela Anikulapo-Kuti and his Koola Lobitos highlife band, who were making regular Ghana tours at the time. Fela was so impressed by the sound of the Uhuru big band that whenever he was on any of his numerous trips to Accra he stayed with Stan Plange at Uhuru House in Asylum Down, Accra. In 1968, Fela reciprocated by arranging for Uhuru to play at both the Glover Memorial Hall and Lisabi Hall in Lagos.

In 1971, my Bokoor band became Uhuru's support band for a while, specialising in pop music. Having a second pop band to attract the youth was a common practice among dance bands like the Tempos and Black Beats from the late 1960s. Bokoor[4] played alongside Uhuru at clubs in Accra and Takoradi, including the famous Zenith Club where Broadway had been the resident band when it was first formed in 1958.

In 1972, Stan Plange left Uhuru and George Amissah took over as the band's director. Plange himself moved on to set up the Obibini Record Company with Faisal Helwani. Later, he became the director of the Ghana Television Corporation's dance band.

It was after this that the music-promoter-cum-diplomat Kwadwo Donkoh again became involved with the band. Donkoh had already composed some of Uhuru's hits, and in 1973 he employed the band to back the flautist Oscar Sulley Braima for an Afrobeat/rock album entitled *Oscar Sulley and the Nzele Afrikana*. The same year, Gyedu-Blay Ambolley made his first single funky-highlife record 'Simigwa Do', with Uhuru personnel under the band name The Steneboofs.

Uhuru with the American king of twist, Chubby Checker, in 1966.
Stan Plange is on Checker's left, singer Charlotte Dada is on his right,
and bassist Slim Bright Amuaku is behind the American. Mac Tontoh
is standing back-right, and Eddie Entrah is crouching on the extreme
right. George Amissah and Teddy Kpakpo Addo are standing second and
third left. (Teddy Kpakpo Addo)

In the mid-seventies Kwadwo Donkoh again worked
with Uhuru[5] on an album called *The Sound of Africa* for his
Agoro label. It was recorded at Ghana Films[6] and consisted
of his own compositions, like 'Biribi', 'Osiakwan', 'Nkobesie',
'Sika', 'Yahyia Me' and 'Awereso'. In 1976–7 Uhuru also became
part of Faisal Helwani's Afrodisia project, a collaboration with
the Decca West African record label in Nigeria. This project
included a once weekly 'Afrodisia Night' at the Tip-Toe Gardens
in Accra which featured Uhuru and other acts such as E.T.
Mensah, Basa Basa, the Bunzus, Bokoor, Abladei, Kwaa Mensah
and Adjo. Faisal also took Uhuru and some of these groups to
Lagos to record.

The Uhuru band continued to operate until the early 1980s. In 1982, the Essiebons' (Dick Essilfie-Bondzie's record company) *Roots to Fruits* film included Joanna Okang and the Ewe singer Efua Dokenoo backed by the Uhuru Band. And well into the 1990s, Faisal Helwani continued to release the Afrodisia recordings as well as other collaborations he did with Uhuru on cassettes and CDs on his Obibini label.

Ebo Taylor

Ebo Delroy Taylor played, at one point, for both the Broadway and Uhuru bands. During his long career, this ace Ghanaian guitarist and composer released seventeen albums, won six national awards and composed evergreen highlife songs like 'Odo Ye Wu', 'Ghana Be Ye Yie', 'Mensu', 'Wofa Nunu' and 'Twer Nyame'. Ebo was born in Saltpond near Cape Coast in 1936 and began learning guitar when he was a fourteen-year-old secondary school pupil at Saint Augustine's College in Cape Coast. There he was intrigued by the performances of local palm wine guitarists from the town, such as Kwame Asare (Jacob Sam) and his nephew Kwaa Mensah. However, it was from the highlife dance band guitarists that the young Ebo first learnt. Particularly important were Eddie Johnson, who at one point had been with the Tempos, Frank Crofi of the Rhythm Aces and Kwamina Kofi of the Black Beats, who specialised in playing double-string solos on the third and sixth notes of the scale.

Whilst still in his final years in secondary school, Ebo was invited to join the Havana dance band, the resident band at the Weekend-in-Havana club.[7] As a result, Ebo never completed his sixth-form studies.

In 1957, Ebo moved to Kumasi to play with the Stargazers

and did some of his first recordings. He composed the hits 'Mensu', 'Onyimpa Neber Ara Nyi' and 'Dance Highlife' for them and in 1960 accompanied them on a tour of Nigeria, Côte d'Ivoire, Togo and Burkina Faso. Then he moved on to the Kingsway Sextet that specialised in jazz as well as highlife.

In 1961, Ebo moved south to join the Takoradi-based Broadway band led by the Nigerian trumpeter Sammy Obot. Bebop Aggrey was their guitarist and he helped Ebo polish his guitar techniques. As Ebo told Titus Arko, the Broadway band was important for his musical development:

> I think it was like a school for me; I learnt a lot from Broadway and its musical director S.S. Ahemah because of the harmony and style of arrangements by foreign writers like Chris Jones and Glenn Miller. By the time I left Broadway, I was a fully-fledged arranger.[8]

Ebo not only became the band's arranger; he also composed highlifes for them like 'Beye Bu Beye Ba' (whatever you do, you will die), 'Wofa Nunu' (there he goes), 'Nsamanfo', 'Dance Marriage' and 'Meja Wu Do' (fatherly love).

In 1962, he obtained a scholarship from Kwame Nkrumah to study at the Eric Guilder School of Music in London. Whilst there, the Ghanaian High Commissioner in London asked Ebo to organise a dance band. It was called the Black Star Band and it included such UK-based Ghanaian musicians as Eddie Quansah, Oscarmore Ofori, George Aikins, the drummer Sol Amarfio and saxophonist Teddy Osei, who later went on to form Cat's Paw and Osibisa. The Black Star Band toured Germany, Spain, Italy, France, Yugoslavia and Romania, but as he explained to Titus Arko, Ebo eventually moved on:

I got fed up with the Black Star Band and so started playing in jazz clubs like Club Tokyo, Flamingo and Ronnie Scotts. That is when I got in contact with Fela Kuti and the trumpeter Mike Falana.[9] I joined them and we played around London.[10]

Whilst in the UK, Ebo was exposed to the jazz of Miles Davis, John Coltrane and Charlie Parker, as well as that of the jazz guitarists Kenny Burrell, Wes Montgomery and Jim Hall. Consequently, he became interested in moving away from the primary three-chord progressions of highlife and enhancing them. One way he did this was to modulate or change key at some point of a song, a technique found in much western music, including jazz. Another that was particularly favoured by modern jazz exponents was the use of passing chords, or complex progressions of multiple substitute chords.[11] Ebo wanted to saturate highlife with jazz and while in London he and Fela Kuti (then also in the UK) discussed various ways this could be done. For both of them, this involved going back home, which Fela did in 1963 and Ebo did in 1965.

On returning to Ghana, Ebo joined Uhuru and, using his modern jazz influences, helped introduce them to modulations and advanced chord progressions. In 1968, he went to Sekondi to play with the Railway Band run by Sammy Lartey, which also included Gyedu-Blay Ambolley, C.K. Mann and Jewel Ackah.

Then in 1972, two of Ghana's leading radio DJs, Mike Eghan and Carl Bannerman, invited Ebo, the guitarist Bob Pinodo[12] and the famous highlife singer Pat Thomas to form the Blue Monks. Ebo and Pinodo left the Blue Monks around 1974 and Ebo became the leader of the Apagya Show Band, the brainchild of music producer Dick Essilfie-Bondzie. This ten-piece band included the Uhuru saxist Ebo Dadson, singer

Joana Okang[13] and the keyboard player Ernest Honey.[14] It released a number of 45 singles on the Essiebons label, some in a funky highlife vein, composed by the group's three principal artists, Ebo, Gyedu-Blay Ambolley and Bob Pinodo.

Two of the Apagya musicians went on to become key players in developing blends of highlife and pop, soul and funk. One is Gyedu-Blay Ambolley who, prior to joining the Apagya Show Band, had played with the Railway Band, Kodjo Donkor's Hugas Extraordinaire and the Tema-based Meridian dance band. In 1973, with Ebo as arranger, Ambolley collaborated with Uhuru (under the name Steneboofs) to make his first record, the still-popular funky highlife 'Simigwa Do'. Ambolley continued in this style with Apagya until he left to form his own band, Zantada in 1979.

The other was Bob Pinodo, who formed his first band, the Silver Bells, in 1969. At the same time, he began experimenting with his 'sonobete' beat, which combined highlife, pop music and the traditional Efutu rhythm of his home town of Winneba, a coastal port city, west of Accra. After the release of his *Sonobete* album in 1973, Pinodo and I formed Szaabu Sounds,[15] after which he moved on to Apagya. Pinodo later became a solo artist and moved to Germany, where he became associated with the so-called Ghanaian 'burger highlife' musicians who, in the 1980s, were combining highlife with funk and disco.

After leaving the Apagya Show Band in the mid-seventies, Ebo Taylor formed the Asase Ase (Underground) band that delved into rootsy Fanti music and proverbial lyrics. However, he also continued releasing albums in the funky highlife style. For instance in 1977–8, working with the saxist George Amissah and trumpeter Arthur Kennedy, he released the album *Ebo Taylor* on the Essiebons label.

During the 1970s he was the Artist and Repertoire (AR)

man for Essiebons. In this capacity he produced and arranged records for Pat Thomas, C.K. Mann, Gyedu-Blay Ambolley, Jewel Ackah and Papa Yankson.

Ebo Taylor around 2008 (Titus Kwabena Ofori Arko)

In the 1990s, Taylor got into the small but evolving Accra jazz scene when, together with George Amissah, he played with the Village Five. Around 2000 he teamed up with his old saxophonist friend Ray Allen to run an Afro-jazz combo called Unconditional Love. In 2002, after a successful interaction with the music students of the University of Ghana's Legon campus,[16] Taylor became artist-in-residence at the school. He taught guitar and helped run the music department's pop band.

By this time, and due to his long musical career, Taylor began to be widely recognised. In 2005, he was given a Lifetime Achievement Award in the African American History/Heritage Month. In 2006, Taylor celebrated his seventieth birthday with a musical bash organised by the Alliance Francaise in Accra.

That same year he played with Nana Kobina Nketsia's Palace Musicians at the Eastern Region's Centre for National Culture. In 2007, Taylor, Ambolley and C.K. Mann played at a garden party in honour of the late Ali Farka Touré, thrown by the musically-inclined World Bank Ghana Country Director, Mats Karlsson and his wife Irena Kunovska.

In 2009, Taylor released his seventeenth album, to coincide with the one hundredth anniversary of Kwame Nkrumah's birth. It was entitled *Abenkwan Puchaa* and was released on the Essiebons label. Artists who appeared on it included trumpeter Osei Tutu, saxophonist Ray Allen and the guitarists Kofi Labayili Kudonu and Koffie 'Fish' Mark Millas of the University of Ghana's music department.

This album launched Taylor's new band, which he called Bonze Konkoma. It included some of the same musicians he used on the album as well as others like the guitarists Henry and William Taylor, the female trombonist Eli Amewode and Taylor's own keyboard-playing son, Ebo Taylor junior. The band explores fusions of jazz, funk, Afrobeat and highlife combined with local asafo, agabdaza, konkoma and adzewa drum rhythms. The group even features the old Fanti konkoma frame drums. In late 2010, Taylor and his twelve-piece Bonze Konkoma went on an extended European tour and released his *Love and Death* CD for the British Strut Records, recorded with the German-based Afrobeat Assembly.

1. 'The Arts Go Pop', *DRUM*, November 1963, pp. 8–9.
2. The band name was suggested by local chief Nana Kobina Nketsia, from the Swahili word for 'freedom'.
3. Stan Plange, personal communication, Napoleon Club, Accra, 15 February 1977. See also Collins, 1996, p.72 .
4. At that time, Bokoor was run by me and the Ghanaian guitarist Robert Beckley. We specialised in the music of Jimmy Hendrix and Carlos Santana as well as local highlifes.

5. At that time, Uhuru consisted of George Amissah (alto sax/leader), George Abunewah (baritone/tenor sax), Kwesi Baiden junior (keyboards), Prince Marco-Bazz and Richard Unegbu (trumpets), Adlib Kwaku Anim (trombone), Max Hammond (drums), Pepper Afful (guitar), Eddie Ntreh and Leo Aggrey-Fynn (vocals) and the percussionists Albert Armah, Stephen Oware and Teiko Foli.

6. The top engineers there were Francis Kwakye, Kofi Archer, Bossman Amoako and Jacob Sedzro.

7. The Havana dance band was formed by Dan Tackie in 1957, after he left E.T. Mensah's third band, the Paramount Stars.

8. Ebo Taylor, quoted in Titus Kwabena Ofori Arko, 'Ebo Taylor: The Man and his Music' (paper written for University of Ghana, 2007/8).

9. During the early 1960s Mike Falana was also involved with percussionist Bayo Martins and trumpeter Peter King of the UK-based African Messengers Afro-jazz outfit.

10. Taylor, quoted in Arko, 'Ebo Taylor', 2007/8.

11. Such as diminished and augmented.

12. Pinodo began his career in the sixties with the Republic Aces band of Agona Swedru and then the Magic Aliens pop band of Accra.

13. After the Apagya Show Band, Joana Okang left Ghana for Sierra Leone, where she sang under the name Joana Naa Awushie Kargbo.

14. Before joining the Apagya Show Band, Ernest Honey (or Honney) was the keyboards man for Dr K. Gyasi's Noble Kings guitar band, which had a huge Essiebons hit album in 1972 called *Sikyi Highlife*.

15. This band, which Pinodo and I ran in 1973 , included guitarist Nat Osamanu, singer Leslie Tex and keyboard player Bob Fiscian. It was managed by Aunty Naomi, who owned the Kyekyeke Club in Accra. Besides sonobete-style songs, the group also played cover versions of soul and reggae.

16. A student paper , 'Ebo Taylor' 2007/8

18

The Ghanaian Highlife Composer Oscarmore Ofori

Twumasi Ankrah 'Oscar' Ofori was one of the most prolific highlife composers in the 1950s and early 1960s, with scores of hit compositions to his credit. He was born on 2 September 1930 in Odumasi Krobo. He was the son of Nana K.T.A. Ofori of the traditional throne of the Royal Ntahera Stool of New Juaben, and Madam Victoria Dale Tawiah Asare, a royal of both the Begorohene Stool and the Manya Krobo Stool. Both his parents were musical: Ofori's father was an organist and accordion player and his mother a chorister. By 1945 Ofori was a drummer in the 'Akro' band of his Old Juaben Senior School and was studying as choirboy under Kwesi Baiden, the school's music master. Being Fanti, Kwesi Baiden also taught the young Ofori to play the guitar, an instrument popular with this coastal ethnic group who were the first in Ghana to develop a local highlife guitar style.

Ofori bought a cheap guitar for two shillings and sixpence, but had to play it when his father was out working or at the palace, because his father believed that all guitarists were drunkards. Despite his father's objections, the young Ofori began playing with the Koforidua Royal Orchestra and in 1950 he moved to Accra to study surveying and draughtsmanship. It was in Accra that he met highlife greats like the Tempos saxophonist Joe Kelly and the trumpeter 'Satchmo' Korley, and his musical career really took off.

Ofori joined Korley's Ranchers dance band for a while in 1953. That year, he also joined the band Kelly had formed after leaving the Tempos, known simply as Joe Kelly's Band, and released his first highlife record hit, 'Sanbra', with them.

Some of the guitarists who impressed and influenced Ofori at the time included Tricky Johnson of the Tempos and Kwamena Crofi of the Black Beats who was an expert in the 'Spanish' (Afro-Cuban son and rumba) double-string solo technique. Another was Kwabena Onyina who ran both a guitar band and his National Trio Concert Party in Kumasi. Onyina was influenced by American ragtime, jazz and the close-harmony music of the Ink Spots. Indeed, Onyina is famous for his early use of advanced jazz chords[1] in guitar highlife, which helped him win the 1961 National Guitar Band Contest.

Oscarmore on double bass, 1960s (BAPMAF, from Oscarmore Ofori)

Ofori became an expert guitarist and sometimes played double bass. It was his popularity on stage as a guitarist that earned him the nickname 'Oscarmore', for his dance fans would shout 'Oscar, Oscar, more, more'. This use of a stage name was quite convenient, as his father really did not want the family's royal name being associated with guitarists. Ofori told me that he was also happy with this name as it resembled the name of Nat King Cole's famous 1937–47 guitarist, Oscar Moore.

In 1954, Ofori joined the Rakers dance band, which was owned by Agyanka Solo and was based at the Tip-Toe Gardens in Accra. It included the singer Bill Snowden, 'Satchmo' Sucaire on alto sax, singer Nat Buckle, 'Big Boy' on trombone, Cano on double bass and an Ashanti percussionist called Opoku. They released several of Ofori's songs for the Parlophone and Decca record labels. But the Rakers broke down financially after a year or so, and so Ofori moved to Kumasi to join the Music Mayors whose leader, Mr Kwakye, taught him the art of musical arrangement.

In 1956 Ofori became the Ghana repertoire manager for Decca Records, which at the time was operating in Ghana, Sierra Leone and Nigeria. In this capacity he got the singer Joss Aikins of Broadway to sign up with Decca. By the mid-fifties Ofori was also composing and sometimes playing for many other bands: Spike Anyankor's Rhythm Aces, Tommy Grippman's Red Spots and Teddy Osei's Comets, with whom Ofori went to Nigeria in 1958–9 to inaugurate Ibadan television. Some of Ofori's many hit compositions included 'Gyae Su', 'Nkae', 'Edusei Okamafo' and 'Bonsu' (with Broadway); 'Gbe Bleoo' and 'Hwe Yie' (Tempos); and 'Akai Man' and 'Me Sere Ham' (Stargazers).

As mentioned in Chapter 14, Ofori also wrote many highlife compositions for the Black Beats. In order to get a wider distribution, King Bruce, who was Ga, would often get an Akan-speaking composer like Ofori to write an Akan highlife for the flip-side of a record that featured one of Bruce's Ga songs. Two particularly popular songs that Ofori did for the Black Beats in the 1950s and released on the Decca label were 'De Ehuo' and 'Agoodzi'. 'De Ehuo' (that which has faded) is about a man advising a woman who wants to move in with him to use lipstick, straighten her hair and wear gabardine, not faded material. 'Agoodzi' is a Fanti slang term for 'money' and in this song a man is assuring his girlfriend that he has plenty of money. In all, Ofori had sixty of his compositions waxed on record by various Ghanaian dance bands.

After an Easter performance in 1958 at the Weekend-in-Havana Club, some of Ofori's friends convinced him to go with them on a high-speed joyride. The drunken driver crashed the car near the army's Gifford Camp and only Ofori was badly injured. As a result, he spent seven months at 37 Hospital with fractured limbs. He was particularly bitter that his drunken friends had left him lying unconscious for hours until a passing army officer had rushed him to hospital, and that none of his friends visited him during all the months he had to spend in recovery. Speaking to Jeremy Smith in 1993, Ofori described what happened and how this resulted in his writing two of his most popular tunes:

> We were eight in the Chevrolet car and coming back from Tema and Labadi and we drove at about a hundred miles an hour through the town. And before I was aware, my legs were hanging at the 37 Military Hospital. These friends never came round. But the Decca engineer came down from Britain when he heard the news, for I was the only eye of the company in West Africa. So they brought me a guitar whilst I was in hospital just to keep myself going. So that's when I decided to write 'Anyanko Goro' and 'Hwe Yie' about untrustworthy friends. I was in hospital for six

months and when I left I went to E.T. Mensah and told him I've got a nice music for the Tempos – and boom, the two songs hit the jackpot.[2]

In 1958, Ofori won a free flight to Britain from the newly inaugurated Ghana Airways for writing them a highlife jingle. He was in the UK for two weeks, during which time he got advice concerning standard music royalty payments from a legal advisor of the British Performing Rights Society. As a result, when he returned to Ghana he was able to get Decca to increase the four pence per record royalty rate given to local West African artists. He went back to London in 1960 to study under Sir Malcolm Sergeant at the Curwen Memorial College of Music, also known as the Tonic Sol-fa College, after winning a scholarship to study music there.

Whilst abroad, he played with Ebo Taylor in a small dance band called the Black Star Band that was patronised by the Ghanaian Embassy in London. In 1962 Ofori decided to develop his skills in both formal music and folkloric studies. That year, he attended the Franz Liszt Academy of Music in Budapest, Hungary and worked under the Hungarian art-composer Zoltán Kodály. When back in London in 1965 he studied at the Trinity College of Music. In London he also became a member of the Royal Institute of Anthropology, studying folk music. Between 1972 and 1975 he became an assistant fieldworker for the International Folk Music Council. In the late 1970s Ofori worked in the United States as a folklore librarian at Oregon University and as a research officer for the New York Black Perspective in Music.

In 1981 Ofori left London to work as a folklorist for the Ghana Arts Council[3] in Koforidua, the capital of Ghana's Eastern Region, becoming its principal cultural officer. As such, Ofori was particularly interested in teaching children traditional music and dancing so that they could take over from the older generation. He also became a member of the Music Syllabus Panel of the West African Examination Council and in 1991 became a Trustee of the National Folklore Board and the Copyright Administration.[4] In the 1990s Ofori became a resource person for both Professor Kwabena Nketia's International Centre for African Music and Dance at Legon and for the BAPMAF Highlife Institute at South Ofankor, Accra, which I had established in 1990. By this time, he had completely shifted from an interest in local dance band music to folk music. In fact, Ofori no longer wanted to be called by his stage name and preferred to be addressed by the name Akora Agyare T.A. Ofori. As he often told me, he had become a folklorist because he thought his musical dance band career had been a waste of time. The following quote from the Ghanaian *Mirror* newspaper of 8 August 1987, reflects Ofori's views on his highlife career:

I regret being a musician. Since I returned from Britain I have vowed not to get involved with any publicity because I feel the country doesn't need me. In Ghana musicians die like church mice because they do not get enough benefits from their work to get them going. It is not likely they will get rich through music. First I set out to create. But then comes a point where one needs to live by ones creative works. But in Ghana that point is cut. So now I am an ordinary civil servant working for my monthly peanuts.[5]

It was not only the financial insecurity of the profession that made him leave this field of music. He was becoming more drawn to studying and promoting his local culture and so was distancing himself from highlife because of its loss of its folkloric roots. As he explained in another portion of the 1987 *Mirror* interview: 'they are destroying the Ghanaian highlife. They are trying to mix it up with western styles which may in the end wipe away the Ghanaianness of highlife.'[6]

In a similar vein this is what Ofori told Jeremy Smith when asked to comment on Afro-rock, burger highlife and other pop-influenced Ghanaian highlife music styles:

> They're adapting western style so I call them the mass production of music, as they're not interested in creating new things from highlife. There is a basic rhythm in highlife and if that is out then you are not playing highlife. If we don't try and come back to where we started, with the rhythm, there won't be any highlife. Today they are all trying to adapt the western thing which I am not into.[7]

With a rekindled interest in traditional music and pursuing his folklorist career, Ofori founded the Dasebre Kete youth cultural troupe in the late 1990s and became the chief atenteben (Akan bamboo flute) player and horn player of the traditional court orchestra of the Omanhene of New Juaben. Ofori also played a vital role in introducing traditional culture into the liturgy of the Anglican Church under the Rt. Rev. Dr Robert Okine, the retired Archbishop of West Africa. In February 2005, Ofori was given a Lifetime Achievement Award during the African American History/Heritage Month at the Du Bois Centre, organised by the US Embassy's Public Affairs Section and BAPMAF. After a protracted illness, Ofori passed away on 25 October 2005, and was buried at Odumase Krobo.

Oscarmore Ofori with John Collins and Serene Danquah in Accra, 1999
(BAPMAF)

1. Diminished, augmented and passing chords.
2. Oscarmore Ofori, personal communication with Jeremy Smith at the Accra National Theatre, 15 July 1993. Smith is a British relative of the Ghanaian Casely-Hayford family, who assisted with the BAPMAF music archives in its early days.
3. By the mid-1980s it was known as the Eastern Region Centre for National Culture.
4. This is when I really got to know Ofori, as I was also a trustee on the Folklore Board and would often travel to Koforidua at the weekends to stay and play guitar with him. He introduced me to the musicians of the New Juaben Royal Palace, as well as the concert party promoter Mr Gambia and the traditional priestess Okomfo Afua Tabiri, who ran the Obuo Tabiri Shrine.
5. Oscarmore Ofori, interview in *The Mirror,* 8 August 1987.
6. Ibid.
7. Ofori, personal communication with Jeremy Smith, 1993.

SECTION FOUR:

The Highlife of Eastern Nigeria

19

Eastern Nigerian Highlife Artists

A s mentioned in Chapter 2, the dominance of highlife in western Nigeria declined with the 1967–70 Nigerian Civil War when many highlife dance bands in Lagos and other Yoruba towns broke up and their Igbo, Efik and Ibibio members returned to their homelands. These include Stephen Osita Osadebe, Rex Lawson, Raphael Amarabem, John Bull, Sony Brown, Sammy Akpabot, E.C. Arinze, Bill Friday, Agu Norris, Enyang Henshaw, Eddy Okonta and Charles Iwegbue. Some of these artists straddled the divide between highlife big band dance music and the unique guitar band style that emerged in this region in the 1970s and 1980s, and inspired a whole generation of eastern Nigerian guitar bands.

Stephen Osita Osadebe

Stephen Osita Osadebe was born in Atani near Onitsha, Anambra State, in 1936. As a child, he was in the church choir and was also exposed to local konkoma, agidigbo and dance band highlife. According to Nwagbo Nnenyelike, Osadebe was inspired to sing by the records he heard of the African American Nat King Cole.[1] Being raised in the east, he was also influenced by the eastern Nigerian palm-wine or native-blues highlife guitar style of Okonkwo Adigwe and Israel Njemanze of the Three Night Wizards. Osadebe began his music career in 1958 as vocalist and percussionist for the Rhythm Skies dance band run by Onitsha-born Stephen Amechi (or Amaechi) and based at Chief Kanu's Empire Hotel in Idi Oro, Lagos. According to

Austin Emielu, as a youngster Osadebe was also a sideman with the highlife dance band run by E.C. Arinze, Eddy Okonta and Charles Iwegbue.[2] In 1959 Osadebe began working with Zeal Onyia's recording group. Zeal taught Osadebe trumpet, chord progressions and big band arrangement. In 1959, Osadebe recorded 'Lagos Life Na So So Enjoyment' with Onyia's Band, followed in 1961 by the Igbo highlifes 'Wabu Ifeukiti' and 'Oyim Kotan' as well as 'Ibale' and 'The Late Patrice Lumumba'.

Osadebe came from a royal family and so his parents frowned on his popular-music activities and tried to divert him from the profession. One way was by sending him to the Soviet Union to study trade unionism and business law. However, this did not deter him and on his return he went back into music and became a singer for the Central Dance Band, run by the trumpeter Eric Onugha (or Onuoha) and based at Chief Fred Osuala's Central Hotel in Yaba. The band included top artists like Easy Kabaka Brown, Tony Babs, Chike Ekwe and the young Maliki Showman. Around 1963–4, after Eric Onugha's departure, this hotel band was reorganised as the Central Modernaires, led by Osadebe with the young guitarists Victor Uwaifo and Fred Coker as co-leaders. Uwaifo had been playing with E.C. Arinze's band. Coker was with Eddy Okonta's and he could sing Trinidadian calypsos in the style of Mighty Sparrow. Other members of the Central Modernaires were the saxists Maliki Showman, Kenneth Obasuyi and Chike Ekwe and the trumpeter Dick Tasin Ubon. In 1964 Osadebe recorded four songs with this group for Philips/Polygram, including 'One Pound No Balance' under the band name Nigerian Sound Makers. This song was so successful that Osadebe began calling himself 'Commander-in-Chief' and took the Nigerian Sound Makers' name to form his own band.

During the war Osabede left Lagos for Igboland but

continued playing. The following is what he told the journalist Nwagbo Nnenyelike in 2004 about the impact of the war:

> Before the Nigerian civil war, when the likes of Dr. Nnamdi Azikiwe, Akanu Ibiam, Dr. Michael Okpara, Aguiyi Ironsi, Obafemi Awolowo were in government, I was playing music in all parts of the country. There was no discrimination and tribalism as we have it today. In fact, there was no part of the Midwest and Yorubaland I did not take my music to. All everybody wanted to dance to was highlife. Nobody cared whether I was speaking Igbo or any other language. It was after the war that tribalism came in and became the order of the day.[3]

With his Nigerian Sound Makers now based in eastern Nigeria he began releasing records in 1972. Although he still used a horn section, by this time his band was playing in guitar band style using traditional polyrhythmic time signatures and call-and-response patterns typical of local Igbo music. In 1975, he released his huge hit 'Osondi Owendi' (one man's meat is another man's poison) on the Polydor label. The album includes seven laid-back songs[4] in both 4/4 and 6/8 time, drawing on various styles: modal 'native blues', minor highlifes, the Ghanaian 'Yaa Amponsah' and the Afro-Cuban son/rumba. Songs were sung in Igbo and pidgin English and included light horn-section passages and muted trumpet solos, polyphonically weaving in and out of the vocals.

During his career, Osadebe released many singles and, later on, full-length albums. By 2000 he had made over seventy albums, mainly released on the Philips/Polygram (now Premier Records) label. Some of his other hit songs were 'No money, No woman', 'Akaraka', 'Enyi Mba Enyi', 'Nnamdi Azikiwe',

'Ononuju Aku', 'Onuigubo', 'Agbala' and 'Makojo'. In 1981 he was awarded a gold disc for the LP 'Onu Kwulonjo'. Chief Osita Osadebe died in 2007 after having released nearly five hundred songs. Many artists passed though his Sound Makers group including St. Augustine Anwuzia, Ali Chukwuma, Prof. Goddy Ezike, Peter Maduagwu and also Vincent Okoroego, who went on to form the Ikenga Super Stars of Africa.

Stephen Osita Osadebe, from a cover of 1977 album released by
Studio 33, Disque Cassettes

'Cardinal' Rex Lawson

Rex Lawson was one of the foremost Nigerian highlife trumpeters and over the years released about thirty records. Indeed, his music is so well loved that, according to Austin Emielu, the government of his home Cross River State has set aside 16 January every year to mark the anniversary of Lawson's death.[5]

Erekosima 'Rex' Jim Lawson was born in 1932 in the town of Calabar. His father was from the Ijaw ethnic group that straddles the Delta and Cross River states, and his mother was an

Igbo. As a result, his highlife music was influenced by local folk rhythms of the region and he was able to speak several Nigerian languages. He attended school at the Christ Army School at Bakana-Kalabari and in his teens he joined Lord Eddyson, who led the Starlite Melody Orchestra of Port Harcourt. Eddyson put the young Rex Lawson under the tutelage of the orchestra's trumpeter Sammy Obot, who later went to Ghana to lead the famous Broadway highlife band in the port town of Takoradi. Four years after joining the Starlite Melody Orchestra, Lawson travelled to Lagos and became a nightclub musician during the 1950s with the Empire Band and the outfits of Bobby Benson, Victor Olaiya, Chris Ajilo and Roy Chicago.

In 1960, Lawson formed the Nigeraphone Studio Orchestra that he renamed the Mayors Dance Band. Raphael Amarabem was his rhythm guitarist from 1963 to 1966 and, as will be discussed below, he later formed the Peacocks guitar band. Another of Lawson's musicians was the conga player Toni Odili who, according to Benson Idonije, 'thrilled the dance floor community in the sixties ... [playing] ... tirelessly for long periods as a solo concession.'[6]

Lawson's eleven-piece Mayors Band was much influenced by the Ghanaian highlife introduced to Nigeria by E.T. Mensah's Tempos' tours in the early and mid-1950s. In fact they used one of E.T.'s numbers as their signature tune. The Mayors Band went on to record a string of hits that included 'So Ala Teme', 'Jolly Papa', 'Love Adure', 'Bere Bote', 'Susana Pango' and 'Peri Special Mbanga', which celebrated the birth of the Rivers State in 1967. The band also combined folk music of the Cross Rivers State people with Ghanaian highlife, as in 'Anate', the traditional moonlight dance of the Ijaw people and 'Wasenigbo' played to a local 6/8 'akpasa' beat.

Like so many Lagos-based eastern Nigerian musicians,

Lawson returned to eastern Nigeria during the period leading up to the 1967–70 Nigerian Civil War. He first went to Onitsha and, with trumpeter Sony (or Soni) Brown, formed the Marine Commando Band. A little later Lawson moved to Port Harcourt to form the Riversmen, where guitarist David Bull and tenor saxist Maliki Showman joined him.

The Riversmen expanded into a group of about fourteen musicians and a large number of artists passed though it, some of whom dated back to Lawson's Mayors Band days. Some of Lawson's other Riversmen were the singer Willie Udoh, the lead/rhythm guitarist Bassey Udoh (or Ordor) and tenor-saxist Augustine Oliseh. On alto-sax was Etim Udo who had played with E.C. Arinze, whilst Lawson's second alto-saxist was Igo Chico Okwuechime who had played with Osadebe's Sound Masters. The Riversmen trombonists were Ben Jack and Okon Jimmy; its trumpeter was Raymond Barber, whilst the band's bassline was supplied by either the double-bassist Bonny Face or bass-guitarist Joseph Uteng. Finally, there was the Riversmen's trap-drummer Asuatang Inoh, with the rest of the percussion section of congas, bongos, claves and maracas played by Anthony Odili, Obubolabra Soloman, Anthony George and Johnson Hamilton. Some of their top songs were, 'Nunfinye Nome Alobo', 'Oko', 'Pay Me My Money Now', 'Yellow Sisi' written by Raymond Barber and 'Gowon Special', which was a tribute to the Nigerian Head of State.

Lawson died tragically in 1971 in a car accident on the Agbor-Warri Road on his way to play at a show in Warri. According to Sony Brown:

> Rex left for Warri where [the] band had an engagement to play. The boys left on Friday and we were to join them on Saturday. I was to travel with Lawson in the same

vehicle but as luck would have it … it was too late in the day to travel. I told him to postpone the journey until the following day, but he went and hired a bus. Unfortunately the bus was involved in a fatal accident on the way and Lawson was taken to Eku Hospital at Warri. As soon as we heard the news, we took off. By the time we reached there Lawson had passed on.[7]

After Lawson's death his sidemen formed the twelve-piece Professional Seagulls in Port Harcourt which was led by David Bull and featured Sony Brown on trumpet.

More than forty years after his death Lawson's music is still fondly remembered. In 1989 the Performing Musicians Association of Nigeria (PMAN) gave 'Cardinal' Rex Lawson a posthumous award for his contribution to Nigerian highlife. Many of his top hits have been rereleased in CD form by Femi Eso's Evergreen Music and Premier Records and Lawson has been honoured at the various Great Highlife Parties that were initiated from 1998 by Benson Idonije, Jahman Anikulapo and Renate Albertsen of the Goethe-Institut in Lagos, with David Bull of the Seagulls band supplying the music for these events. In January 2015, an International Highlife Conference was dedicated to him by the music department of the University of Port Harcourt.

Raphael Amarabem's Peacocks Guitar Band

As mentioned above, Raphael Amarabem was the rhythm guitarist for Lawson's Mayors Dance Band during the mid-sixties. He was born in 1933 in Eziama Ikeduru near Owerri, the capital of Imo State, and played the samba frame drum in his school days. He went to Ghana in 1949 as a young man and became a train driver for the goldfields. During his time in Ghana he was taught guitar by Robert Osuji and joined his Abaraka highlife guitar band. It was after returning to Nigeria in 1962 that Amarabem joined the Mayors band in Lagos. However, he left when it moved to eastern Nigeria during the Nigerian Civil War. Instead of following Lawson to Onitsha, Amarabem went to his home town of Owerri where, in the early 1970s, he formed his Peacocks band.

The Peacocks began recording in 1972 and Amarabem's compositions were heavily influenced by Ghanaian guitar band highlife and sung in various languages: pidgin English, Efik, Igbo as well as the Ghanaian Ewe language. Some of his early hit albums released by EMI (Nigeria) were 'Uba Awuu Nwa' and 'Abiriwa Chapter Two'. One particularly popular tune of 1972 was 'Egwu Mgbashiriko' that lampooned educated women, like lawyers, doctors or nurses who want to wear trousers like a man. Other popular songs included 'Awadada' (about jilted lovers) and 'Eddie Quansa'. However, their biggest hit was undoubtedly the mid-seventies tune 'Sambola Mama' that tried to inspire hope for the Igbo people recovering from the ravages of civil war.[8]

In 1976, a splinter group called the Skylarks International broke off from the Peacocks and by 1978 the band had dissolved altogether, though not before releasing a final batch of albums: *Ije Nde Mma,* *Smash Hits* and *Egiogwu/Ejiogu*. Amarabem briefly reformed the Peacocks in 1981 to record one last album aptly called *The Revived Peacocks*. That year, he became the first chairman of the Imo State Chapter of PMAN. Despite problems with his failing eyesight Amarabem played at the Highlife Parties organised in 1999 and 2000 by the Goethe-Institut and local music organisations in Lagos.

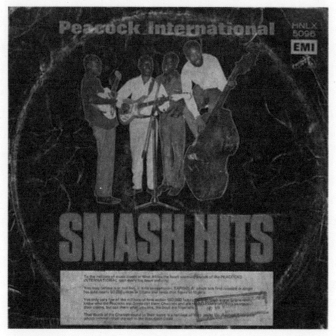

The Peacocks, from the cover of their 1978 EMI/HMV album *Smash Hits*

John Bull and Sony Brown

After Lawson's death in 1971 his sidemen went on to form the twelve-piece Professional Seagulls in Port Harcourt led by guitarist David Bull with Sony Brown on trumpet. Both David Bull and Sony Brown had played with Babyface Paul Osamade's Top Toppers dance band in Lagos in 1958. David Bull then formed his own band in 1964 in Benue State called the Gboka Stars. Sony Brown went to Senegal and Côte d'Ivoire and then, in 1965, moved to Kano to play with the Paradise Band at the Rindan Hotel. While in Kano, he formed his own band with Roy Gabriel, Nat Buckle and Maliki Showman.

Because of the ethnic violence that broke out during the Nigerian Civil War, both Bull and Brown moved to Onitsha in

1967 where they met and formed a band influenced by soul music. They also worked with Lawson, who was in Ontisha running the Marine Commando Band. Brown and Lawson had attended the same school in Bakana-Kalabari and knew each other well. So when Lawson relocated his band to Port Harcourt and renamed it the Riversmen, Brown and Bull moved with him. After Lawson's death Sony formed the Sony Brown Jazz Band in Port Harcourt, and then he too joined John Bull's Seagulls.

The Seagulls members included drummer Peace David, veteran saxist Bonnie Boma, trumpeter Ishmael Njoku, singers Fubara Sekibo and Lonjinus Oparas, conga player Tony Odili, bass-guitarist Victor Uzowulu and keyboard player James Egone. Cyril Bassey was on claves, Johnson Opara on bongos and Fonecha Hamilton on maracas. Later, the Ghanaian vocalist Showboy joined the group. Three top mid-seventies hits by the Seagulls were 'Atabala Women', 'Afro Baby' and 'Smash Hits 77' released by Sound Workshops Records. Others from the late 1970s were 'Peoples Club of Nigeria' and 'Our Lord's Prayer'. In 1981 they had a huge hit with 'Soko Soko'.

In 2000 David Bull's Seagulls was still operating in Port Harcourt, and had produced thirteen albums. Both Rex Lawson's and the newer Seagulls' songs were released by Premier Records on its series of CD releases entitled *Highlife Kings*.

---

1. Nwagbo Nnenyelike, 'Oliver de Coque is my son in music – Osita Osadebe' at http://www.kwenu.com/profile/osita_osadebe.htm (accessed 23 April 2004) .

2. Austin Emielu, 'Nigerian Highlife Music' (PhD thesis, University of Ilorin, 2009), p. 101.

3. Stephen Osita Osadebe, quoted in Nwagbo Nnenyelike, 'Osita Osadebe', 2004.

4. According to Nnenyelike (2004), Osabede gave the name 'Oyolima' to his relaxed style of Igbo highlife.

5.   Emielu, 'Nigerian Highlife Music', 2009, p. 100.
6.   Benson Idonije, 'Highlife: The Music of Independence', *Nigerian Arts Guardian*, 1 October 2008.
7.   Sony Brown, in 'The Great Highlife Party' (Lagos: Goethe-Institut, Lagos, 2000).
8.   Special thanks for the discographical information to John Beadle, Niek Lemmens, Chris Meserve and Kazuya Ogiwara.

20

The Eastern Nigerian Highlife 'Explosion' of the 1970s

Although the Nigerian guitar bands did not employ the full dance band instrumental line-up, this music was profoundly influenced by Nigerian and Ghanaian highlife dance bands and by eastern Nigerians who had played in or run highlife big bands. As discussed in the previous chapter these include Stephen Osita Osadebe, Rex Lawson, Raphael Amarabem, John Bull and Sony Brown.

In fact, eastern Nigerian highlife guitar band music evolved in the 1950s from local palm wine guitar music and native blues infused with Ghanaian/Nigerian dance band highlife. One of the earliest exponents was the Igbo musician Okonkwo. Another was Israel Njemanze and his Three Night Wizards, an acoustic guitar band from Asaba but based in Lagos. Yet another 1950s Igbo band in Lagos was the Rhythm Skies band of the Onitsha-born Stephen Amechi, based at Chief Kanu's Empire Hotel in Idi Oro. This band was formed in the late 1950s as a dance band, but later transmuted into a guitar band when it relocated to the east during the Nigerian Civil War. By the late 1960s other Igbo highlife guitar-bands artists had surfaced, like Paulson Kalu from Aba, Stephen and Aderi Olariechi from Owerri and Michael Eleagha (or Ejiagha) who formed his Paradise Rhythm Orchestra in Enugu, (capital of the former Eastern Region of Nigeria), with the young Efik guitarist and singer Celestine Ukwu as a member.[1]

Celestine Ukwu went on to became a key exponent of eastern Nigerian guitar band highlife. Unlike the pioneering eastern Nigerian highlife musicians mentioned in the previous chapter, who all had to leave western Nigeria during the civil war, Ukwu was always based in eastern Nigeria. He was born Celestine Obiakor Ukwuwas in 1940 in the Niger Delta Region and in 1962 he joined Michael Eleagha's Paradise Rhythm Orchestra. Then in 1966 he started up his own Music Royals group in Onitsha that toured throughout Nigeria until the civil war.

After the war he reformed his group in 1970 as the Philosophers National, which included the saxist Etim Udo and occasionally featured a pedal steel slide guitar. The group played in a relaxed style that was particularly influenced by the Ghanaian guitar band music of Onyina and E.K. Nyame. Some of the Philosophers Nationals singles hits were 'Igede', 'Usondo', 'Ifesinachi', 'Onwuna', 'Uwa bu Olili', 'Ije Emo' and 'Tomorrow is Uncertain'. Celestine Ukwu's most popular album was *Igede Fantasia*, released by Philips in 1976. It included the song 'Money Palaver'. Sadly, Ukwu was killed in a car crash in the late 1970s, at the height of his career.

The Impact of the Civil War on Eastern Nigerian Highlife

Despite the rise of eastern Nigerian highlife guitar bands in the 1950s and 1960s, it was the prestigious highlife dance bands that stole the limelight in the big towns and cities, as guitar bands were associated with low-class dockside bars and palm wine joints. Before the Nigerian Civil War, Lagos was the centre of the country's highlife scene and despite being in a Yoruba area many of the city's top highlife dance bands were run by easterners. Besides Stephen Amechi's Rhythm Skies, there was the Top Ten Aces run by the Efik singer Chief Inyang Nta Henshaw from Calabar who was also an artist and repertoire man for Philips West Africa Records. The Top Ten Aces dance band also included the late Alaba Pedro, who could play in the palm wine style. Another key eastern Nigerian highlife dance band was the Top Aces, run by the Calabari trumpeter Eddy Okonta (or Okunta). It formed in Ibadan in the mid-fifties and relocated to Lagos in 1960.

However, everything changed for eastern highlife artists in Lagos and other parts of western Nigeria during the civil war. These artists belonged to southeastern ethnic groups such as the Ijaw, Efik, Igbo and Ibibio and so had to return to their homelands or relocate elsewhere. One already mentioned in Chapter 7 is the trumpeter E.C. Arinze from Anambra State who played in Lagos from the early fifties and then ran his own dance band until the mid-sixties. He had to quit the city and relocate his band to the Presidential Palace Hotel in Enugu.

Some other easterners who had to move back east during the civil war were Agu Norris, Inyang Henshaw, Stephen Osita Osadebe and Rex Lawson. Charles Iwegbue, an Igbo trumpeter from Ndokwa (Adokwa), Delta State, on the western side of the Niger River, ran his Archibogs dance band in Lagos during the late 1950s and 1960s, but left to form his early Hino Sound band in his hometown in the early 1970s. Although this band included horns, the music it played was in the 6/8 minor highlife or native blues style of local eastern Nigerian guitar bands. Indeed, the group's guitarist was Isaac Rogana Ottah who, as will be mentioned later in this chapter, went on to form his own guitar band.

In fact, there was such an exodus of eastern Nigerian musicians from Lagos from the late 1960s that practically the only highlife dance bands left in the Lagos area were those of Yorubas like Bobby Benson, Victor Olaiya and Roy Chicago – and Chicago's band collapsed when his musicians were drafted into Nigerian army bands. One exception was the trumpeter

St. Augustine Awuzi who was from the Igbo-speaking town of Kwale on the western bank of the Niger River in Delta State. He played with various Lagos dance bands in the 1960s and, although an Igbo, joined the Federal Army during the civil war as leader of the 187th Infantry Battalion Garrison Dance Band. They had a big hit in 1971 with the record 'Ashawo (Prostitute) No Be Work', which gave him the exposure to form his own Lagos-based Rovers Dance Band that released highlife songs like 'Onwu Ama Dike' for Philips during the 1970s.

With the exodus of so many eastern Nigerian musicians during the civil war period, highlife dance band music went into decline in western Nigeria, whilst Yoruba juju music and the later fuji music grew more popular. Nevertheless, highlife continued to flourish in the east of the country despite the ravages of war, which included the destruction of the Philips Records factory in Onitsha, which was bombed by the Federal Air Force. The destruction was so widespread that when I travelled with Victor Uwaifo's Melody Maestros around the Enugu, Onitsha and Aba area in 1975, I saw many damaged bridges and buildings as well as wrecked tanks and airplanes littering the countryside.

As a result of this wartime devastation, and combined with the post-war shortages, many eastern Nigerian highlife musicians moved away from the large expensive-to-maintain dance bands to the smaller and more affordable highlife guitar band format. It was a format that had been established in the fifties and sixties by the bands of Okonkwo Adigwe, Israel Njemanze, Stephen Amechi, Stephen Osita Osadebe, Celestine Ukwu and others.

The Post-War Guitar Band Explosion

Besides Osadebe's Sound Makers, Lawson's Riversmen, the Seagulls and the Peacocks mentioned in the previous chapter, a number of other important artists and groups surfaced in the post–civil war era of the 1970s and 1980s. These are the Ikenga Super Stars of Africa, the Oriental Brothers, Warrios, Rogana Ottah, Douglas Olariche, Oliver de Coque's Ogene band and Nicholas Mbarga's Rocafil Jazz. All these groups drew on pre-existing Nigerian and Ghanaian highlife – some Ghanaian guitar band musicians even worked in Nigeria during the 1970s and 1980s. These also drew on pre-existing Igbo native blues and traditional rhythms, with some being influenced by the Congo jazz (soukous) of central Africa, and the fast makossa guitar band music of the neighbouring Cameroons.[2] These eastern Nigerian guitar bands were composed of two or three guitars, keyboards, trap drums, congas and assorted percussion, sometimes including the Igbo slit-log drum. Some of them also featured muted trumpet or saxophone solos and light horn-section accompaniments, but did not generally focus on a strong horn section as found in highlife dance bands. Incidentally, these highlife guitar bands also influenced the Igbo gospel music of the 1970s and 1980s.

During the Igbo cultural renaissance that took place following the 1967–70 Biafran War, the Ikenga Super Stars of Africa and Oriental Brothers bands pioneered 'ikwokilikwo' or 'ikwokirikwo', a fast-paced form of guitar band highlife that combined elements from the Igbo blues and the imported Congo jazz of Congo-Brazzaville and the DRC. The Ikenga Super Stars of Africa was formed in 1973 by Vincent Okoroego, who had previously played with Stephen Osita Osadebe's Sound Makers. The Ikengas became very popular after they released their huge hit record in 1975 on the Rogers All Stars label called the 'Ikenga of Africa', and this guitar band remained one of the top Nigerian highlife bands of the seventies and eighties.

Other exponents of the fast-paced Ikwokilikwo style from the late 1970s were the Oriental Brothers, the various bands that split away from them, and Fiddey 'Babwire' Onwuneme's Imo Brothers International. The Oriental Brothers was formed in 1974 in the eastern city of Owerri by the three Opara brothers: Ferdinand Dansatch Emeka (aka Dan Satch Opara), Christogonus Ezebuiro 'Dr. Sir Warrior' Obinna and Godwin Kabaka. Feuds between the three of them ultimately led to a split in 1977, resulting in each one forming his own band. The Oriental Brothers itself had two wings; one led by ace guitarist Dan Satch Opara and the other by the vocalist Dr. Sir Warrior, called the Oriental Original. Both, however, were marketed by the Afrodisia label of Decca West Africa. Dan Satch went on recording well into the 1980s, whilst Warrior went on to release about twenty gold and platinum hit records, including his 1978 album *Nwanne Awu Enyi*, which sold almost eight million copies. The third brother, Godwin Kabaka Opara, started his own group, Kabaka International, which released eight albums between 1977 and 1982.

A quite different style of Igbo highlife guitar band music was that of Douglas Olariche's Owerri-based International Guitar Band. This band, like Celestine Ukwu's, did not play in the fast Ikwokilikwo style but was influenced by the slower Ghanaian-inspired guitar band highlife style of Onyina and E.K. Nyame. Moreover, Olariche's band made use of local instruments such as the wooden xylophone and Igbo 'ogene' bells.[3]

Another style of Igbo highlife was created by Anioma musicians from the western side of the Niger River. They were Igbos from the northeastern portion of Delta State and were influenced by neighbouring Edo highlife. One of these was the previously mentioned guitarist Isaac Rogana Ottah from Akoku, Ndokwa. His musical career began in the early 1970s when he played in the bands of Stephen Osita Osadebe and Rex Lawson. Then, in 1973, he joined the Hino Sound band run by fellow Ndokwa native Charles Iwegbue. After Iwegbue's death in 1976, Ottah released a series of 'Oshio Super Series' recordings, beginning with his first album success *Ukwani Special* in 1977. Ottah's guitar band subsequently released around thirty albums and he became known as the 'Oshio Super King'.

The Makossa Connection: Prince Nico Mbarga and Oliver de Coque

By the late 1970s and 1980s, a newer guitar band sound was brewing in southeastern Nigeria from artists like Oliver de Coque and Nicholas Mbarga, or Prince Nico, whose Rocafil Jazz played what he called the 'panko' style of highlife. This was not only a combination of highlife, native blues and Congolese popular soukous, but also the fast makossa guitar band music of the neighbouring Cameroons.

Nicholas or 'Nico' Mbarga was born in 1950, Abakaliki, Anambra State, to a Nigerian mother, and a Cameroonian father who died when Nicholas was very young. He grew up with his mother in Cross River State, amongst the Etura people, and as a youth mastered the traditional wooden xylophone as well as congas, drums and electric guitar in various school bands. He left school in the mid-sixties and in 1969 he and his family fled to the Cameroons to escape the Nigerian Civil War. The following year he joined the Melody Orchestra, a hotel band in the Cameroonian town of Mamfe, playing percussion and then bass, rhythm and finally lead guitar. He was with them for three years and this undoubtedly helped lay the foundation for his later panko style of Igbo highlife, which was heavily influenced by the popular dance music of the Cameroons.

Nico Mbarga returned to Nigeria in 1972 and set up his own group, Rocafil Jazz, based at the Plaza Hotel in Onitsha. Their second single, 'I No Go Marry My Papa', released on the EMI label in 1973, became a regional hit. Then in 1975 Mbarga signed up with the Rogers All Stars Company in Onitsha with whom he released a series of big hits over the next six years. Rocafil Jazz's first smash hit was 'Sweet Mother', released in 1976. It was sung in pidgin English and became one of the top sellers in the history of Nigerian music, selling more than thirteen million copies and earning Mbarga the honoury title of 'Prince'. That year everyone in West Africa began playing 'Sweet Mother', and African prints, nightclubs, chop-bars and local transport vehicles began bearing this name. Cover versions of this song were also popular; in 1977, for instance, the Sierra Leonian producer Akie Deen released a twelve-inch disco single of this song by the Freetown band Sabanoh 75 on the international market. Then in 1994, 'Sweet Mother' and some other top Rocafil Jazz hits were rerecorded by Lokassa and the Soukous Stars on the *Soukous Sound* CD released by the UK-based Sterns African label.

When the British journalist Chris Stapleton asked Nico Mbarga about his 'Sweet Mother' composition, he said it was dedicated to his own mother and indeed all mothers: 'I thought about her suffering and I realised that many before her had suffered and are suffering now'.[4]

Other records by Rocafil Jazz on the Rogers All Star label such as 'Dear Father', 'Free Education in Nigeria', 'Christiana' and 'Simplicity' all sold no fewer than two hundred thousand copies each. Another was 'Music Line' which is literally the story of Mbarga and his band. The song starts with a father warning his son against going into the music business, as he will never be able to save enough money to get married and settle down. But it ends happily with the son becoming so successful through music that he can afford several wives and a big car. According to Stapleton, between 1978 and 1982, Rocafil Jazz released two juju albums called *Aye Elel* and *Dare Jimmi* (Forgive Me) for which Mbarga's group employed a gangan drummer and slide guitarist. This is what he told Stapleton was the reason for him branching out into the juju music of the Yoruba people:

> It is real African music. I cannot begin to blend my music with western music – there's no use trying. And I don't support Africans who play pop, reggae or disco. But juju has the original background of African music.[5]

I met Mbarga in late 1979 when he and I were being interviewed at the BBC's External Broadcasting Centre at Bush House in central London. In person, Mbarga was completely different from his limelight persona, where he looked larger than life. Unlike his boisterous and noisy companions, he was quiet and shy. A wiry, slightly built man with sensitive and finely chiselled features, he used to wear 'stacks' or 'guarantee shoes' that added inches to his short height.

Prince Nico went on to become so successful that he set up his own hotel and club in his hometown of Onitsha, where he also ran a multitrack studio. In 1982 Mbarga went to the UK where he performed with London-based highlife band the Ivory Coasters and the Cameroonian singer Lousiana Tilda and her band. She later rerecorded and released some of Mbarga's greatest hits like 'Sweet Mother', 'Aki Special', 'Money Palava' and 'Family Movement'. Disaster struck Rocafil Jazz in 1983 with the Nigerian Aliens Expulsion Order, which resulted in hundreds of thousands of non-Nigerian Africans without legal papers being suddenly deported. Mbarga lost several of his key Cameroonian musicians. Although he later formed a new version of Rocafil Jazz, it never matched his original group. Nevertheless, Mbarga did extremely well out of his musical career and not only continued to run his hotel, nightclub and studio complex in Onitsha, but also opened the Sweet Mother Hotel in Calabar. Regrettably, Prince Nico Mbarga was killed in 1997 while driving a motorbike.

Prince Nico and his Rocafil Jazz, from the *Sweet Mother* album released in 1976 by Rogers All Stars, Onitsha

Oliver de Coque was another principal eastern Nigerian musician who was influenced by both Congolese and Cameroonian music. He was born Oliver Sunday Akanite in 1947 in Anambra State and learnt guitar from a Congolese guitarist. According to Austin Emielu (2009) he began his musical career playing in Lagos with a series of juju bands: Sunny Agaga's Lucky Stars Band, Jacob Oluwole's Unity Juju Band and Sule Agboola's Moonlight Guitar group.[6] In 1976,

Oliver de Coque also played on Prince Nico Mbarga's album 'Sweet Mother'.

Oliver de Coque (likembe.blogspot.com, July 2010)

In the mid-1970s he formed his own Ogene Super Sounds that combined traditional Igbo music with Congolese soukous, highife and makossa. According to Emielu, De Coque was one of the first Igbo highlife musicians to start using digitally programmed rhythm machines, which made his music more appealing to the youth.[7] De Coque made eighty albums between 1976 and his death in 2009, many being released on his own Ogene Records label that he set up in 1982. His biggest hit was 'Identity', released in 1981 on the Olumu Label. Some of his songs were of a social and political nature, such as his 1979 release (on the Olumu label) 'Jomo Kenyatta Hero of Africa' and his bestselling 'I Salute Africa'. Another was his 1989 'Naira Power', about the perilous state of the economy. De Coque also wrote songs praising eastern Nigerian social clubs such as the Udoka Social Club and the Engerigbo Social Club. Emielu says that, in 1994, De Coque was crowned 'King of Highlife' by the Oba (king) of Oyo, and was awarded an honorary doctorate in music by the University of New Orleans in 2009.[8]

The Rogers All Stars Company

The Rogers All Stars record company and its 24–32 track studio was established in 1977 near Onitsha in Anambra State by the young Igbo music entrepreneur Chief R.E. Okonkwo.[9] It recorded and released numerous eastern Nigerian guitar bands, including the Ikenga Superstars, Prince Nico Mbarga's famous Rocafil Jazz and also the band of Pele Asampete, who had been a member of the Ikenga Super Stars of Africa before moving on to music that combined highlife, juju and Afro-pop. Another famous name linked to the studio was the Igbo musician Muddy Ibe from Onitsha, who ran the Nkwa Brothers band that produced a series of popular albums for the Rogers All Stars label between 1979 and the mid-2000s. Yet another was Super Negro Bantous that, despite its Congolese-sounding name, was an Igbo highlife band led by Elah Elvis, that recorded songs in pidgin English for the Rogers All Stars label from 1977 well into the 1980s. Then there was Bright Chimezie, an Igbo guitarist from Abia State, who called his pop-influenced highlife 'zigima sound'. He began recording for the Rogers All Stars in 1984 as a 24-year-old and continued recording up until the 1990s.

From the late 1970s to the mid-1980s a number of Ghanaian guitar bands also recorded at the Rogers All Stars studio. Some groups toured and even temporarily settled in Nigeria. One reason for this was that Nigeria was already part of the West African highlife zone and so their Ghanaian style of music was appreciated by many Nigerians. Another reason was that Nigeria was going through an oil boom, with plenty of money (petro-naira) available for entertainment and the production of records. The Ghanaian economy and commercial music scene, on the other hand, had collapsed following a sequence of military regimes and so by the early 1980s it was impossible to make records there.

Among those pulled towards Nigeria were Kofi Sammy (Abibrekyireba Kofi Anese) and his Okukuseku band. Kofi Sammy had begun his career in the late 1950s and 1960s with top Ghanaian highlife guitar bands such as E.K. Nyame's, the Jaguar Jokers, K. Gyasi's and Ahamano's Guitar Band, before forming his own Okukuseku Number Two band in 1969. When things began to get difficult in Ghana, Okukuseku began touring Nigeria in 1977, staying in Onitsha for over a year. That was when they recorded the hit song 'Yellow Sisi', which sold like hot cakes in both Nigeria and Ghana. Because of the economic depression in his home country, Kofi Sammy decided to stay in Nigeria permanently in 1979. The band was first based in Lagos where, in the early 1980s, they released the albums *Okponku Special* and *Original Kekako*. Then Okukuseku moved to Onitsha and released half a dozen highlife albums sung in Akan, Igbo and pidgin English for the Rogers All Stars company. These titles included *Yebre Ama Owou*, *Suffer Suffer*, *Take Time*, *Black Beauty* and *Odo Ye De*.

The Konadus was another Ghanaian guitar band that toured Nigeria many times in the late 1970s and early 1980s. It was led by the Ashanti singer/guitarist Alex Kwabena Konadu ('One Man Thousand') who had played with Akwaboah and

Happy Brothers before forming his own band in the early 1970s. On one of his Nigerian trips Konadu lost some of his musicians when the singer-guitarist Big Boy Robert Danso split away in 1979 to form the Canadoes band. The Canadoes stayed in Nigeria and signed up with the Rogers All Stars Company, who produced big hits for them between 1980 and 1985, like 'Oga Sorry', 'Never Lose Hope', 'Afaa Boatemah' and 'Fine Woman'.

Kofi Sammy, 1979 (*Africa Music*, 1, 1980)

Anthony 'Scorpion' Entsie was a Fanti guitarist from the coastal Akan town of Mankesim who stayed in Nigeria between 1977 and 1983. He began his music career in 1971 with Nana Ampadu's African Brothers, and in 1973 he formed his own Beach Scorpions guitar band. In Nigeria he released highlife songs on the Rogers All Stars label (like the 1981 'Original Beach Scorpions') as well as on Ben Okworko's Grover Records. Also linked to the Rogers All Stars was Nana Agyeman Opambuo who had run his guitar band and concert party in Ghana during the 1970s. Following Ghana's economic downturn, he went to live in Nigeria from 1982 to 1984. There, his band, now known as Opambuo's International Band of Ghana, released three albums on the Rogers All Stars label. Yet another Ghanaian guitar band that was associated with the Rogers All Stars label was the Golden Boys Band of Ghana that released 'I Don Tire' in 1984.

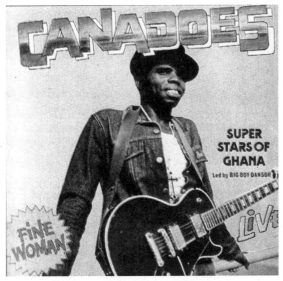

Robert Danso and the Canadoes Band cover of the 'Fine Woman' record released by the Rogers All Stars in 1982

Although he did not record with the Rogers All Stars, another Ghanaian musician who also spent some years in Onitsha was the Kwahu guitarist T.O. Jazz (Thomas Osei Ampoumah) who formed Ampoumah's Guitar Band in 1952. During a 1957–8 tour of Burkina Faso, Ampoumah's band met the Congolese band Bantus Africana, who invited them to the DR Congo to play highlife numbers. Whilst in Kinshasa, T.O. met Franco, the leader of O.K. Jazz. As a result, on returning to Ghana in 1961, he changed the name of his band to T.O. Jazz.

It was with this band that T.O. recorded his 1968 hit 'Aware Bone Asu Manim Ase' (Bad Marriage Has Disgraced Me), for which he was awarded the first Philips West African Golden Disc in 1970. Despite this success, he was still plagued by the economic problems in Ghana at that time, so T.O. and his band decided to relocate to Nigeria for almost two years, staying as the resident group at Stephen Osita Osadebe's hotel in Onitsha. It was while there that T.O. released his album *Ojukwu Welcome*. Produced by Chris Robbin, it was dedicated to the reconciliation and return from exile of General Chukwuemeka Odumegwu Ojukwu, the former leader of the attempted breakaway state of Biafra.

T.O. 'Jazz' Ampoumah, (seated left, with guitar) and his T.O. Jazz band, 1970s (T.O. Jazz)

Many other Ghanaian guitar band musicians operated in Nigeria, sometimes in the eastern region and sometimes in southern Nigeria. One was the Ashanti musician Amakye Dede who began his music career in 1973 with the Kumapim Royals. He then formed his own Apollo High Kings in 1981, after returning from one of his stays in Nigeria, a country he often visited between 1979 and 1983. In Nigeria, Amakye Dede had a number of popular hits in Yoruba, pidgin English and Akan; songs such as 'Kechi', 'Jealousy Go Shame',[10] 'Beautiful Women', 'To Be A Man Na Wa' and 'Taxi Driver'. For a while the Apollo High Kings actually operated in Nigeria as the resident band of the FESTAC Hotel in Lagos.[11] In 1983 Amakye Dede released 'Ifa Anyi Chuku', but that year, like so many other Ghanaians, he had to return home due to the Nigerian Aliens Order. Consequently, he released a song called 'Ye Koe Taba' about his time in Nigeria and the ordeal of having been forced to return home.

Amakye Dede on his *Dabi Dabi Ebe Ye Yie* cassette/album covers
(Dimtex Productions New York)

Another Ghanaian band operating in Nigeria at this time was Eddy Maxwell's Odoyewu Internationals, who released pidgin English and Akan highlifes, such as their album *Smash Hit* for the Nigerian GAB record label in 1982, and *Monkey Chop* on CY Records. Then there was Super Seven, which released the album *Travel and See*, sung in pidgin English. Two others were Paa Bobo and his Three Axes (who produced their *Osaobrokye* album in Nigeria in 1982 on the Janco label), and the Kuul Strangers (who released *Paddle Your Own Canoe* for the Smart label in 1981). Finally, there was the Dytomite Starlite Band of Ghana that recorded in the early 1980s on Tabansi Records, whose 24-track recording studio was set up in Onitsha around 1980 by the Igbo chief Godwin Aloefuna Davison.[12]

Igbo Native Blues and Gospel Highlife

Besides Igbo guitar band highlife, there also arose other forms of Igbo highlife such as those played in the older native blues style and those that blend highlife with gospel music.

The Nigerian guitar highlife bands that play in the native blues style rather than the more contemporary ikwokilikwo, ogene and panko styles draw on indigenous polyrhythmic percussion, traditional proverbs and a modal style of singing that does not follow the verse structure and harmonic progressions of western music. This style also employs traditional instruments like xylophones and thumb pianos.

One highlife musician who drew on this indigenous style in the mid-1970s was the late Nellie Uzonna Uchendu from Enugu who had a varied music career. Her 1977 debut album, *Love Nwantwi*, was a blend of highlife and traditional Igbo blues. In the early 1980s she also worked with the Oriental Brothers and Warrior, then recorded for the soundtrack of the film adaptation of the novel *Things Fall Apart* by Igbo novelist Chinua Achebe.

According to the musicologist Omibiye-Obidike she became acclaimed as the 'Golden Voice of Nigeria'.[13] In 1995, Uchendu switched to gospel music when she released her *Sing Praises* album on the Rogers All Stars label. She was a member of the Association of Female Musicians in Nigeria until her death in 2005.

Since the late 1970s several other eastern Nigeria native-blues-influenced guitar bands have come to the fore. One was Sonny Oti's Band, a small guitar band that produced a number of albums, one of which was called 'Late Night Husband'[14] in which Sonny Oti[15] collaborated with Nellie Uchendu. Two others were the five-piece United Brothers International Band led by Bukana T. Ogudoro and based in Imo State, and Queen Azaka and her Ebiologu Abusu Mma Dance Band. Queen Azaka was an 'Anioma' singer from Ndokwa on the western side of the Niger River, whose band played a variety of highlife influenced by the traditional music from the Ukwuani sub-group of the Igbo. Yet another native blues group was Ibealaoke Chukwukeziri and his Anaedonu Group, which often released cassettes and CDs with traditional Igbo music on one side and guitar band music on the other.

Drawing on both the native blues and the more contemporary guitar band form of highlife was Igbo gospel music. Gospel became big in eastern Nigeria immediately after the Nigerian Civil War and was pioneered by groups such as the Brothers Lazarus and Emmanuel, the Nwokolobia Agwu Gospel Singers and Brother Vincent Onwukanjo's Reconcilers Gospel Band. By the 1980s Igbo gospel artists were multiplying.

One important artist who drew on the fast ogene and panko styles was the guitarist Reverend Patty Obassey and his Charismatics band, which released records on the Tabansi Label. Some others were Anthony Achilike, who released the major hit 'Thank you, Lord', and Ori Okoroh of 'Do you Know His Name' fame.[16] On the other hand, the Brothers Okeke, Elias and Emmanuel Ijioma and His Unshakeable Voices played in the Igbo blues style, which Femi Adedeji calls the 'native' style.[17]

Another popular female artist who, like Nellie Uchendu, drew on local tradition, was Onyeka Onwenu, a singer and film actress from Imo State who released several albums in the 1980s that combined soul, disco and Igbo folk music. She moved fully into gospel music in the 1990s.[18] Some other top gospel artists of the 1990s were Kingsley Ike, who recorded on Kenny Ogungbe's Kenny label, and Stanley Kaosi and the Grace Band that released its debut album 'The Goodness of God' in 1998.

Since the 2000s, Igbo gospel artists have continued to thrive and blend religious music with highlife, although recent artists often employ hi-tech synthesisers, computers and drum-machines. Some of the more popular ones include Brother Obi Obidigbo, Ngozi Chukwu, Chinedu Nwadike, Evangelist Okwara Ezema and his Nightingale Praise Band, Sister Ngozi, Princess Christy Njoku and Sister Ndidiamaka. More recent artists are Princess Oluchukwu Okeke who releases her songs on the Adonai music label, and Princess Njideka Okeke who works with her husband Prince Gozie Okeke. Some of these Igbo gospel highlife artists who sing in pidgin English have also become popular in Ghana. One is Princess Ifeoma Okpala, an excellent stage dancer who released her album *Dependable God* in 2004 and performed in Ghana that year. Another Igbo artist who went to Ghana is Sam Okoro, who played at the Ghana Music Awards in 2003.

The astronomical expansion of gospel highlife, 'native style', 'gos-pop' and other forms of local gospel music[19] throughout Nigeria since the 1980s has resulted in the growth of a commercial recording, promotion and marketing industry based on this music, as well as the formation of gospel unions like the Gospel Musicians Association of Nigeria (GOMAN) and the National Association of Gospel Artistes (NAGA).

1. Benson Idonije, 'Premier Music – Green is the Taste of Veteran Highlifers,' *Arts Guardian*, 26 April 2009.
2. As mentioned in Chapter 1, makossa was a low-class palm wine guitar music born in the port town of Douala in the 1940s/1950s. By the 1960s makossa was crossing over to the more prestigious Cameroonian dance bands of the period like the Black and White Jazz Orchestra and Los Negros. By the 1970s makossa guitar bands had gone electric and were being popularised by Moni Bile, Tity Edima and Sam Fan Thomas.
3. An example is on his 1980 LP 'Me Soro Ibe' (Fontana FTLP 109), which employs these local instruments and whose lyrics are based on Igbo proverbs.
4. Nico Mbarga in Chris Stapleton, 'A Royal Visit', *Black Music and Jazz Review*, (September 1982), p. 23.
5. Ibid.
6. Austin Emielu, 'Nigerian Highlife Music' (PhD thesis, University of Ilorin, 2009).
7. Ibid.
8. Ibid.
9. An article on the Rogers All Stars in *African Music*, 17, (September/October 1983), p. 25.
10. Released on CY Records, (CYLP) in 1982.
11. This hotel was named after the famous Nigerian 1977 Black Arts Festival (FESTAC '77), which was attended by seven hundred scholars and featured fifty plays, eighty films, two hundred poetry and literature sessions, forty arts exhibitions and one hundred and fifty music and dance shows. It drew many popular African artists, including Miriam Makeba, Osibisa, Bembeya Jazz, Les Amazones, Louis Moholo, and Dudu Pukwana. There were also black artists from America: Mighty Sparrow, Gilberto Gil, Stevie Wonder, Sun Ra and Donald Byrd.
12. This chief was a businessman from Anambra State who began his Tabansi Record Company in Kano and Lagos way back in the 1960s.
13. Mosunmola. A. Omibiye-Obidike, 'Women in Popular Music in Nigeria', paper presented at the fourth International Conference of IASPM, Accra, 12–19 August 1987.
14. Released by Afrodisia, in 1979.
15. Incidentally, Sonny Oti was also a playwright and wrote the book *Highlife Music in West Africa*, published posthumously in 2009 by Mailhouse Press, Nigeria.
16. Also Brother Obi Igwe, Pastor Friday U. Okwey and His Masters Servants, Prophetess Helen Nkume, Reverend Father Mbarka and Rosemary Chukwu Onumaegbu.

17. Femi Adedeji, 'Classification of Nigerian Gospel Music Styles', *África: Revista do Centro de Estudos Africanos*, 24/25/26 (March 2009), 235.
18. She also became president of the Association of Musicians in Nigeria and chairperson for the Imo State Council for Arts and Culture.
19. Adedeji (2009, pp. 233–242) says 'gos-pop' is influenced by rock, soul and R&B. In all he mentions twelve varieties of Nigerian gospel that includes 'gospel reggae', 'juju gospel', 'gospel-waka', 'gospel-fuji'. etc.

CODA:

The Highlife Revival

21

The Current Highlife Revival in Nigeria, Ghana and Abroad

Highlife dance band music in Ghana and Nigeria gradually went into decline after its Golden Age during the 1950s and 1960s. One reason was the 1960s ascendency of new forms of foreign music that fascinated the youth, such as rock 'n' roll, soul music and the Congo jazz (soukous) of central Africa. In addition to changes in musical tastes, there were political reasons. In Nigeria there was the impact of the 1967–70 civil war, when many highlife dance bands run by easterners in Lagos and western Nigeria either collapsed or relocated to eastern Nigeria where new highlife bands appeared based on the guitar band model.

Ghana also saw the overthrow of President Nkrumah in 1966. He was a staunch supporter of highlife in all its forms, for not only did the highlife musicians support the independence struggle but Nkrumah used this home-grown, inter-ethnic musical idiom of the urban masses to project a national and indeed Pan African identity.[1] Shortly after Nkrumahs's overthrow the Aliens Compulsion Order was enacted in Ghana in 1969. With just two weeks' notice, hundreds of thousands of non-Ghanaian Africans working or resident in the country were expelled, including those who operated in the highlife arena, like nightclub owners, music promoters and musicians. One example is Ignace De Souza from Benin who, as mentioned in Chapter 12, had to leave Ghana with his Nigerian, Togolese, Beninese and Congolese bandsmen. This, incidentally, was followed in 1983 by a similar Nigerian Aliens Expulsion Order, which abruptly expelled huge numbers of African foreigners.

This included Ghanaian musicians like Amakye Dede who, as discussed in the previous chapter, were based in Nigeria. This same expulsion order gave Nico Mbarga a headache through the sudden loss of the Cameroonian members of his Rocafil Jazz.

Despite the waning of highlife dance bands from the late 1960s, this Nigerian/Ghanaian music helped give birth to new genres of popular music such as eastern Nigerian guitar band highlife. Two others are Afro-rock and Afrobeat that both crystallised as distinct genres around 1970. Afro-rock was created by the London-based Ghanaian group Osibisa, whose key members, Mac Tontoh, Teddy Osei and Sol Amarfio, had all been trained in highlife dance bands such as Uhuru and the Comets. Likewise, Nigeria's Fela Anikulapo-Kuti who fused highlife, jazz, soul and Yoruba music into Afrobeat, had begun his musical career with Victor Olaiya's band and then run his own sixties Koola Lobitos highlife dance band.

Nevertheless, highlife music, particularly the highlife big band variety, continued to decline in both Ghana and Nigeria during the late 1970s and 1980s. One reason was yet another shift in the musical tastes of the urban youth. This time it was towards disco-type techno-pop and music videos with their solo artists, mimed shows and studio bands. Then there were the political and socio-economic factors that worked against live bands during this time. In both Ghana and Nigeria these included military coups, governmental corruption, curfews,[2] austerity measures and a 'brain drain' of talented artists. By the 1980s the youth favoured canned music in discotheques and many in both Ghana and Nigeria were saying that the classical dance band highlife and its live performance venues were dead.

However, since the 1990s both countries have seen something of a revival of dance band highlife, as well as a rise in clubs, venues, promoters, record labels and organisations that cater to this form of local music. It is to this topic we now turn.

Highlife and Dance Band Revival in Nigeria

The first evidence of a revival of old-time, classic big band highlife in Nigeria began with two shows dubbed 'Highlife Parties' in Lagos in 1999 and 2000. They were organised by the Goethe-Institut, Benson Idonije and Jahman Anikulapo. There were two main stage bands at these events. One was the Seagulls led by guitarist David Bull who, as mentioned in Chapter 19, had first played with Babyface Paul Osamade for the Top Spotters band in Lagos in 1958, before moving on to Rex Lawson's Riversmen. The other was the Classic Band of saxophonist Yinusa Akinnibosun who had begun his career with Victor Olaiya, Agu Norris and Bongos Ikwue. These two bands provided the music for a host of old-time highlife stars, including Nellie Uchendu, Victor Olaiya, Chris Ajilo and E.C Arinze who, after operating various highlife dance bands in Lagos in the 1950s and 1960s, relocated to Enugu in the seventies. Also appearing on stage was the guitarist Alaba Pedro and vocalist Tunde Osofisan who had both played with Roy Chicago until his death in 1989. Another artist featured was the guitarist Raphael Amarabem who, as mentioned in Chapter 19, had played with Rex Lawson's Lagos-based Mayors Dance Band, before forming his own Peacocks band in Owerri in 1972.

These Goethe-Institut shows were followed by a series of events in Lagos called 'Highlife Elders Forums' at the O'Jez Club in Yaba and the National Stadium Annex of O'Jez Entertainment. The organisers were the O'Jez Entertainment Company, the Musical Society of Nigeria (MUSON) and the Committee for Relevant Art (CORA). CORA has been particularly important in spearheading the highlife revival. The organisation was created in the late 1990s by artists, art enthusiasts, art promoters and art writers to host local cultural activities. These include the annual Lagos Book and Art Festival, the Lagos Comic Carnival, the open-air Lagos Cinema Carnival and the annual Highlife Elders Forums, also known as Great Highlife Parties.

After the initial highlife events assisted by the Goethe-Institut, these forums or parties continued featuring highlife giants such as Orlando Julius and Steve Rhodes, one-time director of the Nigerian Broadcasting Band. Another ace musician who featured on several occasions for these was Victor Olaiya, the so-called 'evil genius of highlife'. Although in semi-retirement, Olaiya still occasionally played at his Stadium Hotel. However, his son Bayode, a trumpeter, led his father's band at the Club.

According to Benson Idonije these highlife parties and forums continued to honour important figures like Maliki Showman, Fatai Rolling Dollar, Duro Ikujenyo, World Boye, Jimi Solanke (from Roy Chicago's Rhythm Dandies) singer Apapa Jay (from Adeolu Akinsanya's band) and Fela Kuti's Africa 70/Egypt 80 sideman Lekan Animashaun. In December 2007, a Great Highlife Party was held at the Hexagon Hotel in Benin City, Edo State. Tunde Osofisan's Highlife Messengers played, featuring Fatai Rolling Dollar.[3] A positive sign was that many young people attended this show, and indeed two young Edo highlife singers/guitarists made an appearance on stage: Mariam Alile and Oriri Joseph, son of veteran musician Osayomore Joseph who ran the Creative Seven band of the 1970s and 1980s that played Bini highlife.

Some clubs and programmes that still feature old-time

highlife acts in Lagos include the Stadium Hotel, the O'Jez Club as well as the newer Afropolitan Vibes shows, that are held at Freedom Park in Victoria Island.

In addition to these live shows classic highlifes are being rereleased on CD by companies such as Femi Eso's Evergreen Music and Premier Records, and are also being aired on specialist highlife radio programs on FM stations like Radio Nigeria Metro and the Ray Power.

The palm wine guitarist Fatai or Fatayi Rolling Dollar played an important role in this highlife revival. Fatai Olayiwola Olagunju was born in 1928 in Lagos and came from a royal family of the Yoruba town of Ede in Osun State. In 1953, Rolling Dollar became one of the agidigbo thumb-piano players of Julius 'Speedy' Oredola Araba's Rhythm Blues, which played 'toy motion', a combination of palm wine music, asiko, agidigbo and acoustic juju.[4] It was at this time that Rolling Dollar learnt guitar and by 1957 he was ready to form his own eight-piece African Rhythm Band.[5] The African Rhythm Band had some hits for Philips, then moved on to Jofabro/EMI, with whom they recorded over one hundred and fifty singles.

One musician who worked for Rolling Dollar was Orlando Owoh from Osogbo, one of the few Yoruba musicians who went into guitar band highlife. Owoh began his career in the mid-1950s with the Kola Ogunmola Yoruba popular theatre group, as well as dance bands like Kehinde Adex's and Akindele's Chocolate Dandies in Ibadan. After learning guitar from Rolling Dollar, Owoh went on to form his own Omimah Band in 1959, was drafted into the army to train members of the Garrison Band during the Nigerian Civil War and afterwards ran his Kenneries highlife bands.[6] The Civil War also affected Rolling Dollar but in a more negative way – with nightclubs closing down and bands splitting up, his career went into decline. He explains:

The whole band's boys went to join the army, the navy and the air force. One day, we went to play at a club, and an army officer went and smacked one of my boys. The next day he went and joined the army. And so from that time highlife went down, because there was no-one to play it. In the years that followed, new forms of music derived from highlife took over in Nigeria: Juju and Afrobeat.[7]

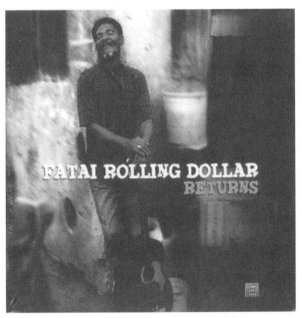

Fatai Rolling Dollar *Returns* album released by Jazzhole Records, 2010

There was more bad luck for Rolling Dollar in 1977 when his house was damaged, as it was close to Fela Kuti's Kalakuta Republic that was razed to the ground by angry soldiers. However, Rolling Dollar was rediscovered in the late 1990s during the highlife revival. Furthermore, in 2008, Rolling Dollar, together with the blind street minstrel Kokoro, and Duro Ikujenyo (ex-keyboardist for Fela Kuti's Egypt 80 band) collaborated on the *Miliki Music* album made by Biodun Ayinde Bakare, the son of the juju pioneer Ayinde Bakare. In 2009, he was still featuring regularly at the O'Jez Club in Lagos. He sadly died in June 2013, aged 86.

A more recent sign of the interest in old-time highlife by academics was a three-day Rex Jim Lawson International Highlife Conference held at the University of Port Harcourt from 21 to 23 January 2015. Local Nigerian scholars attending included Benson Idonije, Doctors B.A. Ejiofor and Austin Emielu and Professors Tunji Vidal, Mosunmola Omibiye-Obidike and Onyee Nwankpa. The ace highlife musician Ebo Taylor and I came from Ghana whilst Professor Mark Levine flew in from the United States. Performances for the event were supplied by the Uniport Band and the Rex Lawson Memorial Band, which included the veteran trumpeter King Sunny Brown and the eighty-six-year-old conga player Chief Anthony Odili.

The Highlife Revival In Ghana

During the military regimes of the late 1970s and 1980s, the live Ghanaian popular music scene collapsed, and into the vacuum came disco-influenced burger highlife. As a result, bands were replaced by solo artists backed by studio musicians, who laid down backing tracks. The disquiet with this state of affairs is reflected in the following comments made to me in 1987 by King Bruce of the Blacks Beats dance band, who was then managing the Elephant Walk recording studio in Accra:

> In the old days when a band had a composition, they rehearsed it and used it at live performances before the public. So by the time the group went into the studio all the musicians would have mastered the music and instrumental solos and have a full idea of the public

reaction to it. It was also better then as recording contracts went to bands. It was rare to get a composer going into a studio with picked-up musicians as in those days there were no session-men.

Nowadays the studio fees are all paid by producers, which is also why we have quite a crop of session-men who don't belong to any particular band and who are always nosing around recording studios. The producers engage these musicians who come from all over the place and because the producers have little time, they are in a hurry to finish everything off. It may be that the session musician's first contact with the composition will be the first day they meet at the studio. They may not know the songs at all. Also, because of the costs, the producers have to limit the number of instruments to the barest minimum. That doesn't do much good for the music.[8]

One of the first signs of a revival of live popular music was in the early 1990s when there was a public outcry against the 'canned' music on local television. This resulted in live televised dance band shows such as *For Your Dancing Feet*. It was also around this time that a new generation of highlife big bands were started up. These included Paapa Yankson and the Western Diamonds; the resident band of Ebo Coker's Westline Hotel in Takoradi; the Ghana Broadcasting Band under former Uhuru leader Stan Plange; and the Golden Nuggets of the Ashanti Goldfields Company. Veteran highlifers also made a comeback: Gyedu-Blay Ambolley, Jewel Ackah, Pat Thomas, C.K. Mann, Nana Tuffour, Kofi Sammy, Amakye Dede, K. Frimpong and A.K. Yeboah.

Besides nostalgia for old-time dance music, another factor that encouraged the formation of live highlife bands was the liberalisation of the economy, when things began to become economically easier in Ghana as it moved back towards democratic civilian rule. This encouraged some of the three million or so Ghanaians who had gone abroad during the 1970s and 1980s hardship to come home. The older returnees generally did not like youthful techno-pop but favoured live jazz, highlife and Afro-jazz played at small exclusive clubs that sprang up, such as Jimmy's Club, Baseline (now called +233), Village Inn and Tonie Maneison's Jazz Tone. These featured bands like Jimmy Beckley's Jazz Combo, Johnny Young's Karmah Jazz Band, Ebo Taylor and Ray Allen's Unconditional Love, Wellington's Magnificent Jazz Trio and also Febeja.[9] There were also individual highlife, jazz and fusion artists such as the trumpeters Osei Tutu, Long John and Mac Tontoh, the singers Rama and Bibi Brew and Cameroonian horn player Fru 'Fats' Tanga.

At the same time, economic liberalisation led to more and more foreign visitors coming to the country, making tourism the third largest foreign-exchange earner for the country after gold and timber.[10] These tourists and 'world music' fans coming to Ghana were seldom interested in local mimed techno music. They sought what they thought was more 'authentic' African music, such as traditional folk music and live dance bands playing highlife and Afro-fusion music. Some of these tourists were African Americans visiting 'home', and in the 1990s the government established special festivals for them, such as PANAFEST located at the Cape Coast and Elmina slave castles, and Emancipation Day, which celebrates the ending of slavery in the Caribbean. Consequently, some African American musicians began to make regular trips or even partially settle in Ghana. These include Stevie Wonder, Isaac Hays and also Rita Marley, who set up a recording studio on Aburi Hill, overlooking Accra.

As a result of all these internal and external factors, more highlife dance bands began to surface during the mid 1990s, such as Ankobra, Avalon Allotey's Gold Coasters, Ozimzim, Megastar and the reformed Marriots. Another was Alpha Waves, based at the Bywels Club in Accra. The band was led by former Black Beats keyboardist Desmond Ababio, and featured E.T. Mensah's trumpeter son Edmund, and the saxist Dan Tackie, who played with E.T.'s second and third bands, the Star Rockets and Paramount Stars, in the 1950s.

From the late 1990s a younger generation of highlife artists' bands entered the growing local live popular music scene, such as Rex Omar, Bessa Simons, Ben Brako, Felix Owusu and Smilin Osei. Another was Nakorex, formed by three young musicians[11] who combined hi-tech with live performance to create a 'world music' brand of highlife.

Another interesting band is Kojo Essah and Cliff Asante's Takashi that combines western and African instruments to play highlife and Afro-fusion. More highlife big bands were also formed, like the Fish Band of former Black Beats leader Sammy Odo, the Vision Band set up in 2003 by the late Komla Amuako and, more recently, Aka Blay's Abiza band. Jerry Hansen's old Ramblers was also reconstituted under the leadership of two of his youthful family members, Felix Amenuda and Peter Marfo. Then in 2002 the university's music department at Legon launched its pop and highlife band under the direction of the highlife veteran Ebo Taylor. This was followed in 2005 by a highlife band being set up at the University of Winneba directed by Bob Pinodo.

Moreover, since 1995, King Bruce's son, Eddie Bruce, has rereleased a string of old evergreen Black Beats highlife hits for the local market on cassette and CD, and in 2009 reformed the Black Beats for a recording project with funds from the

Danish Embassy. I should also add that in the early 2000s the Nigerian highlife horn player Orlando Julius spent some time in Accra where he ran a recording studio, as did the top Liberian female singer Miatta Fahnbulleh, escaping the problems of her war-torn country.

Nat Amanzeba Brew of Nakorex

Various private archival organisations have also been established to document and preserve African music, including old-time Ghanaian highlife. The first two were the African Heritage Library (established in the 1980s at Medie, near Accra, by the ex-Tempos and Afro-jazz musician Kofi Ghanaba), and the Bokoor African Popular Music Archives Foundation (BAPMAF) and its Highlife-Music Institute (which I established in 1990 at South Ofankor, Accra). Other later ones are Professor J.H.K. Nketia's International Centre for African Music and Dance (ICAMD) at the University of Ghana at Legon, Kwame Sarpong's Gramophone Museum in Cape Coast, Kwese Asare's African Cultural Research Centre at Larteh and Koo Nimo's Adadan Cultural Resource Centre in Kumasi.

As in Nigeria, the foreign stimulus to highlife included a positive role by the foreign embassies and their cultural missions. The first instance of this was in 1996 when BAPMAF and the Goethe-Institut in Accra (under Director Sabine Hentzsch) organised a Highlife Month that included seminars, highlife films, the 'Golden Years of Highlife' photo exhibition and performances that featured the Ankobra highlife band and Kofi Ghanaba. This was followed in 2001 when BAPMAF, the Harmattan Company and the French Embassy put on a two-week programme called the 'Story of Highlife' at the Alliance Française in Accra. Then, in January 2002, BAPMAF and the Swiss Embassy organised the launch at the Du Bois Centre of the Basel Mission/UTC compilation CD *Ghana Popular Music 1931–57* (released by Arion Disques). The following month, BAPMAF organised a series of seven lecture-performances on Ghanaian popular music and jazz at the National Theatre for the US Embassy Public Affairs Section's 'Black History Month'. In 2004, the Nigerian Professor Awam Amkpa of New York University and Akonu Dake's Heritage Development Foundation put on a 'Celebration of Highlife' at the National Theatre with seminars and concert performances by the Sappers, Ramblers, C.K. Mann, Wulomei, Mac Tontoh and Castro. In February 2005, BAPMAF and the American jazz percussionist Juma Santos (Jim Riley) co-organised the US Embassy Public Affairs 'African American Heritage/History Month'. Recognising the link between jazz and highlife it gave out Lifetime/Cultural Ambassador Awards to the highlife pioneers Jerry Hansen, Oscarmore Ofori, Stan Plange, Otoo Lincoln,[12] Ebo Taylor, Mac Tontoh, Kofi Ghanaba, Saka Acquaye and Kwadwo Donkoh.

In 2005, the Citi FM Radio Station set up their Music of Ghanaian Origin (MOGO) organisation, which hosts annual shows that have featured Osibisa and highlife acts by Amakye Dede, the Ramblers, Asabea Cropper and Lee Duodu. MOGO's 2012 programme featured A.B. Crentsil and Rex Omar. In October 2006, the first of several 'Highlife Extravaganza' garden parties were held at the house of the then World Bank Country Director Mats Karlsson (himself a cello player) and his wife Irena Kunovska.[13] The events featured highlife performances by Ebo Taylor, Local Dimension,[14] C.K. Mann, Paapa Yankson, Stan Plange, Jewel Ackah, Kwadwo Donkoh, Eddie Soga (former Ramblers bassist) and Kojo Peter Menu who had been the singer for T.O. Jazz.

In 2007 and 2008 the Goethe-Institut organised two 'Made in Germany' festivals that featured live acts by artists involved in the creation in Germany during the 1980s of burger, disco-style highlife. At the same time the University of Ghana at Legon began its annual 'Time for Highlife' programme that has featured the highlife of A.B. Crentsil, Ebo Taylor, the Ramblers, C.K. Mann and Gyedu-Blay Ambolley, as well as new ragga and hiplife acts by Shasha Marley and Obour. Then in 2010 the +233 Jazz Club was opened in Accra for a mature clientele that, despite its name, often features highlife artists; such as Kwame Yeboah, Ackah Blay, Gyedu-Blay Ambolley, Ebo Taylor, Pat Thomas, Della Hayes, Bessa Simmons and A.B. Crentsil.

Local Dimension at Ghana's National Theatre in 2000 with guitarists
T.O. Jazz and John Collins, singer Kojo Menu and xylophonist Aaron
Bebe (Yemo Nunu)

This newfound interest in old-time highlife does not only involve the older generation of Ghanaians and foreigners, as some of the younger post-2000 generation of hiplifers are moving away from borrowing foreign music to utilising highlife. One way they do this is through hiplife stars, like Wutah and Samini, using local beats (including highlife) rather than American ones for the 'jama' style of hiplife. Another way is that some hiplifers are either sampling from old-time highlife records or collaborating with highlife artists.

For instance, Akyeame sampled an old Uhuru one whilst Tic Tac used several of Pat Thomas's tunes. Hiplife–highlife collaborations include Ex Doe and highlife singer Paa Bobo; hiplifer Omanhene and female highlife singer Ewurama Badu; Obour and A.B. Crentsil; and Omanhene Pozo and the leader of the Okukuseku band, Kofi Sammy. Some hiplifers not only rap, but sing in a 'contemporary highlife' mode: artists such as Daasebre Gyamenah, Nana Quame, Slim Busterr, K.K. Fosu, Ofori Amponsah, Kwabena Kwabena and Wunluv. Thus, it's not only elders nostalgic for old sounds and foreigners in search of 'authenticity' who are interested in highlife. Today some young Ghanaian hiplifers are also becoming interested in this home-grown music – which bodes well for the survival, transmission and adaption of highlife.

Nigerian and Ghanaian Bands Playing Highlife in the West

I want to conclude by saying something about the highlife music played by Nigerian and Ghanaian artists who settled outside of their home countries. We will start with Ghanaian artists, one of whom is Nana Tsiboe, whose London-based Supa Hi-Life Band has been operating since the early 1990s and has played at WOMAD world music festivals. This band specialises in acoustic highlife, reflected in its 2003 album *Ahom* (Breath).

Another UK-based Ghanaian band is the ten-piece Yaaba Funk that plays highlife and Afrobeat. Yaaba Funk is led by percussionist/singer Richmond Kwame Kwessie and includes Ghanaian and British musicians, such as ace guitarist Alfred 'Kari' Bannerman and bassist Paul Brett. The Ghanaian musicologist Dr Kwasi Ampene has been running a highlife big band in the US since 2000 called the West African Highlife Ensemble, composed of students of Boulder College of Music in Colorado. Another US-based Ghanaian group that played highlife and Afro-fusion in Portland, Oregon was the Kukrudu band of the Ghanaian master-drummer Obo Addy, who sadly died in 2012.

Still in the States, there is the Chicago-based Occidental Brothers dance band, set up by American guitarist Nathaniel Braddock, together with Ghanaian vocalist/trumpeter Kofi

Cromwell and percussionist Daniel 'Rambo' Asamoah, both of whom obtained their training with the Western Diamonds dance band of Takoradi. In 2009, the Occidental Brothers released their *Odo Sanbra* CD and played in Canada at that year's Afrofest in Toronto. Then, in Toronto, there is the Afrofanto band that also played at Afrofest and includes Theo Yaw Boakye, Paa Joe and Jewel Ackah's son Kofi Ackah. The annual Canadian Afrofest itself, held annually in Toronto, is a long-running music festival started as far back as 1989 by two Ghanaians – Thaddy Uulzen and Sam Mensah of the Highlife World Company.

Europe also hosts some Ghanaian highlife bands. In the Netherlands there is Sloopy Mike Gyamfi's Sankofa Band. The Netherlands is also the home of the annual Afrikafestival Hertme, run by Dr Rob Lokin and his wife, which often hosts highlife acts, like Ebo Taylor's Bonze Konkoma band in 2010. Germany has been the base of many burger highlife musicians such as Rex Gyamfi, George Darko, Daddy Lumba, Allan Cosmos Ade and McGod. In Denmark there are several mixed African and white bands such as Frank Bojestrum's Katamanto Highlife Orchestra and the Highlife N'Gogo Orchestra that at one point featured the Ghanaian artist Afro Moses, now resident in Australia. Incidentally, Australia is also the base of another Ghanaian highlife band called Kotoka Mma, run by the former Koo Nimo percussionist, Little Noah. Furthermore, Australia is the home of the Ghanaian highlife musicians Eddie Quansah and Aweke Yaw Glyman.

Nigeria boasts several artists and bands that play highlife, Afrobeat and juju abroad. In the US there is the veteran Nigerian singer/bassist Babá Ken Okulolo who played with Victor Olaiya and Sunny Ade. From the same pool of Nigerian and Ghanaian musicians he runs three bands in the San Francisco Bay area: the acoustic Nigerian Brothers group, the Kotoja Afro-fusion band and the more highlife-oriented West African Highlife Band. The Nigerian musicians he works with are the trap drummer Lemi Barrow and also Soji Odukogbe; former lead guitarist of Fela Anikulapo-Kuti's Africa 80. The Ghanaians who work with Okulolo's groups are the vocalist Pope Flyne (or Fynne) who previously played with the Sweet Talks, and Nii Armah Hammond who, in the 1970s, was with Faisal Helwani's Hedzoleh Soundz and then went on to record on several of Hugh Masekela's albums. In New York City there is the Asiko Afrobeat Ensemble (formed in 2003 by the Nigerian percussionist Foly Kolade from Ogidi in Anambra State) that combines rock, funk, jazz and West African rhythms.

A Nigerian musician based in the UK is the keyboard player Tunday Akintan from Lagos, who studied music at Goldsmith College London, after which he collaborated with London-based musicians in 2001 to create a style he calls 'Yorubeat': a fusion of highlife, Afrobeat, juju and fuji. His twelve-piece Yorubeat Band released their first DVD in 2007 called *The Genesis of Yorubeat: Live in London* and this group often tours Europe. Berlin has become an important centre for African music through its Afrobeat Academy. This organisation or collective includes Poets of Rhythm, the Cologne-based Schäl Sick Brass Band, Kabu Kabu, the ten-piece Frankfurt RAS band and the Berlin-based Rhythm Taxi.

A key member of the collective is the half-Nigerian, half-German Afro-hiphopper Adé Bantu. Another is former Fela Kuti guitarist Oghene Kologbo, who settled in Berlin in 1978 and joined the Afrobeat Academy in 2005. The Afrobeat Academy often organises tours for Nigerian and Ghanaian acts like the German-Nigerian singer Don Abi (Adiodun Odukoya), the Firedance Crew from Nigeria and, in 2009–2011, Ebo

Taylor and his twelve-piece Bonze Konkoma dance band. As mentioned in Chapter 17, Ebo Taylor was a prolific dance-band highlife composer in the 1950s and 1960s who in later years also experimented with funky highlife and Afro-funk. In his new Bonze Konkoma band, this veteran highlife guitarist has come full circle – by combining dance band highlife and funk with konkoma music, one of the early roots of highlife.

1. John Collins, 'Highlife and Nkrumah's Independence Ethos' *Journal of Performing Arts*, 4:1 (2009/2010) pp. 93-104.
2. Due to armed robberies.
3. Benson Idonije, 'CORA Great Highlife Party', *Nigerian Guardian*, 28 December 2007.
4. See Segun Fajemisin at www.nigeriaworld.com and Daniel Brown at www. mondomix. com.
5. This included the teenaged Ebenezer Obey on maracas. He would later become a famous juju star.
6. Benson Idonije, 'Orlando Owoh. Tribute to a Living Legend', *Nigerian Guardian*, 18 July 2008. Cletus Nwachukwu, 'Orlando Owoh the Kennery is Ill', *Nigerian Guardian*, 4 April 2006.
7. Fatai Rolling Dollar, in Alex Last, 'Nigerians Re-living the Highlife', BBC News, 28 August 2006.
8. King Bruce, personal communication, 1987.
9. With Soroko on keyboards, Cliff Eck on guitar, the Togolese bassist Gautier on bass and Frank Sisi-Oyo (formerly with Fela Kuti) on trap drums.
10. In 2004, 650,000 foreign tourists visited Ghana, bringing $800 million in foreign exchange. By 2012 this had increased 1.2 million tourists bringing $2.2 billion.
11. Nat 'Amandzeba' Brew, Rex Omar and Akosua Agyepong
12. The inventor of the 1960s neo-traditional Ga kpanlogo drum-dance that combines traditional Ga music with highlife, the twist and rock 'n' roll.
13. Incidentally, Mats Karlssen was partly instrumental in getting the Ghanaian government to include the entertainment sector in its Poverty Reduction Strategy.
14. A highlife band based at the University of Ghana set up by myself and Aaron Bebe Sukura in 1998.

PHOTO CREDITS

Photo credits are listed in the captions. Those credits listed as 'BAPMAF' come from the John Collins/Bokooor African Popular Music Archives Foundation, an NGO set up in 1990 to preserve, promote and disseminate Ghanaian/African popular music.

BIBLIOGRAPHY

ABOAGYE, Festus B. 1999. *The Ghanaian Army*. Accra, Sedco Publishing.

ADEDEJI, Femi. 2009. 'Classification of Nigerian Gospel Music Styles', *África: Revista do Centro de Estudos Africanos*, 24/25/26 (**March**), 225–246.

AGHAGHE, Richard. 2009. 'Victor Olaiya: Fifty Years of Ingenious Highlife on Stage', *Nigerian Daily Independent* (online).

AIG-IMOUKHUEDE, Frank. 1975. 'Contemporary Culture' in A.B. Aderibigbe (ed.), *Lagos: The Development of an African City*. Nigeria, Longman Nigeria, pp. 197–226.

AJAYI-SOYINKA, Omofolabo. 2008. 'Calabar', in Carole Boyce Davies (ed.), *Encyclopedia of the African Diaspora: Origins, Experiences, and Culture*, California, ABC-CLIO, p. 526.

AKYEAMPONG, Emmanuel. 1996. *Drink, Power and Cultural Change*, Oxford, James Currey.

ALAJA-BROWNE, Afolabi. 1985. 'Juju Music: A Study of its Social History and Style', PhD dissertation, University of Pittsburgh.

––––––– 1987. 'From "Ere E Faaji Ti O Paria" to "Ere E Faaji Alariwa": A Diachronic Study of Change in Juju Music', paper presented at the fourth International Conference of the International Association for the Study of Popular Music (IASPM), Accra, 12–19 August.

ANYIAM, Charles Anyiam. 1982. 'Life and Times of Bobby Benson', *Africa Music*, 11 (September/October), 12–13.

ARNAUD, Gérald. 2002. 'Bembeya se Réveille', *Africultures*, 1 November.
'The Arts Go Pop', *DRUM*, November 1963, pp. 8–9.

ASHIE, Eric K. II. 1981. 'Why Ghana Ramblers are Consistent', *Africa Music*, 5 (September/October), 32.

BEECHAM, John. 1841. *Ashanti and the Gold Coast*. London, John Mason.

BENDER, Wolfgang. 2004. 'Bayo Martins: Voice of the Drum', Lagos: Music Foundation Nigeria.

'Bobby Benson Hot Showman', *DRUM*, October 1957, pp. 7–8.

BOONZAJER FLAES, Robert. 2000. *Brass Unbound: Secret Children of the Colonial Brass Band*. Royal Tropical Institute, p. 14 and f/n 23.

—— and Fred Gales. 1991. Unpublished manuscript, p.13 and 20, and f/n 20, 22 and 38.

BROOKS, George E. Jr. 1972. *The Kru Mariner in the 19th Century*. Liberia Monograph Studies Series, Department of Anthropology, University of Delaware, No. 1.

Cape Coast Leader, Review of a Magic Costume Ball and Concert. 1 February 1903.

CLARK, Ebun. 1979. *Hubert Ogunde: The Making of Nigerian Theatre*. Oxford University Press.

COLE, Catherine. 2001. *Ghana's Concert Party Theatre*. Bloomington and Indianapolis: Indiana University Press.

COLLINS, John. 1985. *Music Makers of West Africa*. Washington DC, Three Continents Press.

———— 1986. *E.T. Mensah: The King of Highlife*. London, Off The Record Press.

———— 1992. 'Francophone West Africa and the Jali Experience', in John Collins, *West African Pop Roots*. Philadelphia: Temple University Press.

———— 1994. 'The Ghanaian Concert Party: African Popular Entertainment at the Crossroads', PhD thesis, State University of New York.

———— 1996. *Highlife Time*. Accra: Anansesem Press.

———— 2010. 'Highlife and Nkrumah's Independence Ethos' *Journal of Performing Arts*.

Daily Graphic, 25 May 1956.

ECHERUO, Michael J.C. 1962. 'Concert and Theatre in Late Nineteenth Century Lagos', *Nigeria Magazine*, 74 (September), 69–70.

EMIELU, Austin. 2009. 'Nigerian Highlife Music', PhD thesis, University of Ilorin. Published in 2013 by The Centre for Black and African Arts and Civilisation, Lagos.

FARRIS THOMPSON, Robert. *Flash of the Spirit*. USA: Vintage Books, 1984.

FIOFORI, Tam. 1981. 'Zeal Onyia – Trumpet Virtuoso and Music Producer', *Africa Music*, 6 (November/December), 8–11.

GHANABA, Kofi. 1966. *I Have a Story to Tell*. Accra, self-published.

———— 1975. 'Autobiography', unpublished manuscript.

———— 1995. *Hey Baby! Dig Dat Happy Feelin'*. Accra, self-published.

'Ghana's Sweetest Singer', *DRUM*, July 1961, pp. 16–17.

GILROY, Paul. 1993. *The Black Atlantic: Modernity and Double Consciousness*. Cambridge: Harvard University Press.

GMANYAMI, Jonathan. 2007. Jerry Hansen interview, *Ghanaian Spectator*, 3 March, p. 18.

Great Highlife Party. Lagos: Goethe-Institut, 2000, pp. 10–14.

HARREV, Flemming. 1987. 'Goumbe and the Development of Krio Popular Music in Freetown, Sierra Leone', paper presented at the fourth International Conference of the International Association for the Study of Popular Music (IASPM), Accra, 12–9 August, p. 6.

HORTON, Christian Dowu. 1983. 'History of Popular Bands', *African Popular Music*, 14, 12–13.

———— 1984. 'Popular Bands in Sierra Leone', *Black Perspectives in Music*, 12:2, 183–192.

IDONIJE, Benson. 2003. 'Tonight Rains Off Highlife with Roy Chicago's Return', *Lagos Guardian*, 5 February.

———— 2007. 'CORA Great Highlife Party', *Nigerian Guardian*, 28 December.

—— 2008a. 'Legacy of Bobby Benson of Africa', *Lagos Guardian*, 21 May.

—— 2008b. 'Orlando Owoh... Tribute to a Living Legend', *Nigerian Guardian*, 18 July.

—— 2008c. 'Highlife: The Music of Independence', *Nigerian Arts Guardian*, 1 October.

—— 2009a. 'Premier Music – Green is the Taste of Veteran Highlifers', *Arts Guardian*, 26 April.

—— 2009b. 'Echoes of the Sixties', *Lagos Guardian*, 1 October.

JULIUS, Orlando. 2002. *Orlando: The Legendary Orlando Julius Ekemode*. Self-published.

KUBIK, Gerhard. 1999. *Africa and the Blues*. University Press of Mississippi.

LAST, Alex. 2006. 'Nigerians Re-living the Highlife', *BBC News*, 28 August.

Letter from District Commissioner's Office, 16 March 1909, Ghana National Archives, no. 134e.

MAKWENDA, Cecilia Joyce. 1990. 'Zimbabwean Contemporary Music of the 1940s to the 1960s', paper presented at the Audio-Visual Archives Conference, Fayum, Sweden 1–15 July.

MARTINS, Bayo. 1981. 'The Drummer and His Message', *African Music*, 3 (May/June), 10–12.

—— 1984. 'Tribute to Bobby Benson: The Man and his Music', *Africa Music*, 20, (March/April), 11.

—— 2001. 'Remembering the Trumpeter Zeal Onyia', *Lagos Guardian*, 2 May.

—— 2004. 'Zealinjo, Zeal Onyia, "The Hip Cat", 1934–2000', *Ntama Journal of African Music and Popular Culture*, 23 January.

MENSAH, Atta Annan. 1969/70. 'Highlife', unpublished manuscript. There is a copy in the John Collins/BAPMAF music archives Accra.

—— 1971/2. 'Jazz: The Round Trip', *Jazz Forschung/Research* (Universal Edition Graz, Internationalen Gesellschaft Fur Jazzforschung), 3/4, 124-37.

NARCET, Segun. 1981. 'Jazz Scene: Peter King Sax Genius', *African Music*, 2, (March/April), 16–17.

NKETIA, J.H.K. 1968. 'The Instrumental Resources of African Music', *Papers in African Studies*, 3, 1–23.

—— 1973. *Folk Songs of Ghana*. Accra, Ghana Universities Press.

NNENYELIKE, Nwagbo. 2004. 'Oliver de Coque is my son in music – Osita Osadebe'. http://www.kwenu.com/profile/osita_osadebe.htm (accessed 23 April 2004).

NWACHUKU, Cletus. 2006. 'Orlando Owoh the Kennery is Ill', *Nigerian Guardian*, 4 April.

NWACHUKWA, Emeka. 2002. *Lagos Guardian*, 9 November.

OFORI, Oscarmore. 1987. Interview in *The Ghanaian Mirror*, 8 August.

OLWECHIME, Ndubuisi. 1984. 'Highlife Revival Imminent', *Africa Music*, 21 (May/June), 13.

OMBIYE-OBIDIKE, Mosunmola. A. 1987. 'Women in Popular Music in Nigeria', paper presented at the fourth International Conference of the International Association for the Study of Popular Music (IASPM), Accra, 12–19 August.

OPOKU, A. M. 1966. 'Choreography and the African Dance', *African Research Review* 3:1, 53–9.

RAYMOND, Robert. 1960. *Black Star in the Wind*. UK, MacGibbon and Kee.

SACKEY, Chrys Kwesi. 1989. *Konkoma*. Berlin, D. Reimer.

SADOH, Godwin. 2004. 'The Organ Works of Fela Sowande', PhD dissertation, Louisiana State University.

SALM, Steve. 2003. 'The Bukom Boys: Subcultures and Identity Transformation in Accra Ghana', PhD Dissertation, University of Texas.

SERVANT, Jean-Christophe. 2003. *Which Way Nigeria?* Denmark, Freemuse Publications.

STAPLETON, Chris. 1982. 'A Royal Visit', *Black Music and Jazz Review*, September, p. 23.

SUTHERLAND, Efua. 1970. *The Original Bob: The Story of Bob Johnson, Ghana's Ace Comedian*. Accra, Anowuo Educational Publications.

THOMAS, T. Ajayi. 1992. *History of Juju Music: A History of an African Popular Music from Nigeria*. New York, The Organisation.

UWAIFO, Victor. 1998. *Expo '98: Victor Uwaifo – The Legend*. Nigeria, Joromi Organization.

——— and John Collins. 1976. *My Life: The Black Knight of Music Fame*. Accra, Black Bell Publishing.

VEAL, Michael. 2000. *Fela*. Philadelphia, Temple University Press.

WARE, Naomi. 1978. 'Popular Music and African Identity in Freetown Sierra Leone' in Bruno Nettle (ed.), *Eight Urban Musical Cultures*. University of Illinois Press.

WATERMAN, Chris. 1986. 'Juju: The Historical Development, Socio-economic Organisation and Communicative Functions of West Africa Popular Music', PhD thesis, University of Illinois.

——— 1990. *Juju: A Social History and Ethnography of an African Popular Music*. Chicago, University of Chicago Press.

YANKAH, Kwesi. 1984. 'The Akan Highlife Song: A Medium for Cultural Reflection or Deflection?' *Research in African Literatures*, 15:4 (Winter).

ZUESSE, Evan M. 1979. *Ritual Cosmos: The Sanctification of Life in African Religions*. Ohio University Press.

SUGGESTED READINGS

BARBER, Karin, John Collins & Alain Ricard. 1997. *West African Popular Theatre*. Indiana University Press.

BENDER, Wolfgang. 1989. 'Ebenezer Calendar – An appraisal', *Perspectives in African Music*, 9, 43–68.

COLLINS, John. 1992. *West African Pop Roots*. Philadelphia, Temple University Press.

———— 2007. 'The Entrance of Women into Ghanaian Popular Entertainment', in Anne Adams and Efua Sutherland (eds.) *The Legacy of Efua Sutherland: Pan African Cultural Activism*. UK, Ayebia Clark Publishing Ltd, pp. 47–54.

———— 2009. *Fela: Kalakuta Notes*. Amsterdam, Dutch Royal Tropical Institute. Enlarged, updated second edition published by Wesleyan University Press, 2015.

ITA, Chief Bassey. 1984. *Jazz in Nigeria*. Calabar, Atiaya Communications Company.

JEYIFO, Biodun. 1984. *The Yoruba Popular Travelling Theatre of Nigeria*. Lagos, Department of Culture, Federal Ministry of Social Development, Youth, Sports and Culture.

KAZADI, Wa Mukuna. 1992. 'The Genesis of Urban Music in Zaire', *The Journal of the International Library of African Music* (Grahamstown), 7:2, 72–84.

OLATUNJI, Babatunde, with Robert Atkinson and Akinsola Akiwowo. 2005. *The Beat of My Drum – an Autobiography*. Philadelphia, Temple University Press.

PLAGEMAN Nathan. 2013. *Highlife Saturday Night*. Indiana University Press.

SCHOONMAKER, Trevor (ed.). 2003. *Fela: From West Africa to West Broadway*. London, Palgrave Macmillan.

SCHMIDT, Cynthia. 1998. 'Kru Mariners and Migrants of the West African Coast', in Ruth M. Stone (ed.), *Garland Encyclopaedia of World Music: Africa [Vol 1.]*. New York and London, Stone, pp. 370–381.

VAN DER GEEST, Sjaak and Nimrod K. Asante-Darko. 1982. 'The Political Meaning of Highlife Songs in Ghana', *American Studies Review*, 25:1 (March), 27–35.

INDEX

HIGHLIFE GIANTS